THE POLITICS OF DEMOCRATIZATION
IN KOREA *The Role of Civil Society*

THE POLITICS OF

DEMOCRATIZATION IN KOREA

The Role of Civil Society

S U N H Y U K   K I M

University of Pittsburgh Press

Published by the University of Pittsburgh Press, Pittsburgh, Pa. 15261
Copyright © 2000, University of Pittsburgh Press
All rights reserved
Manufactured in the United States of America
Printed on acid-free paper

10 9 8 7 6 5 4 3 2 1

Library of Congress Cataloging-in-Publication Data

Kim, Sunhyuk, 1966–
    The politics of democratization in Korea : the role of civil society /
Sunhyuk Kim.
        p. cm.
Includes bibliographical references (p.   ) and index.
    ISBN 0-8229-5736-1 (pbk.)
    1. Civil society—Korea (South) 2. Democratization—Korea (Soputh 3.
Korea (South)—Politics and government. I. Title.
JQ1729.A15 S58 2000
320.95195—dc21   00-010611

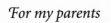

For my parents

Contents

List of Tables and Figures   ix

Acknowledgments   xi

List of Abbreviations   xiii

Note on Transliteration   xv

1 Introduction: Korean Democratization and Civil Society   1

2 Civil Society and Democratization: Conceptual and

Theoretical Issues   9

3 Civil Society in the First Democratic Juncture, 1956–1961   23

4 Civil Society in the Second Democratic Juncture, 1973–1980   50

5 Civil Society in the Third Democratic Juncture, 1984–1987   77

6 Civil Society in Democratic Consolidation, 1988–   105

7 Conclusion: From Protest to Advocacy   137

Notes   151

Bibliography   165

Index   179

List of Tables and Figures

Tables

Table 2.1 Dimensions and Characteristics of Civil Society   15
Table 2.2 Three Democratic Junctures in Korea: Periodization   19
Table 3.1 Policies of the USAMGIK toward Civil Society and
           Political Society, 1945–1947   27
Table 3.2 Trade Unions and Labor Disputes, 1956–1961   40
Table 4.1 GNP Growth Rates, 1962–1968   53
Table 4.2 Results of Presidential Elections, 1963 and 1967   53
Table 4.3 GNP Growth Rates, Gross Investment Ratios, and
           Labor Disputes, 1969–1972   56
Table 4.4 Changes in the Class Structure, 1960–1980   70
Table 4.5 Civilians and Soldiers-in-mufti in the Executive, 1948–1993   72
Table 4.6 Civilians and Soldiers-in-mufti in the Legislature, 1948–1993   72
Table 5.1 GNP Growth Rates, 1980–1983   81
Table 5.2 Results of National Assembly Elections, 1985   85
Table 5.3 Trade Unions and Labor Disputes, 1983–1987   93
Table 6.1 Citizens' Movement Groups, 1945–1993   108
Table 6.2 Social, Women's, and Youth Groups, 1980–1993   109
Table 6.3 Results of National Assembly Elections, 1988   113
Table 6.4 Environmental Groups, 1960–1993   124
Table 7.1 Civil Society and Democratization in Korea: Chronology   140
Table 7.2 Civil Society and Democratization in Korea: Analysis   145

Figures

Figure 2.1 Civil Society and Other Societal Spheres   14
Figure 2.2 Three Dimensions of Civil Society   16
Figure 2.3 Three Democratic Junctures in Korea: Different Paths   18

Acknowledgments

This book is a product of guilt. During the tempestuous years of democratization in Korea in the mid-1980s, I was an undergraduate student at Seoul National University, Korea. For various reasons, I did not join many of my friends who were actively involved in the antigovernment student movement for democracy. I hope this book compensates for my silence at the time. I also hope my book provides condolence to all those who lost their lives during the long and tortuous journey toward democracy in Korea.

In writing this book, I have been blessed to receive help from many people. Most of all, I am immensely indebted to my mentors at Stanford University—Philippe Schmitter (now at the European University Institute), Larry Diamond, and Daniel Okimoto—for their unstinting support and guidance during and after my graduate years there.

I am deeply grateful to Doh Chull Shin at the University of Missouri at Columbia for his help and encouragement through the revision process of this book. I also thank Chae-Jin Lee at Claremont-McKenna College, Hagen Koo at the University of Hawaii, and HeeMin Kim at Florida State University for their insightful comments on earlier drafts and chapters of my book.

I want to express my gratitude to some of my teachers, colleagues, and friends in Korea and in the United States who provided me with counsel, encouragement, and inspiration. I thank Hee-Yeon Cho, Jang Jip Choi, Jungug Choi, Bong Y. Choy, Dae-Hwa Chung, Sung-joo Han, Eun Mee Kim, Young Rae Kim, Sukjoon Lee, Sung-Jong Lee, Hyun Chin Lim, Sunung Moon, Ho Sung Park, and K.W. Rowe.

At the University of Southern California, I have been surrounded by many supportive and knowledgeable colleagues. I especially thank the chair of my department, Sheldon Kamieniecki, for his untiring support throughout the process of writing this book. In addition, some of my students at USC assisted me with my research and writing. I thank Mark Carpowich, Jonathan O'Hara, Steven Cade, Steve Gribben, Yong Wook Lee, and Chong Hee Han.

I profoundly thank my parents in Korea. My father, Nakjung Kim, was one of the most careful and critical readers of my manuscript. As an activist who survived all those tumultuous years of Korean democratization, he wrote me hundreds of letters to comment on my book. I learned a lot from his criticisms and suggestions. My mother, Namkee Kim, was one of the greatest supporters of my project. I admire her optimism, humor, and political acumen.

My book would not have been possible without the love, patience, sacrifice, and support of many other members of my family. My heartfelt thanks go to my parents-in-law, Deuk San Choi and Jong Lim Kim, to my two little boys, Jonathan Hongsoon and Christopher Iksoon, and most of all to my wife, Hye-Won Choi.

I deeply thank the two anonymous reviewers who evaluated my manuscript for the University of Pittsburgh Press. My book benefited tremendously from their insightful comments and suggestions. I also thank Eileen Kiley and Ann Walston of the press for their enthusiasm and effectiveness in helping to bring this book to fruition.

List of Abbreviations

AFPP	Association of Families of Political Prisoners (Minjuhwa silch'ŏn kajok undong hyŏbŭihoe or Min'gahyŏp)
CCEJ	Citizens' Coalition for Economic Justice (Kyŏngje chŏngŭi silch'ŏn simin hyŏbŭihoe or Kyŏngsillyŏn)
CCFE	Citizens' Council for Fair Elections (Kongmyŏng sŏn'gŏ silch'ŏn simin undong hyŏbŭihoe or Kongsŏnhyŏp)
CMPD	Council of Movement for People and Democracy (Minjung minju undong hyŏbŭihoe or Minminhyŏp)
CPAJ	Catholic Priests' Association for Justice (K'at'ollik chŏngŭi kuhyŏn chŏn'guk sajedan)
DJP	Democratic Justice Party (Minju chŏngŭidang or Minjŏngdang)
FKTU	Federation of Korean Trade Unions (Han'guk nodong chohap ch'ong yŏnmaeng or Han'guk noch'ong, formerly Taehan noch'ong)
KAPMA	Korea Anti-Pollution Movement Association (Konghae ch'ubang undong yŏnhap or Kongch'uryŏn)
KCCM	Korea Council of Citizens' Movements (Simin tanch'e hyŏbŭihoe or Siminhyŏp)
KCIA	Korea Central Intelligence Agency (Chungang chŏngbobu; renamed National Security Planning Agency in 1980, renamed National Intelligence Service in 1999)
KCTU	Korean Confederation of Trade Unions (Chŏn'guk minju nodong chohap ch'ong yŏnmaeng or Minju noch'ong)
KFEM	Korea Federation for Environmental Movement (Hwan'gyŏng undong yŏnhap or Hwan'gyŏngnyŏn)
KTEWU	Korea Teachers' and Educational Workers' Union (Chŏn'guk kyojigwŏn nodong chohap or Chŏn'gyojo)
KTUC	Korean Trade Union Council (Chŏn'guk nodong chohap hyŏbŭihoe or Chŏnnohyŏp)
LCNS	Legislative Council for National Security (Kukka powi ippŏp hoeŭi)

LP   Liberal Party (Chayudang)
NADUK   National Alliance for Democracy and Unification of Korea
            (Minjujuŭi minjok t'ongil chŏn'guk yŏnhap or Chŏn'guk
            yŏnhap)
NCDR   National Congress for Democracy and Reunification (Minju
            t'ongil kungmin hoeŭi or Kungmin hoeŭi)
NCUSC   National Coalition of University Student Councils (Han'guk
            taehak ch'ong haksaenghoe yŏnhap or Hanch'ongnyŏn)
NDP   New Democratic Party (Sinmindang)
NKDP   New Korea Democratic Party (Sinhan minjudang or
            Sinmindang)
NMHDC   National Movement Headquarters for Democratic Constitution
            (Minju hŏnbŏp chaengch'wi kungmin undong ponbu or
            Kungmin undong ponbu)
NSL   National Security Law (Kukka poanbŏp)
PMCDR   People's Movement Coalition for Democracy and Reunification
            (Minju t'ongil minjung undong yŏnhap or Mint'ongnyŏn)
PSPD   People's Solidarity for Participatory Democracy (Ch'amyŏ minju
            sahoe simin yŏndae or Ch'amyŏ yŏndae)
RDP   Reunification Democratic Party (T'ongil minjudang)
USAMGIK   United States Army Military Government in Korea (Migunjŏng)
YCDM   Youth Coalition for Democracy Movement (Minjuhwa undong
            ch'ŏngnyŏn yŏnhap or Minch'ŏngnyŏn)

Note on Transliteration

In general, Korean words and names in this book conform to the McCune-Reischauer transliteration system. Exceptions were made for those individuals who had their own idiosyncratic renderings (for example, Syngman Rhee, Park Chung Hee, Chun Doo Hwan). Family names preceded given names and given names were not hyphenated, except for some individual authors in the bibliography who preferred hyphenation of their given names.

Introduction
Korean Democratization and Civil Society

In Korea, Burma, Taiwan, Thailand, Pakistan, the Philippines, Bangladesh, Sri Lanka, and other countries, democracy has been frustrated at times, even suspended. Nevertheless, most of these countries have democratized, and in all of them, a resilient 'people power' has been demonstrated through elections and popular movements.

KIM DAE JUNG, 1994

The contribution of protest to Korean democracy cannot be overstated. . . . Particularly in the 1980s . . . Korean students, workers and young people brought into the public space uniquely original and autonomous configurations of political and social protest.

BRUCE CUMINGS, 1999

Korean Democratization

MORE than twelve years have passed since democratization began in earnest in South Korea (hereafter referred to as Korea) in 1987. During the past decade, there have been a number of prominent changes in Korean politics. First of all, political contestation has become much fairer.[1] Today, there are no longer undemocratic "gymnasium elections" (*ch'eyukkwan sŏn'gŏ*). Under the previous authoritarian regimes, the president was elected indirectly by members of the national electoral college, who gathered in a large athletic gymnasium and voted nearly unanimously for the designated authoritarian ruler. Since 1987, however, opposition party candidates' chances of getting elected have increased considerably, which explains in part the election of Kim Dae Jung, a longtime opposition leader who had run for the presidency four times, as president in 1997.

Furthermore, civil liberties have been substantially expanded.[2] The Basic Press Law (*Ŏllon kibonbŏp*), a sophisticated and comprehensive system of press censorship enacted in 1980 by the Legislative Council for National Security (*Kukka powi ippŏp hoeŭi*), was abolished. A number of labor laws, which had severely restricted the exercise of labor rights, were overhauled. The dissident national peak association of labor unions, which had been outlawed and harshly suppressed by the preceding authoritarian regimes, was finally recognized by the government. The intelligence agency (National Intelligence Service, Kukchŏngwŏn; formerly known as the National Security Planning Agency and originally called the Korea Central Intelligence Agency), which had served the past authoritarian regimes by monitoring opposition politicians and suppressing dissident movements, pledged to end domestic surveillance and to shift its focus to intelligence operations related to counterterrorism and foreign criminals who threaten the national security of Korea. Many political prisoners and prisoners of conscience were amnestied and released, which has noticeably improved Korea's international standing on human rights and political freedom.

In addition, civilian control over the military has been considerably augmented. Given that "elected officials must be able to exercise their constitutional powers without being subjected to overriding opposition from unelected officials," civilian control over the military is integral to the practice of democracy.[3] The elite Hanahoe faction of the Korean Military Academy, whose members had intruded in politics under earlier authoritarian regimes, has been effectively subdued. Measures have been taken to downgrade the influence of the military's intelligence division, banning civilian surveillance and making a relatively low-ranking officer head the division. Numerous navy admirals and air force generals were discharged for accepting bribes to promote junior officers.[4]

With increased fairness in political contestation, expanded civil liberties, and augmented civilian control of the military, Korea has successfully accomplished its transition from authoritarian rule to democracy and has now become one of the leading nascent democracies in Asia.

Explaining Korean Democratization

Several different explanations have been presented about Korean democratization.[5] Some have highlighted the role of external factors, particularly the posture and policies of the United States, in facilitating Korea's democratic transition. According to this explanation, diplomatic maneuvers by the United States government, pro-democracy resolutions by the United States Senate and House, and the continued attention paid by the United States mass media to the "Korean crisis" significantly helped to prevent another military coup and promoted a smooth democratic transition in Korea in 1987.[6] In this regard, the role of the United States in 1987 was somewhat similar to the one it had played in 1960, when the United States refused to give support to the civilian dictatorship of Syngman Rhee, which eventually resulted in Rhee's resignation and a democratic transition in that same year.

Few would dispute the significance of international factors in Korea's democratic transition. But most studies on Korean democratization to date have put a greater emphasis on domestic factors. External factors may have played an important role—but not a decisive or primary one. This also conforms with the prevailing consensus in the existing literature on democratization. Except for a few cases of "imposed democracy" resulting from, for example, a defeat in a war, external factors have played only a marginal and supplementary role in most of the cases in the recent wave of global democratization. The existing literature asserts that "the reasons for launching a transition can be found predominantly in domestic, internal factors."[7] The case of Korea, in fact, does not drastically deviate from this central finding in the existing literature. In other words, the democratic transition in Korea was largely a result of internal political developments.

Some of those espousing the primacy of domestic factors have argued that the democratic transition in Korea in 1987 was chiefly—if not entirely—driven by a series of elite calculations and interactions.[8] The focus of this interpretation is the proposition of an eight-point democratization package made by Roh Tae Woo, the chairman of the ruling Democratic Justice Party, on June 29, 1987. According to such an elitist paradigm, the June 29 Declaration originated from and stood for a grand compromise between the softliners (*blandos*) and the hardliners (*duros*) in the ruling bloc. In other words, the transition was possible because the softliners, who believed that democratization was unavoidable, predominated over the hardliners. In this regard, what happened in Korea in 1987 surprisingly resembled what had happened earlier in some South European and Latin American countries. The dominant paradigm in the literature on democratic transition and consolidation, primarily based on South European and Latin America experiences, maintains that "there is no transition whose beginning is not the consequence of important divisions within the authoritarian regime itself, principally . . . between hardliners and softliners."[9] The Korean case hence is another verification of the elitist paradigm that contends that "elite dispositions, calculations, and pacts . . . largely determine whether or not an opening [would] occur at all."[10]

Serious criticisms have been raised, however, about the elitist paradigm in general and its application to the Korean case in particular. In general, the elitist paradigm has received objections for three reasons. One reason is because the visibility of elite interactions does not necessarily mean that they are causal. Also, excessive focus on elites tends to overlook the fact that elites' interactions are subject to structural constraints. Furthermore, strategic choices that mass publics make sometimes prompt elites to move.[11]

Whether there existed a genuine chasm between the hardliners and the softliners in the ruling bloc in Korea's case remains extremely dubious.[12] Many analysts have argued that there was no serious split within the ruling bloc. Rather, the ruling regime at the time was quite united and resolved not to concede to the popular uproar for constitutional revision and democratization. Chun Doo Hwan's power and influence in the ruling bloc stayed consistently strong and there were no visible anti-Chun "softliners" who dared to challenge or mitigate Chun's recalcitrance.

Moreover, the elitist explanation of Korean democratization is unduly myopic in that it chooses to focus only on the immediate causes of the transition. On the surface, the democratic transition in Korea in 1987 was set in motion with the June 29 Declaration by the ruling elite. But it is misleading to assume that the elite's decision, which immediately *preceded* the democratic transition, also *caused* it. Temporal proximity is entirely different from causality. The elitist explanation of Korean democratization tends to neglect, either intentionally or inadvertently, that there had been a series of massive, intense, and protracted pro-democracy popular movements prior to June 29, 1987. There were hundreds of public gatherings, street demonstrations, and signature-collection campaigns in 1986 and 1987, ultimately culminating in the June uprising in 1987. In June 1987 alone, millions of Koreans participated in these pro-democracy protest campaigns.

This is why, by far, most scholars of Korean democratization have subscribed to the view that Korea's democratic transition was primarily mass-driven. According to this explanation, it was principally the civil society, "the realm of organized social life that is voluntary, self-generating, (largely) self-supporting, and autonomous from the state," that significantly facilitated, if not directly caused, various phases of democratization in Korea.[13] In particular, analysts have emphasized that student groups, labor unions, and religious organizations had waged intense pro-democracy struggles since the early 1970s. United under the leadership of several national umbrella organizations, these social groups mobilized a formidable democratic alliance against the authoritarian regime in 1987.[14]

In comparative perspective, therefore, the transition in Korea was different from some cases in Southern Europe and Latin America because conflicts, negotiations, and "pacts" among political elites were not the primary determinants of democratization. Rather, similar to the cases in some East European and African countries, it was the civil society groups that initiated and directed the entire process of democratization by forming a pro-democracy alliance within civil society, by creating a grand coalition with the opposition political party, and by eventually pressuring the authoritarian regime to yield to the "popular upsurge" from below.[15]

Themes and Organization of This Volume

The main purpose of this book is to develop and refine a civil society paradigm to analyze and explain the politics of democratization in Korea better. Although there has been a general consensus among Korean experts on the centrality of civil society in Korean democratization, so far there have been no serious attempts to establish and develop a comprehensive and systematic civil society framework. In this book, through a comparative-historical analysis of three "democratic junctures" in Korea, I demonstrate that Korean democratization has consistently been initiated and promoted by civil society groups. Groups in civil society significantly precipitated—if not directly caused—authoritarian breakdowns, facilitated democratic transitions, and, to a large extent, also determined the dynamics of posttransitional politics in democratic consolidation.[16] I particularly focus on how and why the pro-democracy alliance of civil society groups became more extensive, more organized, and more powerful over the three selected periods.

In chapter 2, which is a theoretical and conceptual chapter, I first review the intellectual and historical context in which civil society emerged as a critical variable in the study of democratic transition and consolidation. Then, after briefly discussing the definitions of democracy, democratization, and civil society, I present a synopsis of the case, the argument, and the analytical framework. In chapters 3, 4, and 5, I examine the Korean case in detail. Specifically, I analyze the role of civil society in three different "democratic junctures": 1956–1961, 1973–1980, and 1984–1987. In each chapter, I first describe the internal configuration of civil society at the given period, focusing on important cross-temporal changes. The role of civil society groups in authoritarian break-down and democratic transition is reviewed next. Then I explain the role of civil society in democratization according to my analytical framework. In chapter 6, I examine the current stage of Korean democratization, highlighting how civil society has been transformed after the democratic transition and how the transformed civil society, in turn, has affected the ongoing democratic consolidation since 1988. Finally, in chapter 7, based on the empirical findings in chapters 3 through 6, I discuss some theoretical implications of the Korean case and reflect on the future of civil society and democracy in Korea.

Civil Society and Democratization
Conceptual and Theoretical Issues

*In this third wave of global democratization, no phenomenon
has more vividly captured the imagination of democratic scholars,
observers, and activists alike than "civil society."*

LARRY DIAMOND, 1994

*The presence of a civil society contributes (positively) to the
consolidation of democracy.*

PHILIPPE C. SCHMITTER, 1997

Global Democratization and the Civil Society Paradigm

WHAT is labeled "the third wave" of global democratization[1] or "the global resurgence of democracy"[2] has been characterizing our times. Over the past two decades or so, this "democratic revolution"[3] transformed numerous parts of Southern Europe, Latin America, Asia, Africa, and eventually engulfed the entire Soviet bloc.[4] Authoritarian regimes and totalitarian party-states unraveled one after another, and transitions to democracy ensued. Although widely dissimilar in terms of timing, mode, pace, and degree, transitions from totalitarianism and authoritarianism in general have significantly increased the number of democracies on the globe.[5]

Considering the impact of the third wave on the present and future of the post–Cold War era, it is not very surprising to discover that political scientists as a whole and comparativists in particular have strived over recent years to comprehend the causes, to explicate the processes, and to predict the consequences of the global democratization.[6] Scholars have generated an impressive amount of works on various aspects of democratic transition and consolidation—for example, leadership and legitimacy, elite strategies and interactions,

7

civil-military relations, socioeconomic structure, political culture, ethnic and regional cleavages, institutional design, electoral and party systems, constitutional arrangement, the issue of "dual transitions," and international factors.[7] As a consequence, theories of democratic transition and consolidation, or what experts call "transitology" and "consolidology," have been established as two of the most important subfields of comparative politics.[8]

In transitology and consolidology, two competing and, to a greater degree, conflicting paradigms have been prominent and dominant.[9] The first is the "preconditions paradigm." This paradigm argues that there exist a set of preconditions necessary for democratization. One such precondition, for instance, is economic development. As Lipset affirms, "The more well-to-do a nation, the greater the chances that it will sustain democracy."[10] Another precondition is "civic culture."[11] Certain cultural traits, such as mutual trust, tolerance, accommodation, and compromise, are essential to democratization.[12]

The second is the "contingency paradigm."[13] According to this paradigm, democratization is characterized by a high degree of uncertainty. Consequently, the dynamics of democratization necessarily revolve around and gravitate toward strategic interactions among actors with uncertain power resources. Contingency implies that political outcomes in the process of democratization depend less on objective structural conditions than on subjective rules surrounding strategic choices made by the elite.[14] Primarily, the contingency paradigm is a voluntaristic rebuttal to the overly structuralist tone of the preconditions paradigm.

More recently, a third paradigm has emerged. One of the most distinctive features of the latest round of discussions and debates on global democratization is that "civil society," hitherto "relatively uncharted frontiers in the study of democratic development," has been in unprecedented vogue.[15] Civil society has occupied an important, if not the most important, position in the analyses of the actual processes and future possibilities of democratization in Southern Europe and Latin America,[16] Asia,[17] Africa,[18] Eastern Europe,[19] and the Middle East.[20]

The existing literature on civil society and democratization is, to a great extent, focused on the role of civil society in democratic transition and consolidation. Although analysts differ on what civil society is exactly—that is, on how to define civil society—they do not differ very much on whether civil society is beneficial to democratization. A broad and strong consensus that civil society plays a very positive role in democratization appears to exist. Most analysts agree that civil society is crucial in promoting, protecting, and preserving democracy.[21]

In Southern Europe and Latin America, civil society was "resurrected" as soon as the first steps toward political liberalization had been made, and the subsequent "popular upsurge" precipitated the demise of authoritarian rule, "pushing the transition further than it would otherwise have gone."[22] In Eastern Europe, the independent and "reconstituted" civil society served as a necessary, if not sufficient, condition for transition.[23] Also, in Asia, the growth of civil society has played a critical role in transition because the impetus of the political progress primarily came from the conflict and compromise between the increasingly organized citizenry and the ruling party.[24] In Africa, too, civil society's "politics of protest" has played a decisive role in the struggle for democratization, and it is highly unlikely that a viable democracy can survive without a civil society.[25]

Furthermore, it is also envisioned that civil society will play equally significant roles in consolidating and institutionalizing many of the fledgling democracies. For example, civil society inculcates conceptions of interest and civic norms of behavior; disseminates information and empowers citizens in the collective pursuit and defense of their interests and values; stabilizes expectations within social groups; structures and provides multiple channels for the identification, articulation, expression, and representation of interests; and serves to govern the behavior of its members with regard to collective commitments. They also reduce the burden of governance for both public authorities and private producers; supplement the role of political parties; recruit and train new political leaders; give the citizens respect for the state and positive engagement with it; and contain the power of democratic governments by providing important reservoirs of potential resistance to arbitrary or tyrannical action by rulers.[26]

The principal goal of this book is to confirm, develop, and expand the thesis that civil society contributes positively to democratization—what may be called the "civil society paradigm." The theoretical argument I make and develop is that the civil society paradigm can effectively combine the two existing—and more or less clashing—paradigms in the study of democratization. On the one hand, by probing how structural factors such as economic development and cultural traits affect the configuration, shape, and characteristics of civil society over time, I show how the civil society paradigm can incorporate the significance of prerequisites outlined by the structuralists. I also illustrate how the civil society paradigm can accommodate the importance of choices and contingencies underlined by the voluntarists by examining the interactions between civil society and the state.

The empirical case I examine is Korea. As I have stated earlier, most of the existing studies on Korean democratization have emphasized that Korea is an excellent testimony of the civil society paradigm. Characterizing Korean democratization basically as the triumph of civil society over the authoritarian state, many Korean scholars as well as foreign observers have argued that civil society has been a major determinant of democratization in the country. Yet there has not been much effort to support and demonstrate such a claim empirically. In this book, I intend to transform this casual claim into a substantive argument through a comparative-historical analysis of the specific processes and trajectories of Korean democratization.

Before I switch to the case of Korea, however, I identify two definitional questions that appear to demand immediate answers: What is democracy? and, What is civil society?

Democracy and Democratization

Throughout history, various philosophers and political scientists have presented different and virtually innumerable definitions of democracy. However, recent studies on democracy and democratization show a considerable degree of consensus on what constitutes the "procedural minimum" of democracy. The studies show that the procedural minimum of democracy encompasses, among other things, "secret balloting, universal adult suffrage, regular elections, partisan competition, associational recognition and access, and executive accountability."[27] This procedural minimum is equivalent to Dahl's eight "institutional requirements," which include: "(1) freedom to form and join organizations; (2) freedom of expression; (3) right to vote; (4) eligibility for public office; (5) right of political leaders to compete for support and votes; (6) alternative sources of information; (7) free and fair elections; (8) institutions for making government policies depend on votes and other expressions of preference."[28] Such definitions of democracy based on the procedural minimum are broader than earlier minimalist definitions and therefore avoid what Schmitter and Karl call the "fallacy of electoralism."[29]

In considering Korean democratization, I adopt a definition of democracy focused on the procedural minimum or the institutional requirements. From the beginning of the Republic in 1948, Korea had elections and political competition. Under the authoritarian regimes, however, those elections and political competition were neither free nor fair and were severely constrained by the lack of various democratic freedoms. Therefore, the presence or absence of the procedural minimum or the institutional requirements, which emphasizes numerous civil liberties, serves as a good litmus test for whether a regime is democratic or authoritarian. Specifically, I define democracy as "a political system in which, first, decision-makers are chosen through relatively free, fair, and regular elections in which virtually all the adult population is eligible to vote, and second, there exists a considerable level of civil and political liberties—for example, freedom of thought and expression, freedom of the press, freedom of assembly and demonstration, freedom to form and join organizations, and freedom from terror and unjustified imprisonment."[30]

Democratization is a nonlinear, complex, prolonged, and dynamic process in which a nondemocratic political system moves to a democratic one. As such, democratization involves roughly three conceptually distinguishable—but empirically overlapping—stages. The first stage involves the demise or termination of the nondemocratic regime (authoritarian breakdown). The second occurs when the procedural minimum of democracy is established or recovered and the democratic regime is inaugurated (democratic transition). The third phase involves, on the one hand, the prevention of an authoritarian regression and, on the other, the protection, preservation, and deepening of the democratic system (democratic consolidation).

Authoritarian breakdown is a process in which an authoritarian regime chooses or is forced to carry out a set of democratic reforms due to various factors, including an internal split between hardliners and softliners in the ruling bloc or a massive popular upsurge. In the democratic transition phase, new rules and procedures of citizenship are agreed upon, established, and extended to persons and political institutions previously not subject to citizen participation.[31] In democratic consolidation, a democracy becomes so broadly and profoundly legitimate among its citizens that it is very unlikely to break down.[32] Political rights are also extended more broadly to accommodate traditionally marginalized segments of the populace.

What Is and Is Not Civil Society

Like many other terms in political science, including democracy, the concept of civil society is also subject to diverse interpretations. Political scientists have presented so different conceptions of civil society that it becomes a formidable, if not impossible, task to establish a universal definition.[33] However, at least three important threads common to these various conceptions of civil society exist. In this section, I will explain what can be called the three dimensions of civil society and extract the defining characteristics of civil society in terms of each dimension based on some of the latest theories on what constitutes civil society.

The Organizational Dimension

According to the existing literature, civil society refers to the organized aspect of society. This is the organizational dimension of civil society. The actual form and degree of organization may vary—they may be planned or spontaneous, enduring or temporary, tight or loose, formal or informal. Nevertheless, civil society comprises diverse interacting human collectivities, such as groups, organizations, associations, movements, and institutions. Hence, analysts define civil society, for instance, as "the realm of organized social life," "[the arena of] manifold social movements and civic organizations," "a range of social groups," "the organization of interests," "an associational realm," "a complex of institutions," or "an aggregate of institutions."[34]

What defines civil society in the organizational dimension is the fact that civil society groups are self-organized and operate within the public sphere.[35] To a great extent individuals organize voluntarily or join civil society groups to express their needs and passions, articulate their concerns, and represent their interests. However, civil society groups differ from parochial groups, which principally converge around private needs of group members. Civil society relates to the public, the community, and the collectivity.[36] In this respect, then, civil society is "the self-organization of society, the constituent parts of which voluntarily engage in public activity."[37]

The Relational Dimension

Civil society forms and maintains a set of relationships with other societal spheres. This is the relational dimension of civil society. Specifically, this dimension involves civil society's external relations with the state, private units of production and reproduction, and political society. What defines civil society in terms of the relational dimension is civil society's relative autonomy from these three societal spheres.

First of all, civil society is independent of, and often in conflict with, the state. Civil society is "outside the state in an increasingly independent social sphere," "engaged primarily in a complex of non-state activities," and it is "not regulated, dominated, or controlled by the ruling regime," often "resisting the incursions of the state."[38] In other words, civil society is "distinctly different from the state and largely in autonomy from it."[39] Therefore, under state corporatism, where the authoritarian state organizes, sponsors, funds, subsidizes, monitors, subordinates, mobilizes, and controls corporatist groups, with a view to cooptation, incorporation, repression, and domination, civil society, if it exists at all, is considerably limited.[40]

Furthermore, civil society is also separate and autonomous from the private units of production and reproduction in a society—namely, businesses and families and clans.[41] Civil society is independent of the profit-making enterprise of individual business firms.[42] Civil society derives, among other things, its membership, resource, and support from the basic units of society—that is, families and clans—in return for representing, defending, and promoting their needs, concerns, and interests. However, a group that is penetrated and manipulated by certain families or clans cannot be regarded as a part of civil society. Thus, civil society can be considered as an intermediary sphere between the private sphere and the state. These two types of autonomy—autonomy from the state and autonomy from the basic units of production and reproduction —comprise what is termed the "dual autonomy" of civil society.[43]

Lastly, civil society is also differentiated and autonomous from political society. Political society is "the arena where various political actors compete to gain control over public power and the state apparatus"[44] and is principally composed of political parties and their affiliated networks, organizations, and campaigns.[45] Even though civil society and political society may be intimately interconnected through multilevel channels, the two entities are conceptually different. Most of all, civil society, unlike political society, does not seek to replace state agents.[46] Instead, civil society seeks to engage and to influence the state. Groups in civil society may form coalitions with political parties, but if they become captured by political parties, they cannot be considered as part of civil society.[47]

To sum up, civil society is largely separate from and independent of the state, basic units of production and reproduction, and political society. As figure 2.1 shows, civil society, together with political society, is the intermediary sphere and the representational domain that connects the state and the basic units of production and reproduction and that represents the concerns and interests of firms and families to the state.[48]

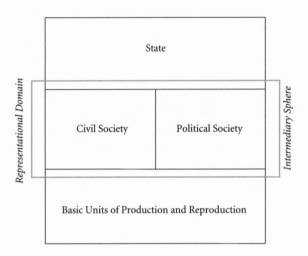

Figure 2.1. Civil Society and Other Societal Spheres

The Normative Dimension

According to the existing literature, civil society engages in collective actions according to a certain set of shared norms and rules. This is the normative dimension of civil society. In this dimension civil society groups respect pluralism and self-governance. In their interactions with other civil society groups, they act according to "a widespread pattern of refined or civil manners."[49] They honor diversity and partialness and do not seek to represent all individual or community interests: instead, different groups represent various interests. If an organization seeks to monopolize the entire civil society by claiming that it represents the only legitimate path, it contradicts the pluralism and diversity of civil society,[50] the irreducible condition that makes a civil society "civil."[51]

Two different possibilities exist in respect to civil society's relations with the state. On the one hand, when state authority is based on the rule of law, and the state honors the self-governance of civil society, groups in civil society agree to act within the context of a legally defined state-society relationship, where "civil society and the state are bound together by the constitution and by traditions which stress the obligations of each to the other as well as their rights vis-à-vis each other."[52] In this case, civil society, legally guaranteed, legitimates state authority.[53] On the other hand, however, when the state itself is lawless and contemptuous of the self-governance and autonomy of civil society, groups in civil society often do not consent to the legitimacy of the existing order, but attempt to annul and alter the norms and rules themselves, either by crafting informal arrangements invisible to the authorities or by substituting the existing state-society relations with new ones. In this case, "civil society is potentially a highly subversive space, a space where new structures and norms may take hold to challenge the existing state order."[54]

Table 2.1 summarizes the defining characteristics of civil society in terms of the organizational, relational, and normative dimensions. Although civil society is largely self-organized, public, autonomous, pluralistic, and self-governing, these characteristics of civil society are not absolute in nature. Civil society in reality can only be *relatively* so; only the relative degree to which these characteristics occur matters.

Figure 2.2 represents visually the three dimensions of civil society. The organizational dimension (OD) concerns the overall constitution and configuration of civil society. The relational dimension (RD) refers to civil society's relations with the state (RD1), basic units of production and reproduction (RD2), and political society (RD3). The normative dimension (ND) deals with the norms and principles governing both the interrelations among civil society groups and civil society's external relations with other societal spheres.

Synthesizing the defining characteristics in the organizational, relational, and normative dimensions, I define civil society as "a set of self-organized groups and movements in society that are relatively autonomous from the state, basic units of production and reproduction, and political society, and are capable of political activities in the public sphere to express their concerns and advance their interests according to the principles of pluralism and self-governance." Thus, civil society is composed of, but certainly is not limited to, trade unions, business associations, religious groups, environmental organizations, student organizations, women's movement groups, human rights movement groups, and so forth.

TABLE 2.1
Dimensions and Characteristics of Civil Society

Dimension	Characteristics
Organizational	Self-organization and publicness
Relational	Independence and autonomy
Normative	Pluralism and self-governance

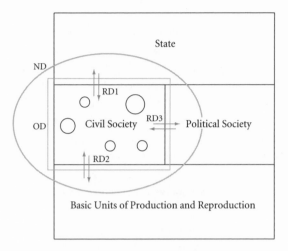

Figure 2.2. Three Dimensions of Civil Society

The Case, the Argument, and the Analytical Framework

Until the Asian economic crisis in 1997, many East Asian countries, including Korea, attracted scholars' attention primarily because of their impressive economic growth from the 1960s through the 1980s. Scholars focused on, for example, what kind of industrialization strategies and policies were adopted and carried out in these countries, what role the state played, how the state interacted with business and labor, and whether the East Asian development model is applicable to and replicable in other areas of the developing world and how. Since 1997, analysts have been trying to explain what has gone wrong in the "miracle economies" in East Asia. In addressing both economic developments and economic crises, however, scholars have ignored the political and social aspects to a great extent. I have written this book largely to rectify these scholars' oversight by highlighting the political and social dynamics of democratization in Korea.

Specifically, I look at three different periods in the history of Korea since 1948: 1956 to 1961, 1973 to 1980, and 1984 to 1987. These three periods, which I call "democratic junctures," are the periods in which an authoritarian regime collapsed and a transition to democracy *actually* occurred or could have *potentially* occurred but failed to do so because of a military coup. My concept of "democratic juncture" is similar to Collier and Collier's notion of a "critical juncture," or "a period of significant change, which typically occurs in distinct

ways in different countries and which is hypothesized to produce distinct legacies."[55] Also, my concept of democratic juncture is close to the "essential moments" of civil society in Africa—that is, "junctures when high levels of
popular participation, engagement and commonly articulated interests have
coincided with the weakening of established state structures and the redefini-
tion of political regimes."[56]

In the first democratic juncture, which occurred in Korea between 1956
and 1961, Syngman Rhee's authoritarian regime was overthrown by a series of
massive student protests across the country in 1960 called the April Uprising.
As a result, a democratic transition ensued when a democratic regime led by
Chang Myŏn was brought to power in August 1960. However, the Chang
regime soon collapsed as a result of Park Chung Hee's military coup on May
16, 1961.

The second democratic juncture happened between 1973 and 1980.
Antigovernment struggles by students, labor unions, and religious groups
starting in the mid-1970s generated a serious split within the top leadership of
Park Chung Hee's authoritarian regime, which ultimately resulted in Park's
assassination. But military hardliners designed and carried out a multiphased
coup, first taking control of the military and then gradually undermining
and eventually replacing the caretaker government of Ch'oe Kyu Ha. On May
17, 1980, the military hardliners, led by Chun Doo Hwan, extended the
existing martial law to the entire nation and virtually took over the entire state
apparatus.

In the third democratic juncture, which occurred between 1984 and 1987,
a succession of massive and violent pro-democracy demonstrations and
protests pressured Chun Doo Hwan's authoritarian regime to agree to revise
the constitution , adopt a direct presidential election system, and promise democratic reforms. A new democratic government emerged through the founding
elections.

From 1988 to the present, various democratic reforms have been drafted
and implemented. In 1992, a genuine civilian (not a military general-in-mufti,
who retires from the military to take a public office) became Korean president
for the first time since the early 1960s. In 1997, an opposition candidate was
elected to the presidency for the first time in Korean history. Currently, democracy is being consolidated behaviorally, attitudinally, and constitutionally in
Korea. Behaviorally, no significant social group pursues the overthrow of the
democratic regime. Attitudinally, the majority of the Korean people believe

that political change must emanate from the parameters of democratic formulas. Constitutionally, most political and social actors concur that political conflict should be resolved according to the established norms.[57]

To sum up, the three democratic junctures in Korea took different paths. The first juncture went through authoritarian crisis → authoritarian breakdown → democratic transition → authoritarian regression. The second juncture went through authoritarian crisis → authoritarian breakdown → authoritarian regression. The third juncture went through authoritarian crisis → authoritarian breakdown → democratic transition → democratic consolidation. Figure 2.3 summarizes these different paths taken in each democratic

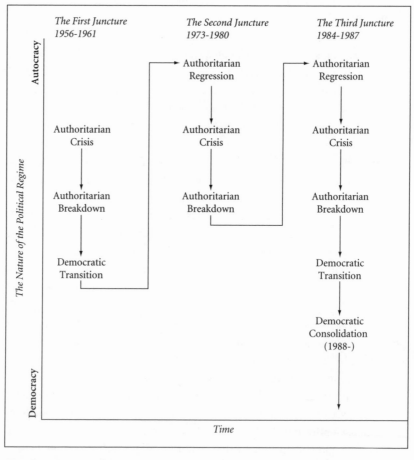

Figure 2.3. Three Democratic Junctures in Korea: Different Paths

juncture. Table 2.2 shows the specific periods in each juncture matching various stages of democratization.

This book is a comparative-historical analysis of these three democratic junctures in Korea. Through a crosstemporal comparison of these three critical periods, I argue that civil society has consistently been a crucial factor determining Korean democratization. This argument, which ultimately confirms the civil society paradigm, or the thesis on the positive contribution of civil society to democratization, consists of three different but closely interrelated subarguments. The first argument I make is that in all three democratic junctures civil society groups directly caused or indirectly facilitated authoritarian breakdown and democratic transition. It has consistently been the mobilization and protest politics of civil society groups that precipitated the demise of the authoritarian regime and the subsequent transition to democracy. In addition, over the three democratic junctures, civil society became more extensive, more organized, and more powerful. This in large measure explains why there was no authoritarian regression in the third democratic juncture. Finally, civil society groups have also been playing an important role in posttransitional politics of Korea. In particular, shifting alliances of various civil society groups have been pressuring the regimes to further democratic consolidation and deepening.

In examining the role of civil society in these three democratic junctures and at different stages of Korean democratization, I will particularly focus on the following three categories of research questions. Each category of questions

TABLE 2.2
Three Democratic Junctures in Korea: Periodization

	1st Juncture	2nd Juncture	3rd Juncture
Authoritarian crisis	1956– April 1960	1973– October 1979	1984– June 1987
Authoritarian breakdown	April 19, 1960	October 26, 1979	June 29, 1987
Democratic transition	April– August 1960	n/a	June– December 1987
Authoritarian regression	May 16, 1961	May 17, 1980	n/a
Democratic consolidation	n/a	n/a	1988–

roughly corresponds to each dimension of civil society I used above to define civil society. Admittedly, this is not an exhaustive list and, therefore, there can be other questions worth considering. Also, the questions on the list are not completely mutually exclusive. Some questions overlap. Nevertheless, this list provides us with a useful analytical framework to examine systematically the relationship between civil society and democratization.

1. *Actors.* Issues in this category primarily address the overall constitution and configuration of civil society. What are the main groups in civil society? What are the pro-democracy groups? How and why do they initiate and promote democratization?

Civil society is neither a monolithic nor a homogeneous entity: it is by definition composed of diverse elements. It is therefore rare that civil society *as a whole* contributes to democratization; rather, only certain elements or constituents in civil society do so. For example, in many of the earlier democratizing countries in Western Europe, it was principally the newly emerged bourgeois class that challenged monarchy and aristocracy and ultimately brought about democratization. Hence, the maxim, "no bourgeoisie, no democracy," could serve as a general statement about the democratization process.[58] By contrast, in some Latin American countries, it was not the business class but mainly the working class that promoted democratization.[59] In this regard, it is essential to identify main pro-democracy actors in civil society (and their alliances) and evaluate their roles in various phases of democratization. Questions regarding actors in civil society roughly correspond to the organizational dimension of civil society that highlights the organized nature of civil society (OD in figure 2.2).

2. *Interactions.* Questions in this category address the characteristics of civil society's relations and interactions with other societal spheres. As already pointed out, civil society is distinct and autonomous from other societal spheres such as the state, political society, and basic units of production and reproduction. At the same time, however, civil society engages and interacts with these societal spheres. What kind of relations do civil society groups form and maintain with the state? How do civil society actors characterize and engage the state? How does the state, in response, deal with civil society? On the other hand, what characterizes the relationship between civil society and political society? How does the movement by civil society groups get politicized? How do civil society groups and political parties build and expand a grand pro-democracy coalition? How do they organize, coordinate, and mobilize different ele-

ments in civil society and political society? These questions primarily concern the relational dimension of civil society that focuses on civil society's relations with other societal spheres (RD1 and RD3 in figure 2.2).[60]

3. *Issues.* Questions in this category primarily have to do with the specific contents of civil society's interactions with other societal spheres. What issues are raised and suppressed by civil society groups in their movement? What explains the selection and suppression of those issues? How do civil society groups manage their agendas? What kind of movement strategies, tactics, methods, and styles do civil society groups employ to engage the state and political society and to promote their causes, interests, and goals? Because management of issues and choice of strategies fundamentally reflect the norms and principles governing civil society groups in general, these questions largely correspond to the normative dimension of civil society (ND in figure 2.2).

In each category, there are some important comparative-static questions to be asked. In the actors category, for example, what are the main changes in the general configuration of civil society over time? Comparing the pretransition and posttransition periods, what are similarities and differences? How does the pro-democracy alliance change over time, in terms of its composition, power, and character? How do structural factors, such as economic development or culture, affect the configuration of civil society? In the interactions category, how do state–civil society and political society–civil society relations change over time? How do civil society groups redefine and reformulate their relations with the state and political society over time, particularly in the aftermath of the democratic transition? In the issues category, how and why do the issues raised by civil society groups change over time? How and why do the strategies, tactics, methods, and styles of civil society groups change over time, particularly before and after the democratic transition? Do civil society actors undergo a process of "political learning"? If so, how does political learning affect the strategies and behaviors of civil society groups?

Summary and Conclusions

In this chapter, I dealt with some of the theoretical and conceptual issues related to my analysis of Korean democratization in this book. I first reviewed the intellectual-historical context in which the concept of civil society emerged as a major variable in the study of democratic transition and consolidation. I introduced the civil society paradigm and highlighted the thesis on the positive contribution of civil society to democratic transition and consolidation. The purpose of my book is to confirm and develop this thesis using the case of Korea.

Next, I presented my definition of democracy focused on procedural minimum or institutional requirements. Also, I differentiated and defined the three main stages of democratization: authoritarian breakdown, democratic transition, and democratic consolidation. According to the recent literature on civil society and democratization, I then distinguished three dimensions of civil society—organizational, relational, and normative—and summarized defining characteristics of civil society in each dimension. The characteristics include self-organization, publicness, autonomy, pluralism, and self-governance.

Last, I introduced the case of Korea. I selected three democratic junctures in the history of Korea since 1948 and described their dissimilar paths. Then I stated my thesis and developed a list of analytical questions in terms of actors, interactions, and issues. In the following chapter, on the basis of the theoretical and conceptual issues discussed in this chapter, I turn to the Korean case and analyze the role of civil society in Korea's first democratic juncture between 1956 and 1961.

Civil Society in the First Democratic Juncture, 1956–1961

Now, the mortal agony of the dictatorship is stifling and threatening the freedom and life of our entire people. . . . If we do not purify this dirty history containing extreme vice and immorality, we will be eternally condemned to generations of curse. . . . Today, we should raise a torch of rebellion to achieve the true ideal of democracy.

KOREA UNIVERSITY STUDENTS, 1960

The history of democracy is a history of struggles for liberty, which demonstrates that any form of dictatorship is merely a brittle "paper tiger" in front of the masses. . . . The basis of modern democracy is liberty. . . . We take great pride in striking the bell of liberty in the midst of dark silence.

SEOUL NATIONAL UNIVERSITY STUDENTS, 1960

I N this chapter, I investigate how civil society affected democratization in the first democratic juncture of Korea from 1956 to 1961. This period, after an evanescent democratic respite, was followed by a military coup and ultimately by an authoritarian regression. During this period, however, groups in Korean civil society—particularly student organizations—played crucial roles in bringing down the authoritarian regime of Syngman Rhee and in pressuring the succeeding governments to pursue democratic reforms. In section 1, I explain how the internal constitution of Korean civil society was historically shaped and changed up to 1956, focusing on some important precolonial and colonial legacies as well as postcolonial developments. In section 2, I analyze the role of civil society in the process of the authoritarian breakdown leading to Syngman Rhee's resignation and exile in 1960. In section 3, I examine how civil society groups affected the politics of democratic transition during the Hŏ Chŏng interim government and the Chang Myŏn regime. In section 4, I review Korean civil society during this period according to my analytical framework.

Configuration of Korean Civil Society, 1945–1956

Legacy of Japanese Colonialism

One of the most important and consequential historical legacies of Japanese colonial rule in Korea from 1910 to 1945 was the emergence and development of a pattern of "conflictual engagement" between the repressive state and the resistant civil society.[1] Above all, Japanese imperialism installed a powerful colonial state in the Korean peninsula. The colonial state, far stronger than the traditional monarchy in precolonial Korea and centered on the governor-generalship, was granted unlimited power over legislative, judicial, administrative, and military affairs.[2] The colonial state, responsive only to the orders and directions from the Japanese metropole, stood above and presided over the indigenous society and population of Korea.

On the other hand, Japanese imperialism also created a highly resistant and militant civil society. The onslaught of Japanese capital drastically altered the class composition of Korea. Domestic capitalists and landlords were considerably weakened and marginalized. In contrast, the number and power of labor and peasant classes substantially increased.[3] In 1924, despite harsh state suppression, strengthened labor and peasant classes succeeded in organizing the Korea Federation of Workers and Peasants (*Chosŏn nonong ch'ong tongmaeng*), which later evolved into the Korea Federation of Workers and the Korea Federation of Peasants, respectively. Through these organizations, Korean workers and peasants waged violent struggles against Japanese capitalists and imperialism throughout the colonial period. It was these outlawed and underground revolutionary unions of laborers and peasants that came to symbolize the Korean people's untiring battle against Japanese colonialism.[4] Many Korean students who had been influenced by socialism during their study in Japan also joined and often led anti-Japanese organizations of laborers and peasants. However, owing to the extensive network of police and security forces, and the collaboration of some pro-Japanese groups of Koreans, the colonial state was to a large extent able to preempt, contain, and suppress the rebellious civil society during this period.

Civil Society after the Liberation

Although the violent anti-Japanese struggles by Koreans in and outside of Korea contributed in part to the liberation of Korea in 1945, the freedom was chiefly "given" externally by the United States and the Allied Forces. External factors—particularly the beginning and development of the Cold War—not only determined the independence of Korea, but also the political unfoldings in the postindependence period. Following Japan's surrender, the Japanese colonial state in Korea rapidly unraveled. Initially, Japanese authorities transferred its power to Yŏ Un Hyŏng, a centrist with closer ties to leftists. Yŏ organized the Preparatory Committee for Establishing a New State (*Kŏnjun*) to replace the Japanese state apparatus. Within two weeks, the Preparatory Committee established 145 local offices. On September 8, 1945, it inaugurated the People's Republic of Korea (*In'gong*), and the existing local offices were converted to people's committees (*Inmin wiwŏnhoe*). These people's committees were quite effective in providing basic state services and supplies such as security, food, and order.[5]

In creating and developing various organizations to replace the existing colonial state structures, the Preparatory Committee for Establishing a New State recognized and accommodated the explosive expansion of civil society at the time, which was most pronounced in the unprecedented proliferation of labor and peasant organizations. After a long period of coerced hibernation under Japanese colonialism, during which unions were completely outlawed and harshly suppressed, laborers and peasants vigorously and openly formed their organizations. Workers demanded, for example, the right to manage their factories, job security, and pregnancy benefits. Peasants organized self-governing agricultural committees (*Nongjang chach'i wiwŏnhoe*) and protested against the arbitrary sales of their land. Moreover, numerous social organizations representing youth, students, women, cultural activities, and religious sects were also created.[6]

Communists played a particularly instrumental role in the formation and multiplication of these labor, peasant, and other social organizations. Korean communists, who had led a number of illegal and underground struggles against Japanese imperialism in and out of prison during the colonial period, officially inaugurated the Korean Communist Party (*Chosŏn kongsandang*) on September 11, 1945. Responding to and capitalizing on the spontaneous grassroots activism of laborers and peasants, the Korean Communist Party played crucial roles in organizing the National Council of Labor Unions (*Chŏnp'yŏng*) and the National Federation of Peasant Unions (*Chŏnnong*) on November 5 and December 8, 1945, respectively. The National Council of Labor Unions consisted of professional movement activists released from prison immediately after the independence. It started with 15 industrial unions and 180,000 members. Within a couple of months, it grew to an organization with 223 local offices, 1,757 local unions, and 550,000 members. The National Federation of Peasant Unions started with 556 representatives from local peasant unions.[7] In addition, the Korean Communist Party took the initiative in organizing the Korean Democratic Youth Federation (*Minch'ŏng*), the National Women's Union (*Puch'ong*), the Communist Youth Federation (*Kongch'ŏng*), the Writers Alliance, and the Scientists Alliance. As of February 15, 1946, the number of diverse social organizations reached thirty-five.[8]

Although communists played crucial roles in organizing them, these civil society groups were not entirely under the influence and control of communists. Civil society groups in this period were characterized by their high degree of functionality and autonomy. What may be called "associational explosion" was already in place, and the communists only took advantage of the existing and ever-increasing popular demand for organizations to reflect and represent the people's interests and aspirations. Partly in response to these " procommunist" organizations, rightist elements in civil society, which in most of the cases had been also pro-Japanese during the colonial period, organized their own groups, such as the Korean Patriotic Women's Association (*Han'guk aeguk puinhoe*), the Korean Youth Association (*Taehan ch'ŏngnyŏndan*), and the Women's Alliance for Independence (*Kŏn'guk punyŏ tongmaeng*). As a result, Korea witnessed two sharply contrasting trends—aggressive proliferation and expansion of bottom-up "leftist" organizations on the one hand, and reactive but expeditious construction of top-down rightist organizations on the other. Overall, however, immediately after the national independence in August 1945 Korean civil society was dominated by the former trend.

United States Army Military Government in Korea and Its Legacy

The arrival of the United States Army Military Government in Korea (US-AMGIK, *Migunjŏng*) in September 1945, however, terminated the dominance of the bottom-up organizations and dramatically changed the whole political landscape in Korea. Appalled by the close connection between diverse civil society groups and communists in Korea, the USAMGIK decided to stem the explosion of civil society. The newly created groups in civil society were systematically suppressed and depoliticized. On October 10, the USAMGIK denied the status of the People's Republic of Korea altogether, saying that the so-called People's Republic did not have any authority, power, or existence. Afterwards, the USAMGIK promulgated several laws to prohibit labor and peasant movements. Also, it forcibly dismantled grassroots organizations in both the cities and the countryside. Groups in civil society, led by the National Council of Labor Unions and the National Federation of Peasant Unions, responded to the oppressive policies of the USAMGIK with violent strikes and demonstrations. For example, there were a series of peasant rebellions and labor strikes across the country between August and October 1946.[9] Despite these protests,

TABLE 3.1
Policies of the USAMGIK toward Civil Society and Political Society, 1945–1947

Date	Policy
October 10, 1945	USAMGIK releases a statement denying the status of the People's Republic of Korea
December 27, 1945	USAMGIK announces a document entitled "Regarding the Organization of the National Police"
January 15, 1946	USAMGIK orders dispersal of private military groups (including those of the People's Republic of Korea), and instead installs its own security forces
February 23, 1946	Political parties—leftist parties in particular—are required to register with USAMGIK
March 29, 1946	Expansion of state bureaucracy
April 23, 1946	Closing of leftist newspapers like *Inminbo* (People's News), *Chayu sinmun* (Freedom Paper), *Hyŏndae ilbo* (Contemporary Daily)
May 18, 1946	Suspension of *Haebang ilbo* (Liberation Daily)
September 1946	Arrests of notable leftist leaders such as Pak Hŏn Yŏng, Yi Chu Ha, and Yi Kang Kuk
August 11–14, 1947	Closing of the National Council of Labor Unions' central committee office; arrest of 1,000 leftists

Source: Kwang Sik Kim, "8–15 chikhu han'guk sahoewa migunjŏngŭi sŏnggyŏk," 56.

however, the USAMGIK continued its Cold War policies, disbanding leftist parties, closing and suspending leftist newspapers, and arresting and imprisoning leftist leaders. Table 3.1 summarizes the systematic efforts of the USAMGIK to install pro-American state structures and arrest the expansion of "procommunist" civil society groups. The USAMGIK also encouraged and sponsored formerly pro-Japanese and rightist elements in Korean society to organize a variety of social organizations. Rightists rallied around the flag of anticommunism and anti-Sovietism raised by the USAMGIK.[10]

When the Republic of Korea (South Korea) was established in 1948, therefore, most of the civil society groups that had emerged immediately following the liberation in 1945 were destroyed by the USAMGIK and pro-American political forces. Those groups were either completely disbanded or forced to go underground; some even defected to North Korea. In this respect, the two interrelated ideological preferences of the USAMGIK—anticommunism and pro-Americanism—left an enduring, if not indelible, birthmark on the subsequent unfoldings of Korean politics. Later, the theme of anti-communism was frequently exploited and appropriated by different Korean governments to suppress the opposition and civil society groups. The inauguration of a pro-American regime in Korea also meant that the regime, however flimsy or hypocritical, needed to maintain the facade, if not the substance, of liberal democracy based on the "American model." Major political crises and resistance from civil society always centered around the practice and content of liberal democracy. In all three democratic junctures in Korea, authoritarian crises began either when the regime downright disregarded and violated the basic rules of liberal democracy or when the regime's attempt to affect minimally the appearance of liberal democracy produced unintended consequences. In this respect, pro-Americanism served as a double-edged sword for the subsequent Korean governments: while it was the ideological basis for anticommunism that was frequently used to muffle political dissidence, American democracy was also a political model that ideal Korean governments were pressured to emulate.

Civil Society in the 1950s

During the tenure of Syngman Rhee, the despotic founder of Korea who ruled the country from 1948 to 1960, Korean civil society was characterized by relative quiescence. Syngman Rhee's regime employed a dual strategy toward civil society: it actively sponsored the conservative, anticommunist, and rightist groups while severely suppressing the "radical," "procommunist," and "leftist" groups. This strategy was in large measure a continuation of the USAMGIK's policies. The progovernment groups included anticommunist and ultrarightist organizations, state-corporatist labor and peasant unions, and ad-hoc proregime campaigns and movements. The regime controlled and mobilized these groups to win elections, alter the constitution, maintain social order, and suppress political opponents.

Most of all, the ruling Liberal Party (LP, *Chayudang*), established in 1951 for Rhee's reelection, was principally based on the organization and membership of five progovernment groups: the Korea People's Association (*Taehan kungminhoe*), the Korea Youth Organization (*Taehan ch'ŏngnyŏndan*), the Federation of Korean Trade Unions (FKTU, *Taehan nodong chohap ch'ong yŏnmaeng*), the Federation of Farmers' Unions (*Nongmin chohap ch'ong yŏnmaeng*), and the Korea Women's Association (*Taehan puinhoe*).[11] These groups were highly dependent on and supportive of the Rhee regime. From the very beginning, Syngman Rhee effectively used these groups to consolidate and to maintain his authoritarian regime. In 1951, Syngman Rhee, seeing no possibility of being reelected (indirectly) by the opposition Korea Democratic Party (*Hanmindang*) in the National Assembly, proposed a constitutional revision to allow direct presidential elections. But this proposal was rejected by the National Assembly. In response, in 1951 and 1952, Rhee mobilized various state-corporatist organizations to initiate a massive popular campaign for "recalling those legislators who betrayed people's wishes by opposing Rhee's proposal." Eventually, after the arrests of many opposition politicians on charges of procommunist activities and the imposition of martial law in the wartime capital Pusan, on July 4, 1952, the National Assembly passed the proposal for direct presidential elections.

Although there were a few labor disputes in the cities of Pusan (1952) and Taegu (1956), the labor class as a whole was under the tight control of the FKTU, which functioned as a reliable arm of the Rhee regime. Throughout the Rhee regime, the FKTU waged a number of progovernment demonstrations and frequently threatened to initiate pro-Rhee strikes. For instance, in 1956, when Syngman Rhee pretended to harbor no intention to seek a third term, the FKTU decided to have a general strike in case Rhee would not run for reelection, staging a massive street protest parade.[12] Likewise, peasants were under the constant supervision of the Federation of Farmers' Unions.[13]

Meanwhile, as noted above, those groups in civil society that could have posed fundamental challenges to the authority and legitimacy of the Rhee regime had already been decimated by the USAMGIK prior to the birth of the Republic of Korea. The USAMGIK, against the backdrop of the rapidly unfolding Cold War conflict between the United States and the Soviet Union, vigorously sponsored pro-American rightist groups and systematically suppressed radical social organizations. A relatively small number of radical and centrist groups in Korean civil society and political society, having managed to survive the USAMGIK period, had to face another series of intensive anticommunist offensives by the Rhee regime. Rhee's favorite weapon was the National Security Law (NSL, *Kukka poanbŏp*), passed by the National Assembly in 1948 after an allegedly communist-led sedition in Yŏsu and Sunch'ŏn. The NSL defined sedition in such a broad and vague way that the Rhee government could use the law to suppress "virtually any kind of opposition."[14]

The Korean War from 1950 to 1953 dealt a final blow to the remnants of progressive groups in Korean civil society. The war, initiated by the communist North, significantly bolstered Rhee's anticommunist position. In the second National Assembly elections held immediately before the Korean War, a number of progressive parties—for example, the Socialist Party (*Sahoedang*) and the National Independence League Party (*Minjok chaju yŏnmaeng*)—fared quite well, and numerous radical and centrist politicians were elected. However, in the third National Assembly elections held after the war in 1954, most candidates converged on the themes of anticommunism and liberal democracy, and communism began to be regarded as taboo in Korea's political discourse.[15] Anticommunism was firmly established as a national ideology, and the authoritarian regime's systematic suppression of the antigovernment groups in civil society was in large measure justified and tolerated in the name of national security and political stability.

Even students, who would later spearhead antigovernment movements, remained relatively silent during the 1950s. University students were regimented by the government into the Student Defense Corps (*Hakto hoguktan*) and were tightly controlled. Several government-sponsored student demonstrations even occurred as students were mobilized on various occasions by the government to show their support for government policies.[16]

In summary, Korean civil society from 1948 to 1956 remained relatively quiescent. Owing to the policies of the USAMGIK and, later, of the Syngman Rhee regime, radical elements were removed and repressed, and civil society was depoliticized. All major segments of civil society—laborers, peasants, and students—were incorporated and controlled by the Rhee government and the ruling LP.

Civil Society and the Politics of Authoritarian Breakdown

The 1956 Presidential Election

Toward the late 1950s the relative quiescence of Korean civil society—or the absence of any noticeable antigovernment groups—gradually began to change. The authoritarian crisis that ultimately resulted in the demise of the Rhee regime in April 1960 started with the 1956 presidential election.

In this election, Syngman Rhee, despite his victory, was surprised to discover that his popularity as the "father" of the Republic of Korea had been substantially eroded. In the election, the opposition candidate, Sin Ik Hǔi, posed a formidable threat to Rhee. Sin's campaign rally in Seoul before the elections attracted between 100,000 and 200,000 people, the largest gathering of voters in Korean history up to that point. Unfortunately, however, Sin died of a heart attack one week before the elections. But, despite Sin's sudden death, Rhee obtained only 56 percent of the vote, a significant decline from the 74.6 percentage Rhee had received four years earlier. Particularly, in Seoul, the capital city of the country, the invalid votes (either blank or for Sin; 40.4 percent) were more than the votes Syngman Rhee garnered (29.2 percent).[17] The huge number of invalids evidently indicated voters' sympathy with and support for the deceased opposition candidate, Sin. That same year, the vice-presidency went to the opposition candidate, Chang Myŏn, who defeated the ruling party candidate, Yi Ki Pung.

As the election results in Seoul illustrated, the decrease in the electoral popularity of the ruling LP was most conspicuous in cities. The opposition fared better than the ruling party not only in Seoul but also in Taegu and other major cities of the country. Rural areas became the support base for the ruling party, whereas urban sections became a bastion for the opposition. This phenomenon—the ruling party in the countryside and the opposition in cities (*Yŏch'on yado*)—became one of the enduring characteristics of the voting behavior of Koreans.[18] In the 1958 National Assembly elections, the opposition Democratic Party won in fourteen out of sixteen electoral districts in Seoul, whereas the LP won only one district.[19]

Why did the voters, especially urbanites, gradually turn their back on the Rhee regime? During the early 1950s, the regime tried to abide by the principles and procedures of liberal democracy (at least in appearance). As I discussed earlier, the Rhee regime revised the constitution to introduce a direct presidential election system to facilitate Rhee's reelection in 1952. But at the time, the regime could justify its actions in the name of liberal democracy by arguing that the "general will" of the entire people dictated the implementation of the direct presidential election system. However, in 1954, the authoritarian regime went one step further. The Rhee regime, using almost nonsensical logic, amended the constitution to abolish the term limit for Syngman Rhee. Initially, the ruling LP's proposal for a constitutional revision was defeated in the National Assembly by a vote of 135 out of 203 (136 being the two-thirds needed). However, when the National Assembly reconvened, the LP declared that the constitutional amendment had passed, 135 being counted as the necessary two-thirds by rounding to the nearest decimal place. This happening in the National Assembly caused considerable political cynicism amongst Korean citizens. Voters, especially urbanites with higher education levels, keener political consciousness, and greater exposure to information, grew increasingly tired of Rhee's attempts at extending, if not actually perpetuating, his tenure.[20]

The Rhee Regime's Anticommunist Campaigns

Seriously threatened by its ever-decreasing electoral popularity, particularly in the cities, the authoritarian regime resorted to another anticommunist offensive. First, in December 1958, the ruling LP hastily passed a new and strengthened NSL while three hundred military police incarcerated the opposition legislators in the basement of the National Assembly Hall. The ruling LP allegedly intended for this new NSL to augment the ability to investigate procommunist activities, but their real intention was to suppress the opposition party and control the antigovernment press, thus preparing for the next presidential and vice-presidential elections.[21] Then, in May 1959, the government ordered the shutdown of one of the major newspapers in Korea at the time, *Kyŏnghyang Daily*. The regime argued that the shutdown was for national security and for a "more desirable" development of journalism. But the government's real intention was to suppress the *Kyŏnghyang Daily* because the newspaper had been very critical of the authoritarian regime throughout the 1950s. Finally, in July 1959 the regime executed Cho Pong Am, the head of the Progressive Party (Chinbodang), on various charges of espionage and for what the regime deemed as "procommunist" activities. Previously, Cho had run a very close race with Syngman Rhee in the 1950 presidential election. Additionally in 1956, Cho surprised the LP by garnering more than 30 percent of the total vote and winning a majority in major cities including Taegu, Ch'ŏngju, Mokp'o, Chinju, and Chŏngŏp in the presidential election. The Rhee regime charged that Cho and his progressive party had colluded with North Korea and therefore executed Cho eight months before the 1960 presidential election.

Emergence of Antigovernment Forces

In 1960, however, anticommunist measures by the Rhee regime, which had been relatively powerful in the early 1950s immediately after the Korean War, proved no longer effective. To most Koreans, anticommunist propaganda sounded increasingly hollow. Although the regime repeatedly stressed that the goal of the NSL was to defend the country against the North Korean threat, it became more and more evident that the goal was rather to defend and protect the authoritarian regime against the challenges from political opponents and antigovernment civil society groups *within* South Korea. The misuse and abuse of the NSL by the Rhee regime thus began to enrage many Koreans.

Particularly, the educated urban elite in Seoul began to lose patience with the existing political system. University students started to criticize the hypocrisy and to challenge the legitimacy of the authoritarian regime. Numbering 100,000 in 1960, college and university students were the only elements in civil society extensively exposed to and influenced by Western political ideas such as liberty, equality, human rights, and democracy. To many students, what the Rhee regime had perpetrated throughout the 1950s—arbitrary and frequent revisions of the constitution to extend Rhee's tenure, the passage and misuse of the repressive NSL, and the persecution and execution of political opponents—was too far from the ideals of liberal democracy, such as constitutionalism, tolerance of ideological diversity, and fair political competition, they were taught at school. Frustrated and angered by the authoritarian regime's repeated variances from the principles of liberal democracy, students started to identify themselves as guardians or vanguards of democracy.[22] They organized various antigovernment groups, searching for ways to restore liberal democracy in Korea.

Moreover, on the labor front, a movement against the existing state-corporatist FKTU was launched in earnest. A second national peak organization of trade unions, the Korea Trade Union Council (KTUC, *Chŏn'guk nodong chohap hyŏbŭihoe*), was created in August 1959. Denouncing the corruption, lack of autonomy from the state, and dictatorship of the existing FKTU, this new organization proclaimed it would lead a new labor movement that would be genuinely free and democratic in nature, thereby contributing to the democratization of Korea.[23] To the embarrassment of the FKTU and its sponsor, the Rhee regime, numerous high officials and member unions of the FKTU subsequently defected to the KTUC, and the competition and confrontation between the FKTU and the KTUC intensified. For instance, within the period of only one month (May 1960), the KTUC attracted 160,000 laborers to its ranks. The Rhee government was in a special political quandary in its relations with the KTUC because most of the activists who formed the KTUC were anti-communists who had contributed to the annihilation of leftist labor unions under the National Council of Labor Unions immediately after the liberation in 1945. KTUC leaders had been an important part of the FKTU and were still, in general, supportive of Syngman Rhee. Therefore, the government could neither attack nor suppress them as procommunists.[24]

The Regime's Response—Election Rigging

Faced with the emergence and expansion of student groups and new labor unions on the one hand and steadily decreasing electoral popularity on the other, the Rhee regime resorted to massive election rigging in March 1960 to preserve its power. At a daily meeting with police chiefs, city mayors, and province governors, the Minister of the Interior at the time advised: "Using whatever illegal emergency measures, we should make sure to get Syngman Rhee elected. Historically, have you ever heard of a lawsuit in connection with a presidential election? Winning the elections is vital and [its] legality is only secondary."[25] The Ministry of Finance and the Bank of Industry illegally generated political funds for Rhee's reelection, using the money to buy votes and fund the election campaign.[26]

Also, unsurprisingly, state-corporatist groups were widely mobilized and deeply involved in the rigged elections. The FKTU created a committee for re-electing Rhee in preparation for the election and actively supported the extension of the authoritarian regime.[27] In addition, the Korean Anticommunist Youth Association (Taehan pan'gong ch'ŏngnyŏndan), which was originally established in August 1951 and had strongly demanded a death sentence for Cho Pong Am, contributed to the election rigging by organizing special "election squads" that pressured and threatened voters to vote for Rhee.[28]

To protest the massive and systematic election rigging, students launched violent demonstrations. In Masan, citizens and opposition party politicians, shocked by the massive election rigging, declared on March 15, 1960, that they would pull out from the elections. That same evening, about 10,000 students marched to Masan city hall, calling for a new, fair election. The police shot at the crowd, resulting in dozens of casualties and injuries.[29] The Rhee government, to nobody's surprise, characterized the antigovernment demonstrations as leftist uprisings instigated by underground communist organizations and announced that they had already launched an investigation into the communists' involvement in the demonstrations. However, such an anticommunist offensive by the government only proved more and more ineffective. Despite the government's announcement, a series of sympathy student demonstrations spread in major cities, including Taejŏn, Ch'ungju, Suwŏn, Osan, and P'ohang, supported by journalists, lawyers, and academics.

The April Uprising and the Demise of the Authoritarian Regime

The antiregime protests rapidly spread across the country, particularly after the body of Kim Chu Yŏl, with fragments of a tear-gas bomb in his eyes, was recovered from the seashore of Masan city. Kim was a high school student who had participated in the antigovernment demonstrations on March 15. Apparently, he had been fatally struck by a tear-gas canister, and his body had been dumped into the bay by the police. The discovery of Kim's corpse immediately prompted the citizens of Masan to pour into the streets, providing the spark that ignited the rest of the country. Antigovernment protests by students, sympathetic professors, and ordinary citizens began to spread all over Korea. Kim's death disclosed the violence of the Rhee regime and elevated the goal of antigovernment demonstrations from criticism of the election rigging to the overthrow of the illegal government.

The Rhee regime, still believing in the efficacy of previously powerful anticommunism, claimed that communists had masterminded the student activity. Simultaneously, the regime also broadly mobilized the police, state-corporatist groups, and even gangsters to buttress their anticommunist offensive and to offset the antigovernment protests by student groups. On April 18, 1960, the Rhee regime encouraged the ultrarightist Korean Anticommunist Youth Association to lynch student demonstrators from Korea University, resulting in dozens of injuries. After this attack, students from Seoul National University, Yonsei University, Konkuk University, Chungang University, Kyunghee University, Dongguk University, and Sungkyunkwan University, who had prepared a massive antigovernment demonstration, set April 19 as their action day. On this day ("Bloody Tuesday"), some 30,000 university and high school students, the harsh suppression by the authoritarian regime and the collaboration of the corporatist groups notwithstanding, marched toward the presidential mansion in Seoul, shouting, "Banish the enemies of the state! What is really enemy-benefiting: demonstrators or despotism? Re-hold March 15 elections!" The police fired upon the peaceful and unarmed student demonstrators, killing 21 and injuring 172 people.[30] The students in Seoul then began to riot and were joined by other outraged students and ordinary citizens in major cities. By the end of the day, around 130 students were killed and another 1,000 were wounded in Seoul alone. The antiregime street demonstrations became so extensive and uncontrollable that the government had to declare martial law in the major cities of the country.[31]

On April 21, 1960, Syngman Rhee attempted to end the protests by making all cabinet members and LP officers resign. Furthermore, on April 24 Rhee announced that he would resign from the presidency of the ruling LP. But these cosmetic measures did not satisfy demonstrators. Rather, on April 25, three hundred university professors conducted demonstrations in front of the National Assembly Hall in protest of the government, calling for the resignation of Rhee himself. Following the professors' protests, student demonstrations revived, eventually winning over the military: the Martial Law Command under General Song Yo Ch'an refused to fire on the demonstrators and turned its back on the authoritarian regime. Meanwhile, the United States was also pushing Rhee to resign. On April 19, 1960, the U.S. Secretary of State delivered to Korea's ambassador a number of possible solutions to the April Uprising, including the "holding of re-elections according to democratic means and guarantee of the freedoms of expression and assembly." Also, on April 20 the State Department released a statement calling for democratization of Korea.[32] Syngman Rhee, with neither the military nor the United States on his side, finally had no choice but to step down on April 26. He went into exile in Hawaii in May, marking the end of his authoritarian regime.

Civil Society and the Politics of Democratic Transition

Civil Society under the Hŏ Interim Government

Primarily owing to a series of student demonstrations, assisted by the military's betrayal and the external pressure from the United States, the Syngman Rhee regime fell. The collapse of the Rhee regime, however, did not lead to a smooth democratic transition. Despite the great popular demand for democratic reforms, the interim government of Hŏ Chŏng (April–August 1960) carried out a set of antidemocratic measures. First, the Hŏ government arrested numerous members of student groups, such as the April Revolution Youth-Student Alliance (*4-19 ch'ŏngnyŏn haksaeng tongmaeng*) and the Federation for the Promotion of National Reunification (*Minjok t'ongil ch'okchin yŏnmaeng*). Then it attempted to prevent or slow down the decorporatization process of the FKTU by strengthening governmental labor committees, intervening in labor disputes, and repressing any new labor movement. Next, the Hŏ government delayed the punishment of corrupt bureaucrats, politicians, police officers, and military officers in the Rhee regime.[33] Alarmed by the Hŏ government's reactionary moves, student groups and other antigovernment organizations in civil society that had been crucial in overthrowing the authoritarian regime of Syngman Rhee continued their pro-democracy struggle. On June 11, 1960, for example, the April Revolution Youth-Student Alliance, the Federation for the Promotion of National Reunification, and the Association of the Wounded in the April Revolution (*4 wŏl hyŏngmyŏng pusang tongjihoe*) held a mass rally in Seoul denouncing the counterrevolutionary measures of the Hŏ government.[34]

Civil Society during the Chang Regime

In July 1960 a general election was held, and the new government of Prime Minister Chang Myŏn was launched in August. Koreans believed that the new government, different from Hŏ Chŏng's interim government, could and would implement democratic reforms. Rather than meeting the popular request for democratization and making a clear break with the authoritarian past, however, the Chang regime (August 1960–May 1961) disappointed the Korean people once again by imposing antidemocratic measures. For example, arguing that a retroactive law to punish those associated with the previous government could be neither enacted nor applied, the Chang regime released most of the bureaucrats and politicians of the LP who were involved in the election rigging and the suppression of the April Uprising. In response, enraged citizens and students occupied the National Assembly Hall on October 10, 1960. The Chang government subsequently agreed to pass a special law to punish those who committed unlawful acts in connection with the March 15 elections and who committed grave antidemocratic acts.

Also, a so-called purge of the police and the military by the Chang regime was incomplete and inappropriate. Those who were involved in the election rigging and the suppression of the uprising were simply dismissed without any prosecution or punishment. In the military, young officers, rather than the older, more corrupt generals, were removed. Most of the dismissed young officers had been supportive of internal reforms of the military, and therefore they were outraged by the inappropriate purging, which ultimately contributed to the military coup of May 16, 1961.[35]

Immediately after the collapse of the Rhee regime, some of the student movement groups changed their goals and strategies. In the latter half of 1960, some student groups, under the slogan of "students back to their campus," concentrated on nonpolitical issues like the "new life movement" or "intracampus democratization." Consequently, the reform tasks were delegated to the new government of Chang Myŏn. However, in early 1961, dissatisfied with the scope and the pace of the democratic reforms by the Chang regime, student groups and youth organizations returned to political issues and continued their pro-democracy struggle, forming a coalition with progressive politicians. A number of progressive parties emerged before the 1960 general elections. On May 13, 1960, the Socialist Mass Party (*Sahoe taejungdang*) was established, "based on peasants, laborers, working intelligentsia, businesspersons, and conscientious capitalists, in support of democratic socialism." Exactly two weeks later, the Federation of Progressive Comrades (*Hyŏksin tongji ch'ong yŏnmaeng*) was established, and on June 14, 1960, the Korea Socialist Party (*Han'guk sahoedang*) was created.[36] During the election period, students supported these progressive parties and helped their candidates. However, in the elections, these progressive parties failed miserably, only yielding five winners (6.6 percent of the total votes) in the lower house and three winners (3.3 percent of the total votes) in the upper house.[37] Despite the defeat, students maintained their coalition with progressive politicians and mobilized it in the pro-democracy campaign under the new government. Specifically, the Youth Alliance for Democracy and Nationalism (*Minju minjok ch'ŏngnyŏn tongmaeng*), the Youth Alliance for Reunification and Democracy (*T'ongil minju ch'ŏngnyŏn tongmaeng*), numerous university national reunification student leagues (*Minjok t'ongil yŏnmaeng*) and fronts (*Minjok t'ongil chŏnsŏn*), and progressive labor unions like the Teachers' Labor Union (*Kyowŏn nojo*) formed a coalition with progressive parties and spearheaded a series of intense antigovernment struggles.

Pro-Democracy Movement by Students and Progressive Politicians

Under the Chang Myŏn regime, student groups, radical trade unions, and progressive politicians concentrated on three key issue areas. The first was Korean–United States relations. Seventeen political parties and civil society groups organized a joint committee opposing the Korean–United States economic agreement. Participating groups included student organizations from major universities and various social groups.[38] The Korean–United States economic agreement at issue, if passed, would allow United States authorities unlimited access to plans and records regarding the use of United States aid to Korea, and also permit the United States government to halt the aid without any prior notice. Student groups and progressive parties believed that this was a serious infringement on the sovereignty of Korea and were thus intensely opposed to the agreement. To many civil society groups in Korea, a democratic government should be more responsive to its populace, not to a foreign country. However, in response to the vigorous antigovernment activism by civil society groups and progressive political parties, the "democratic" Chang regime, copying Syngman Rhee's tactics, widely mobilized the state-corporatist groups to stage demonstrations supporting the agreement and eventually succeeded in ratifying it.

The second key issue was the Chang government's attempt to pass two antidemocratic laws that would have seriously restricted democratic freedoms. The two proposed pieces of legislation were the "anticommunist special law (*Pan'gong imsi tŭkpyŏlbŏp*)" and the "demonstration regulation law (*Temo kyujebŏp*)." The anticommunist special law, together with the existing NSL, would have added more restrictions to the freedoms of expression and assembly. The National Committee for Fighting against the Antidemocratic Laws (*Chŏn'guk akpŏp pandae kongdong t'ujaeng wiwŏnhoe*), composed of numerous progressive parties, eleven youth groups, and sixteen student organizations, staged and spread massive protests across the country. On March 22, 1961, a huge crowd of demonstrators gathered in Seoul, continuing violent protests through the night. Confronted with the protest by civil society groups and progressive political parties, the Chang regime abandoned the two proposed laws.[39]

Third, student groups and progressive parties waged a vigorous reunification campaign. The idea of the "communist" threat posed by North Korea was misused and abused many times by the Rhee regime to muffle and suppress its opposition. Civil society groups began to believe that genuine democracy in Korea would be impossible to achieve without reconciliation between the two Koreas. On May 3, 1960, student groups from Seoul National University proposed a conference between North and South Korean students. Across the nation, a series of public gatherings followed, welcoming and supporting the proposal. Progressive parties such as the Socialist Mass Party and the Unification Socialist Party (*T'ongil sahoedang*) formed separate organizations solely

devoted to national reunification and closely cooperated with student movement groups such as the student leagues for national reunification at many
universities to promote the reunification movement. Most important, on February 25, 1961, the Central Council for Independent National Unification
(*Minjat'ong*) was established by four progressive parties (the Socialist Party, the
Socialist Mass Party, part of the Reform Party, and part of the Tonghak Party),
thirteen civil society groups (such as the Democratic Nationalist Youth Federation, the Professors' Council, press unions, and the Teachers' Labor Union),
and other regional groups.[40] Under the leadership of the Central Council for
Independent National Unification and other organizations, student groups
and progressive parties caustically criticized the conservative reunification
policies of the government and encouraged direct talks and contacts with
North Korea.[41]

The Labor Movement during the Chang Regime

Meanwhile, labor unions concentrated on deliberating, articulating, and ex-
pressing their sectoral interests, which were repressed during the preceding authoritarian regime of Syngman Rhee. An explosive increase in the number of
trade unions and labor disputes occurred under the Chang regime. Labor disputes in 1960 amounted to 227, more than double the number in 1959 (see
table 3.2). Particularly conspicuous were the formation and expansion of
white-collar unions such as teachers' unions, bank unions, and journalist
unions.[42]

Significantly, the FKTU, which had been consistently progovernment during the Rhee regime, apologized for their state-corporatist past and strived for
autonomy from the state. In the middle of the April Uprising, the FKTU had
announced that it would sever its relationship with the ruling LP. After the de-

TABLE 3.2
Trade Unions and Labor Disputes, 1956–1961

	1956	1957	1958	1959	1960	1961
Trade unions	578	572	634	558	914	960
Labor disputes	32	45	41	95	227	n/a

Sources: Nak Chung Kim, *Han'guk nodong undongsa*, 187, 189; Sŏnk Chun Kim, *Han'guk
sanŏnphwa kukkaron*, 333.

mise of the Rhee regime, the FKTU merged with rival KTUC and created the new Korea Federation of Labor Unions (*Han'guk nodong chohap ch'ong yŏnmaeng*) in November 1960, pledging to lead an autonomous and democratic labor movement in Korea.

Many state-corporatist groups, which had been silent temporarily owing to the dramatic expansion of student and youth groups during the April Uprising, began to reassert themselves. The Association of Anticommunist Groups (*Pan'gong tanch'e yŏnhaphoe*) and other rightist groups, encouraged and mobilized by the Chang Myŏn government, vehemently reproached the reunification movement and other pro-democracy struggles by students and progressive politicians.[43] In addition, seventy-eight business leaders hastily created the Korea Economic Council (*Han'guk kyŏngje hyŏbŭihoe*) in January 1961 to deal with and counteract the rapid growth of the labor movement.

The Breakdown of the Chang Regime

The tragedy of the Chang regime came in the decision of the "democratic" government, which was deeply indebted to the April Uprising for its existence, to not align itself with the pro-democracy groups in civil society to carry out democratic reforms.[44] Instead of responding to and accommodating the popular demand for democracy, the Chang government stalled and countered the pro-democracy movement by resurrecting and mobilizing old state-corporatist groups. Student groups, youth organizations, and progressive party politicians persistently requested a speedy transition to democracy. Most of all, they called strongly for a revolutionary break with the authoritarian past through the proper punishment of the former officials of the Rhee government. But the Chang regime did not accept and honor this popular request. Rather, it sabotaged the officials' punishment and instead solicited help from the state-corporatist and antidemocratic groups that had previously had close connections with old bureaucrats, politicians, and the military. These groups fiercely opposed the pro-democracy campaigns by the students and progressive politicians and attempted to maintain the status quo or, if possible, preferred to revert to the status quo ante.[45] Various rightist groups and organizations held huge nationwide gatherings, trenchantly condemning the "procommunist" activities by "leftist" elements in society. The Chang regime was neither able nor willing to resolve such ideological polarization. Rather, the democratic regime itself aggravated it. There was a constant fear among Korean people of a big showdown between the two opposing camps; this showdown finally materialized on April 2, 1961, when the two camps violently clashed in Taegu city, resulting in the injury or arrest of a large number of people.[46]

Student groups, youth organizations, and progressive politicians restrained themselves from waging massive antigovernment demonstrations after the Taegu incident. But it was already too late when they detected a clandestine design of the military to intervene to "terminate social turmoil" and "restore order and stability." A military coup occurred in May 1961 under Park Chung Hee and aborted the democratic transition in this first democratic juncture. Immediately after the coup, its leaders dissolved the national and local assemblies and prohibited activities of all political parties and social organizations. As a consequence, 15 political parties and 238 social groups were disbanded. At the same time, the military government created the Korea Central Intelligence Agency (KCIA, *Chungang chŏngbobu*), which would become a powerful organization to control and monitor civil society at large.

Analysis of the First Democratic Juncture

Actors

Japanese colonialism in Korea brought about both a strong, overdeveloped state and a contentious, rebellious civil society.[47] Immediately after Korea's liberation from Japan in 1945, various sectoral organizations and movement associations, many of whom were closely connected to and assisted by communists, proliferated in Korean civil society. The development of the Cold War and the installment of the USAMGIK ultimately defused such an associational explosion and rapidly depoliticized civil society in Korea.[48]

The Syngman Rhee regime inherited and basically reproduced the US-AMGIK's two-pronged policy toward social groups. While it suppressed and attempted to uproot the progressive, "leftist" elements in Korean civil society it also incorporated, sponsored, and mobilized state-corporatist, rightist organizations. Consequently, civil society in Korea throughout the 1950s remained rather quiescent. Strictly speaking, civil society was virtually nonexistent during this period: most elements in Korean civil society at the time were tightly controlled and monitored by the Rhee regime and therefore were not autonomous from the state. In this regard, the system of interest intermediation under the Rhee regime was much more than corporatism.[49] It was actually closer to a model called "monism," or "a system of interest representation in which the constituent units are organized into a fixed number of singular, ideologically selective, noncompetitive, functionally differentiated and hierarchically ordered categories, created, subsidized and licensed by a single party and granted a representational role within that party and vis-à-vis the state in exchange for observing certain controls on their selection of leaders, articulation of demands and mobilization of support."[50] Also, this period in Korea was similar in nature to the first "moment" of civil society in Africa in the late 1950s through the early 1960s in which "state domination and societal quiescence contravened the engagement of an autonomous societal realm."[51]

It was Korea's students who broke this quiescence of civil society. Student groups were the main elements that contributed to the collapse of Syngman Rhee's authoritarian regime in 1960. This is why the April Uprising in 1960 is also called April *Student* Revolution.[52] After the demise of the authoritarian rule, student groups, in close cooperation with progressive parties, continued their various movements for democracy and reunification. Why did students, who had been largely silent throughout the 1950s, emerge as the main antigovernment force in the first democratic juncture in Korea? There are several reasons for this occurrence. First, of all the elements of Korean civil society at the time, student groups were the most broadly exposed to the influence of theories and practices of liberal democracy from the West. They were simply better informed about what Western democracies were about and how they worked. Therefore, in the eyes of students, the repeated constitutional revisions made by the regime to extend Rhee's tenure and suppress the opposition did not appear by any means to be hallmarks of democracy. Their perceptions of a gap between Korean democratic reality and the ideal of Western democracy greatly frustrated and angered the students.

There were also economic reasons for the emergence of student groups as the main antigovernment force. From 1948 to 1960, the number of institutions of higher education had doubled, and student enrollments had increased by a factor of twelve. Meanwhile, economic development during the 1950s, particularly compared with what happened in the 1960s, was meager. As a result, about 60 percent of graduates were finding it difficult or impossible to obtain employment, and even those who did find work often ended up with jobs they considered unsatisfactory.[53] The gap between the growth of universities and university students and the expansion of the economy substantially aggravated student dissatisfaction and frustration with the Rhee regime.

In addition, underlying historical and cultural factors affected students' increased political activism. Korea had long been a Confucian society. In the Chosŏn Dynasty (1392–1910), Confucianism served as state ideology and religion. One of the most salient characteristics of the Confucian system in Korea was the respect accorded to scholars. Confucian scholars, who often entered the officialdom through state examinations, were highly regarded by the populace as a whole, and scholar-officials occupied the top rung of the Confucian social hierarchy in traditional Korea. Meanwhile, scholars had moral obligations to evaluate critically state policies and to remonstrate with the royal court and the public officials.[54] University students, the modern embodiment of Confucian scholars during the Chosŏn Dynasty, were thus a socially privileged and respected status group and consequently were morally expected to speak up against the dictatorship of Syngman Rhee.[55]

Because the main actors in civil society during this democratic juncture were students—a *status group* rather than a social class—there was no real substantive basis for the April "revolution."[56] Students failed to forge alliances with other civil society groups and as a result mass participation was conspicuously absent in the students' various campaigns during the Hŏ and Chang governments. In this regard, when the military coup happened in 1961, it was no surprise that students found no strong allies or extensive support in civil society to resist the authoritarian regression.

Interactions

The relationship between civil society and the state during the first democratic juncture was primarily confrontational and conflictual. During the first half of the 1950s, the state incorporated, monitored, and controlled virtually all social groups. However, beginning with the revolt of students and intellectuals in 1956, the pattern of incorporation rapidly shifted to the mode of conflictual engagement between civil society and the state. Throughout the authoritarian breakdown, the Syngman Rhee regime was viewed by civil society as illegal, immoral, incompetent, and therefore something to overthrow. Civil society entertained a rather dichotomous, and to some degree Manichean, view of the political configuration at the time: it perceived the conflict as one between an evil state and a good civil society.

What is notable during this democratic juncture is that such a hostile view of the state by civil society continued into the democratic transition. During the Hŏ interim government and Chang government, students and other civil society groups continued to harbor a profound suspicion about the state. They were appalled and disappointed by some of the reactionary and antidemocratic policies of these two governments and consequently highlighted the similarities between the Syngman Rhee regime and these two regimes. In particular, students and other groups in civil society were dismayed to witness that even the Chang regime, a putatively democratic one, widely and unabashedly mobilized state-corporatist groups to oppose and oppress civil society groups.

From the viewpoint of students, therefore, continuing the pro-democracy struggle against the state was a defensive—and therefore largely justifiable—move to protect and preserve the valuable fruits of the April Uprising. As a result, no other modes except for conflictual engagement could emerge. On the other hand, progovernment groups, which were not even part of civil society because they lacked autonomy from the state, were not just in a cooperative engagement with the state: they were basically part of the state in a state-corporatist political arrangement. This political configuration—namely the intense conflict between civil society on the one hand and the state and state-corporatist groups on the other—was to last for a long time through the later democratic junctures in Korea. The military capitalized on this confrontation between the two opposing sides to stage a military coup in 1961, resulting in the breakdown of the democratic regime.[57] The legacy of this political pattern of conflictual engagement between civil society and the state, as I will highlight in chapter 7, is among the factors affecting and constraining the consolidation of Korean democracy.

In terms of civil society-political society interactions, there was no notable cooperation in the process of authoritarian breakdown. The April Uprising was largely led by students. Opposition politicians did not play any significant role in the demise of the authoritarian regime. Following the collapse of the Rhee regime, however, and under the Hŏ interim government and the Chang regime, students actively cooperated and collaborated with politicians. In particular, student groups aligned with politicians from various progressive parties that had emerged after the authoritarian breakdown. Party politicians actively sought alignment with student groups in elections. But progressive parties during this democratic juncture failed to garner much popular support. Because of their own political marginality and precarious existence, their alignment with civil society was neither solid nor durable. Some joint organizations were supposed to unite and to coordinate the cooperation between civil society and political society,. but these organizations were ad hoc, temporary groups organized to draft and announce protest statements.

The lack of any prominent and significant alignment between civil society and political society during this democratic juncture was due in part to the lack of a viable, strong opposition in political society. The LP, which had been the ruling party during the Rhee regime and had been seriously discredited during the process of authoritarian breakdown, was the opposition. But the LP was obviously not an appealing partner for civil society groups in their continued struggle for democracy. Lack of a viable opposition in political society prompted student groups to collaborate with various progressive parties that were politically too marginal.

Issues

One issue civil society groups raised throughout the authoritarian breakdown and the democratic transition during this democratic juncture was idea of liberal democracy. The liberal democracy supported by students and intellectuals at the time was close to the procedural minimum of democracy discussed in chapter 2. However, some radical student groups idealized and supported socialism and most progressive parties supported different versions of social democracy. Overall, however, Western-type liberal democracy, centered around the procedural minimum or Dahl's institutional requirements, was the movement's main goal at the time. Radical and socialist versions of democracy failed to receive any serious attention from movement groups in civil society and the general public both. The issues raised and promoted by civil society groups during this juncture—free and fair elections, no arbitrary constitutional revisions, guarantee of civil liberties—are all basic, essential components of liberal democracy. Unlike what occurred during the third democratic juncture, which I will analyze in chapter 5, the concept of democracy entertained by civil society groups during the first democratic juncture did not involve any "substantive" issues such as socioeconomic equalities.

The other two prominent issues raised by civil society groups during this juncture—national reunification and self-assertive foreign relations (particularly with the United States)—were also closely linked to the issue and goal of liberal democracy. In fact, these two issues were supported and pursued because of their close connections to the establishment and consolidation of liberal democracy. The issue of national reunification was crucial because the Rhee regime had frequently justified its suppression of political opposition and restriction of civil liberties by pointing to the national division and the resulting communist military threat from North Korea. National division was a great misfortune for Korean people as a whole, but ironically it served as a magic wand, not only for the Syngman Rhee regime but also for later authoritarian regimes. By reciting the "special" security situation on the Korean peninsula owing to the national division and by repeatedly conjuring up the image of a formidable North Korea on the brink of launching another Korean War, the authoritarian regimes could desensitize Korean citizens in general to the widespread political repression and restrictions on civil liberties.[58] From the viewpoint of civil society groups, liberal democracy would continue to exist as a mirage as long as the nation was divided and the regime could appeal to the deep-seated sense of insecurity and fear in the minds of the Korean people. This was why civil society groups pursued the issue of national reunification simultaneously with the issue of liberal democracy.

The issue of self-assertive diplomacy was also deemed essential to the achievement of liberal democracy. A democracy, by definition, should be responsive and accountable more to its own domestic citizenry than to a foreign citizenry. According to the analysis of student groups during this democratic juncture, however, the Korean government, whether it was Rhee's authoritarian government or Chang's "democratic" government, consistently ignored the Korean people and instead tried to curry favor with the United States. In the opinion of civil society groups in Korea at the time this "humiliating diplomacy" was just another ugly side of political authoritarianism in Korea. In short, the three main issues raised by civil society groups during this democratic juncture—liberal democracy, national reunification, self-assertive foreign relations—were all closely intertwined and almost inseparable and continued to be pivotal through the second and the third democratic junctures.

In pursuing these issues, student groups and party politicians largely relied on popular demonstrations. These groups did not hesitate to resort to violence if necessary. Most civil society movement groups were not greatly concerned with the illegality of their methods. As far as the illegal and immoral issues are concerned, according to civil society groups the authoritarian government of Syngman Rhee and the subsequent "democratic" government of Chang Myŏn were greater transgressors, as they passed and reinforced numerous antidemocratic laws, arbitrarily amended the constitution for personal interests, and harshly suppressed political opposition. Furthermore, both the Rhee and Chang regimes mobilized various progovernment state-corporatist groups, composed of gangsters in some cases, to threaten, pacify, and lynch political dissidents. If the state, with all of its power and organization, resorted to unjustifiable violence, it was reasonable that civil society groups used violence to defend themselves. Injustice and immorality were more important concerns than illegality. Civil society groups perceived themselves to be far more just, legitimate, and moral than the state, which largely justified and exonerated to a certain extent the violence they exhibited through the movement.

Summary and Conclusions

In this chapter, I analyzed the role of civil society groups in the authoritarian breakdown and democratic transition in Korea between 1956 and 1961. I began by reviewing some of the historical factors affecting the internal configuration of Korean civil society prior to this period, tracing the origins of the harsh confrontation between a repressive state and resistant civil society to Japanese colonialism. I then showed how civil society groups were resurrected and explosively expanded immediately after the liberation and how they were later repressed and destroyed by the United States Army Military Government in Korea. I also explained how the Korean War and the state-corporatism of the Syngman Rhee regime produced the relative quiescence of Korean civil society during the 1950s.

Next, I examined the role of civil society groups in the authoritarian demise of the Rhee regime. I examined how the authoritarian regime's continued disregard for the basic rules of liberal democracy and its abuse of anticommunist sentiment to suppress the opposition enraged voters, particularly urbanites. I also explained how students were mobilized and how a series of massive student demonstrations finally led to the collapse of the authoritarian regime.

Third, I analyzed the role of civil society groups in the democratic transition under the Chang Myŏn regime. Student groups, aligned with progressive politicians, waged struggles against the reactionary and antidemocratic measures of the interim government of Hŏ Chŏng and the Chang regime. I argued that the inability and unwillingness of Chang's "democratic" regime to accommodate and honor the legitimate pro-democracy demands of civil society ultimately led to an authoritarian regression.

Finally, I provided an analysis of this democratic juncture in terms of actors, interactions, and issues. Students were prominent actors in civil society owing to several social, economic, and cultural reasons. Civil society–state interactions throughout the period remained consistently hostile and antagonistic, principally owing to the perceived similarities between the democratic regime and the preceding authoritarian regime. Civil society–political society interactions were collaborative but failed to produce any politically meaningful results, mainly because of the marginality of the political parties involved. Issues raised by civil society were an amalgam of liberal democracy, reunification, and self-assertive foreign relations because civil society groups believed that these three issues are organically interconnected. In the next chapter I examine the configuration of Korean civil society and the role of civil society groups in democratization during the second democratic juncture, from 1973 to 1980.

C H A P T E R **4**

Civil Society in the Second Democratic Juncture, 1973–1980

"Abide by the Labor Standard Laws!" "We are not machines!"
"Do not waste my life!"

CHŎN T'AE IL, 1970

The tree of democracy grows on blood. Listen, friends! Why do
you hesitate to dedicate your holy blood to make the green leaves
of democracy thrive?

KIM SANG CHIN, 1975

Responding to people's demand and partaking in the workers'
sufferings is to practice love, which is God's most important
order, to join Jesus' suffering of the cross, and to realize God's just
rule in this world.

KOREA NATIONAL CHRISTIAN CHURCH COUNCIL, 1979

I N this chapter, I shift to Korea's second attempt at democratization between 1973 and 1980. This democratic juncture began with a series of antigovernment demonstrations in the aftermath of the proclamation of a highly authoritarian political system named Yusin and ended with a multiphased coup in 1979 and 1980. In section 1, I examine the internal configuration of civil society in the 1960s. I particularly focus on some of the important changes in comparison with the first democratic juncture. In section 2, I analyze how civil society groups affected the authoritarian breakdown of the Park Chung Hee regime in 1979. In section 3, I examine the role of civil society groups in democratization until the transition was forcibly aborted by a military coup in May 1980. In section 4, I analyze this democratic juncture in terms of my analytical framework.

Configuration of Korean Civil Society, 1961–1973

Student Activism

The first democratic juncture of Korea (1956–1961) ended with a military coup in May 1961. The coup leaders, reneging on their initial promise that they would relinquish power to a civilian government in due course, created their own political party, the Democratic Republican Party (*Minju konghwadang*) in February 1963. One of the top coup leaders, Park Chung Hee, retired from the army, joined the Democratic Republican Party, and ran in the 1963 presidential election. He won the election and was sworn in as the fifth president of Korea in December 1963.

As seen in the preceding chapter, Korean civil society during the 1950s was in large part quiescent. But this was not the case in the 1960s. There were several significant incidents in which groups in civil society actively criticized and challenged the legitimacy and authority of the ruling regime. The military coup in 1961 did not completely terminate various pro-democracy forces that had emerged in the brief democratic intermission of 1960–1961.

There were a series of intense antigovernment demonstrations in the mid-1960s. Students, dissident intellectuals, and opposition politicians protested against Korean-Japanese normalization in 1965, criticizing the government for engaging in a "humiliating diplomacy" with the former colonizer. On June 3, 1964, students overwhelmed the police and almost took over major government offices. The government declared a state of emergency, closed universities, started press censorship, and arrested and imprisoned those involved in the incident.[1]

Then there was strong opposition to the government's decision to send Korean soldiers to the Vietnam War in August 1965. A series of student demonstrations broke out, protesting the regime's submissiveness in dealing with the United States. Although the issues raised in the antigovernment protests in 1964–1965 were primarily about international relations and not necessarily about domestic politics, the demonstrations were an extension of the previous pro-democracy movement because civil society groups criticized the heavy-handed ways in which the authoritarian regime of Park Chung Hee handled crucial foreign policy decisions. Civil society groups also opposed Park Chung Hee's attempt in 1969 to revise the constitution to enable him to be elected for the third time. Park had been reelected in the 1967 presidential election and, according to the Korean constitution at the time, was not allowed to run for a third term.

Lack of Mass Participation

Overall, however, these antigovernment protests by civil society groups in the 1960s failed to pose any systematic challenge to the authoritarian regime. All of these incidents were ephemeral and intermittent. The Park regime responded by enforcing martial law, garrison decrees, and closings of university campuses; these suppressive measures were to a great extent powerful enough to contain the social protest. Most of the antigovernment protests were led by students and a limited number of dissident intellectuals. Although there were several ad hoc nationwide organizations of student groups and other antigovernment groups, the movements were largely disorganized and did not draw large-scale support from other sectors of civil society. Throughout the 1960s the student movement remained "within the confines of urban intellectual life, with no affiliation to political parties or any other social groups."[2]

What, then, accounts for the fact that while student activism continued, other sectors of civil society did not lend their support to the protests against the Park regime? With respect to the continued activism of student movement, the explanation lies in the self-contradictory nature of the Park Chung Hee regime. Although the May 16 coup's engineers originally claimed that they staged the coup not to subvert the April Uprising but to support and succeed it, it became clear that the military regime and the subsequent pseudo-civilian government of Park Chung Hee in fact undermined and destroyed the democratic ideals of the April Uprising. From the students' perspective, then, the achievements of the April Uprising had been negated by the military coup, and therefore it seemed essential to continue their struggle for democracy. Through their protests against Korean-Japanese normalization and against the dispatch of Korean soldiers to the Vietnam War, student groups focused their energy on exposing the external dependence of the authoritarian regime on foreign powers.[3] At the same time, as they had done during the Syngman Rhee regime, students criticized and opposed the frequent and arbitrary changes of democratic rules by the authoritarian regime in their struggle against the constitutional revision in 1969.

Meanwhile, three factors impeded the massive support and participation of other sectors in the movement led by students and intellectuals. First, having seized power through a military coup in 1961, Park Chung Hee resolved to purchase political legitimacy through economic development. Under the leadership of the renovated Economic Planning Board (*Kyŏngje kihoegwŏn*), the Park regime designed and implemented an ambitious export-oriented industrialization strategy, which resulted in impressively high growth rates in the 1960s (table 4.1). Economic development, as anticipated, secured Park a considerable degree of electoral popularity and political legitimacy (table 4.2). Voters, impressed by Park's performance in economic development, elected him by a large margin in the presidential election of 1967. "Development first and democracy later" became firmly entrenched as a national motto.

Secondly, although the Park regime was authoritarian in nature, it kept its facade as a liberal democracy. The military government formally transferred political power to a "civilian" government led by Park Chung Hee, who was a general-turned-president. Elections were held regularly and—despite widespread corruption—relatively freely. Voters felt that they could influence, if not alter, the regime by participating in presidential and National Assembly elections. As long as the economy was on the rise and the minimal liberal democratic institutions were maintained, other sectors of civil society did not have much incentive to join the antigovernment demonstrations led by student groups and other dissident intellectuals.

Thirdly, the authoritarian regime of Park Chung Hee employed a set of institutional mechanisms to repress the expansion of antigovernment groups. Most of all, the powerful Korean Central Intelligence Agency (KCIA, *Chungang*

TABLE 4.1
GNP Growth Rates, 1962–1968

	1962	1963	1964	1965	1966	1967	1968
GNP Growth Rate (%)	3.5	9.1	8.3	7.4	13.4	8.9	13.3

Source: EPB, *Han'guk t'onggye yŏn'gam*, 100–101.

TABLE 4.2
Results of Presidential Elections, 1963 and 1967
(In percentage of votes cast)

	1963	1967
Park Chung Hee	42.61	51.40
Yun Po Sŏn	41.19	41.00

Sources: NEC, *Taehan min'guk sŏn'gŏsa*, 491; RGKP *Han'guk chŏngch'isa*, 349.

chŏngbobu) effectively forestalled and controlled the "unrest" by student groups or labor unions. Established in June 1961 with Kim Jong Pil as its head, the KCIA was granted powers that went far beyond those of the American CIA and included domestic as well as international surveillance besides the right to investigate other intelligence agencies. One of the first tasks of the newly formed KCIA was the screening of 41,000 government employees, 1,863 of whom were found to have been involved in corruption and "antirevolutionary" activities.[4] Within three years, the KCIA had established an extensive network of agents in Korea and abroad. It was this organization that eventually came to symbolize the sophisticated and systematic repression of the Park era.[5]

Also, the existing antidemocratic laws were reinforced. In July 1961, the Anti-Communist Law was reinforced, and in September 1962, the National Security Law was strengthened.[6] The antigovernment movement was severely punished for "encouraging and praising communism" and creating an "antistate organization." On the basis of these fortified legal regulations, the KCIA periodically "disclosed" pro-North "revolutionary parties," terrorizing the entire civil society with nationwide anticommunist campaigns. For example, the People's Revolutionary Party (*Inmin hyŏngmyŏngdang*), allegedly composed of fifty-seven politicians, journalists, professors, and students, was discovered in 1964, and the Reunification Revolutionary Party (*T'ongil hyŏngmyŏngdang*), allegedly consisting of intellectuals and Seoul National University graduates, was uncovered in 1968.

Remobilization of State-Corporatist Groups

On the other hand, Park Chung Hee, like Syngman Rhee in the 1950s and Chang Myŏn in 1960–1961, created and mobilized various state-corporatist progovernment groups. First, the Park regime organized or refurbished a number of anticommunist and rightist groups and employed them as the mass base for the ruling Democratic Republican Party. These groups included the National Headquarters for Reconstruction (*Chaegŏn kungmin undong ponbu*), the Korea Youth Association (*Han'guk ch'ŏngnyŏnhoe*), the Korea Women's Association (*Han'guk puinhoe*), and 4H Clubs.

Then the regime used the existing or new interest associations to control the bourgeois class. Organized as the Federation of Korean Industries (*Han'guk kyŏngjein hyŏphoe*, later *Chŏn'gyŏngnyŏn*), the Korea Chamber of Commerce and Industry (*Taehan sanggong hoeŭiso*), and the Korea International Trade Association (*Han'guk muyŏk hyŏphoe*), Korean capitalists, under the guidance and leadership of government ministries, thrived as a subsidiary partner to the authoritarian developmental state.[7] Originally, the military regime promised to punish severely the businesspersons involved in the past corruption. But because of their urgency to pursue economic development, they abandoned their original idea and decided to use these capitalists to build the Korean economy, letting them serve as the crusaders of economic development. The military and the business circles emerged as a major alliance in Korean politics.[8]

In addition, the Organizing Committee for the Reconstruction of Korean Labor Groups (*Han'guk nodong tanch'e chaegŏn chojik wiwŏnhoe*), whose nine members were directly appointed and intensively trained by the military regime, reestablished the Federation of Korean Trade Unions in August 1960.[9] As a result, the democratic labor movement that had flourished during the 1960–1961 period came to an end. Once again, the FKTU, which was the only legal and official representative organization of all workers in Korea, degenerated into an instrument of the authoritarian regime and the ruling party.

Emergence of Labor and Other Dissident Groups in Civil Society

Toward the early 1970s, however, the situation gradually but significantly changed. Labor unions emerged as an important antigovernment force in civil society. There were several labor disputes earlier in the late 1960s. Examples include protests by miners' unions in 1967, by railway workers' unions in 1968, and by stevedores' unions in 1969. However, the labor movement at the time basically focused on economic and welfare issues and did not challenge the political legitimacy of the Park regime. But labor struggles dramatically intensified after the death of Chŏn T'ae Il, a tailor and labor activist at the P'yŏnghwa [Peace] Market in Seoul. Chŏn immolated himself for labor rights and better working conditions in November 1970. Raising fundamental questions about the official slogan of "development first and democracy later," workers began to demand, among other things, the guarantee of basic human rights.

What is the reason for the emergence of labor as a major antiregime force in this period? Most of all, the initial euphoria over the impressive economic performance of the Park regime evaporated as the economy suffered from numerous troubles toward the beginning of the 1970s. In 1969, 45 percent of the business firms in Korea, including many funded by foreign loans, were declared bankrupt. Also, beginning in 1972, foreign debt amounted to $2.6 billion, or 26.5 percent of the total GNP. The GNP growth rate and gross investment ratio began to fall steadily (table 4.3). Severely hit by these economic problems, industrial laborers began to amplify their resistance against the Park regime.

Industrial laborers were not alone in their protest against Park's authoritarian rule. In 1971, starting with *Tonga ilbo* (Tonga Daily), journalists also launched their pro-democracy movement for the freedom of the press. Moreover, in July 1971, judges in Seoul district courts resigned en masse, supporting the movement to protect the independence of the judiciary. Later that same year, college professors strongly demanded independence of colleges and universities from state control and intervention. In summary, compared to the 1960s, when students and dissident intellectuals were alone in their antigovernment struggles, more and more elements in Korean civil society began to express their discontent with the authoritarian regime toward the 1970s.

Civil Society and the Politics of Authoritarian Breakdown

Establishment of the Yusin System

In examining the first democratic juncture between 1956 and 1961, I pointed out that Syngman Rhee's authoritarian regime to a large extent precipitated its own demise by becoming increasingly arbitrary and violating basic principles of liberal democracy. Specifically, the regime amended the constitution twice to enable Rhee's reelections, exploited anticommunist slogans to attack and suppress the opposition, and perpetrated massive election rigging. The basic dynamics of authoritarian breakdown in the second democratic juncture were not significantly different. In 1969, Park Chung Hee also revised the constitution to facilitate his reelections and resorted to anticommunist campaigns. The only difference between Rhee and Park was that Park was more risk-aversive, perfectionist, and authoritarian. Rhee at least maintained the facade of liberal democracy by allowing and preserving a certain degree of political competition. In contrast, Park sought to guarantee and perpetuate his power by elimi-

TABLE 4.3
GNP Growth Rates, Gross Investment Ratios, and Labor Disputes, 1969–1972

	1969	1970	1971	1972
GNP growth rate (%)	13.8	7.6	9.4	5.8
Gross investment ratio (% of GNP)	28.8	26.8	25.2	21.7
Number of labor disputes	130	165	1,656	346

Sources: EPB, *Han'guk t'onggye yŏn'gam*, 73; KNCC, *1970 nyŏndae nodong hyŏnjanggwa chŏngŏn*, 123.

nating political competition altogether. To him, even sustaining the minimal appearance of liberal democracy was too disagreeable.

In 1969, despite violent antigovernment protests by student groups and opposition politicians, Park Chung Hee managed to revise the constitution to allow a third presidential term for himself. In the 1971 presidential election, however, he ran a very close race with opposition candidate Kim Dae Jung, who would later become president of Korea (1998–present). Park garnered 6,432,828 votes (53.2 percent), whereas Kim gathered 5,395,900 votes (45.3 percent). The margin was significantly closer than the previous presidential election in 1967 (table 4.2). In 1967, Park successfully defeated his opponent because his economic development strategy succeeded and his fresh image as a "young turk" against old and corrupt politicians impressed the voters. In 1971, however, the economy was in deep trouble and his image was considerably damaged by the hardly justifiable constitutional revision in 1969. After the election, Park Chung Hee realized he would not be able to survive another presidential election and resolved to devise a way to bypass political competition as much as possible. Because the constitution he revised in 1969 allowed only three terms for a president, he needed a new, drastic way to extend his tenure.

Therefore, in 1972, Park Chung Hee proclaimed an emergency decree called October Yusin (Revitalization), which was basically a coup-in-office or an executive coup. The Park regime dissolved the National Assembly and replaced it with an emergency cabinet, prohibited all activities of political parties, and revised the constitution. The new constitution—the Yusin Constitution—called for indirect presidential elections by a national electoral college and abolished term limits for president, as Park desired. In addition, the president was given the power to appoint one-third of the members of the legislature. Thus, political power came to be excessively concentrated in the hands of one person, Park Chung Hee. One of the reasons Park provided to justify Yusin was the need to achieve "Korean democracy" that would allegedly avoid "waste" and "inefficiency." Yusin was graphic evidence that Park abhorred or, more exactly, feared the rules, procedures, and institutions of liberal democracy. "Korean democracy" à la Park Chung Hee was outright authoritarianism without real political competition or popular participation. The declaration of Yusin, with its emphasis on "Korean democracy," signaled that Park was now completely ready to abandon the onerous principles and mechanisms of liberal democracy and to suppress civil society at his will.

Emergence of Chaeya

With the establishment of Yusin, a highly repressive and authoritarian political system, the hope of liberal democracy was all but extinguished in Korea. Yusin, however, neither preempted nor arrested the expansion of pro-democracy forces in Korean civil society. Ironically, it was during the dark moments under Yusin that many civil society groups emerged, gained greater influence, and moved toward unity. Above all, Yusin provided the groups in Korean civil society with an unprecedentedly focused picture of the status quo they felt compelled to resist. The nature of Yusin—that is, a wholesale denial of liberal democracy in the name of "efficiency" and "national security"—manifestly recapitulated and eloquently stated to the antigovernment groups in civil society the illegitimacy, illegality, immorality, and violence of the Park regime. Civil society groups thus escalated their anti-Park and anti-Yusin campaigns. In this respect, the declaration of Yusin was the beginning of the authoritarian breakdown.

The pro-democracy movement against Yusin, which began in earnest with student demonstrations in early October 1973, was led by a number of national associations in civil society. National movement associations were not a new phenomenon in Korea. Several national committees and organizations existed that represented movement groups in the early 1960s, during the first democratic juncture. But at the time these organizations were ad hoc, irregular, short-lived, and limited in membership. It was through a series of antigovernment struggles in the 1960s—against the Korea-Japanese normalization, against the dispatch of Korean troops to the Vietnam War, and against the constitutional revision to allow a third term for Park—that the national movement associations became more stable, permanent, and extensive. These national associations eventually grew into what is called *chaeya* (literally "out in the field," "out of power," or "in opposition"), a loose assemblage of dissident groups composed of social movement activists, politicians, writers, youth groups, journalists, and lawyers.[10] Where the established, legal political arena was completely monopolized by the authoritarian state and the ruling party, the emergence of an alternative, second political space outside of the legal framework was both natural and inevitable.[11]

Despite continuing threats and severe suppression by the Yusin regime, *chaeya* movement associations were continually created. In November 1974, the National Congress for the Restoration of Democracy (*Minju hoebok kung-*

min hoeŭi) was founded. Later, in 1978–1979, the pro-democracy movement was represented by two other peak organizations, the National Coalition for Democracy (*Minjujuŭi kungmin yŏnhap*) in 1978 and the National Coalition for Democracy and Reunification (*Minjujuŭiwa minjok t'ongirŭl wihan kungmin yŏnhap*) in 1979. Participating organizations included religious groups (for example, the Catholic Priests' Association for Justice), intellectual groups such as the Council of Dismissed Professors, human rights organizations like the Korean Council for Human Rights Movement, and writers' groups (the Council of Writers for Practicing Freedom, for instance).[12] The leadership of these national *chaeya* organizations included such renowned dissident activists as Yun Po Sŏn, Kim Dae Jung, Ham Sŏk Hŏn, Mun Ik Hwan, Chi Hak Sun, Ham Se Ung, Pak Hyŏng Kyu, Kye Hun Che, Paek Ki Wan, and Han Wan Sang. These individuals were former politicians, religious leaders, scholars, and other professionals and were widely respected for their morality, integrity, experience, and caliber. Consequently, in waging anti-Yusin campaigns, these movement organizations frequently underlined their moral superiority over the repressive authoritarian regime. While their movement called for the restoration of morality and legitimacy by the ruling regime, it also focused on organizing civil society groups as an alternative power to the ruling regime. In this respect, the nature of their movement was a combination of both dissidence and opposition.[13]

Under the leadership of such highly respected and moral individuals, these national *chaeya* associations persistently challenged and resisted the authoritarian government. Despite a series of Presidential Emergency Measures (*Kin'gŭp choch'i*) and harsh suppression, they consistently tried to rely on nonviolent methods, such as the announcement of antigovernment statements and signature collection campaigns. For example, they announced the "Democratic People's Charter" (1975), the "Democratic Declaration to Save the Nation" (1976), the "Democratic Charter to Save the Nation" (1977), and the "March First Democratic Declaration" (1978). Their "One Million Signature Campaign for Constitutional Change," which started in December 1973, posed a significant challenge to the authoritarian regime. Through these statements and campaigns, these national dissident organizations demanded an end to the Yusin system and a return to liberal democracy; abolition of the Presidential Emergency Measures; release of political prisoners; guarantee of the freedoms of the press, publication, and assembly; restoration of the National Assembly; and independence of the judiciary.

Religious Organizations and the Formation of the Triple Solidarity

Particularly critical in the expansion of anti-Yusin pro-democracy movement was the role of religious organizations. Many renowned Catholic priests and Protestant pastors joined the leadership of *chaeya* movement associations. Churches and their related organizations became a very crucial component of the pro-democracy movement. Prior to Yusin, the Korean Christian community had hardly been active as an antigovernment force. Rather, it either supported the ruling regime or remained indifferent to politics, citing the separation of politics and religion as justification. However, after the flickering flames of liberal democracy were extinguished by Yusin, some of the more politically conscious and progressive priests and theologians took upon themselves the role of public advocates of human rights and democracy.[14] They could no longer overlook the brutal suppression and persecution of workers and students by the Park regime. As church activists were also arrested and incarcerated for their opposition to the government, angry protest movements spread through the then-rapidly growing Christian community, arousing it to what the persecuted church leaders considered the plight of the country.[15] For instance, Catholic churches held sixty-three "Prayer Meetings for the Nation" in 1974. Almost 100,000 priests and believers participated in these prayer meetings, which frequently developed into street demonstrations against the authoritarian regime. Churches had certain advantages in waging antiregime struggles. They were comparatively immune to anticommunist ideological attacks by the authoritarian regime owing to their belief in God—an anathema to communism. In addition, they had a solid organizational base and could rely on international support—both moral and financial.

The church was also very instrumental in facilitating the formation and development of the "triple solidarity" of students, workers, and churches. Religious organizations aligned with student groups and dissident intellectuals through, for example, the Korea Student Christian Federation (*Han'guk kidok haksaeng ch'ong yŏnmaeng*), Korean Ecumenical Youth Council (*Han'guk kidok ch'ŏngnyŏn hyŏbŭihoe*), and the Korean Christian Academy. They also actively supported labor unions through various movement groups such as Young Catholic Workers (*K'at'ollik nodong ch'ŏngnyŏnhoe*) and the Urban Industrial Mission (*Tosi sanŏp sŏn'gyohoe*).[16] In close cooperation with traditionally active student organizations and rapidly strengthening labor groups, the church became a guardian of young full-time dissidents, mostly composed of expelled students from colleges and universities, and a care-provider for labor activists.

The church-student and church-labor alignments, together with the already developing student-labor alignment, constituted a triple solidarity of students, laborers, and churches. This union, or "people's movement camp" (*Minjung undonggwŏn*), as its elements identified themselves later, would become a crucial, leading component in the pro-democracy coalition during the third democratic juncture.[17]

Formation of a Hardline Opposition in Political Society

Meanwhile, in political society, the major opposition party, the New Democratic Party (NDP, *Sinmindang*) also waged anti-Yusin campaigns. The NDP intensified its opposition to the authoritarian regime particularly after it was disclosed that Kim Dae Jung, a leading opposition politician who had run a very close race with Park Chung Hee in the 1971 presidential election, was brutally kidnapped from Japan by the KCIA in August 1973. At the time, Kim had been in exile in Japan delivering stinging anti-Yusin speeches. The kidnapping incident, which vividly illustrated the intolerance and violence of the authoritarian regime, prompted the NDP to launch their anti-Park struggles in earnest. Under the slogan of "Replace the Yusin Constitution with a New Democratic One," the NDP started the One Million Signature Campaign for Constitutional Change in late 1973. As I pointed out earlier, various national movement associations participated in this nationwide campaign. Despite government warnings and threats, the citizen participation in the campaign was impressive. In January 1974, the number of collected signatures exceeded 300,000, which posed a great moral threat to the authoritarian government.[18]

However, it was not until the return of Kim Young Sam to the NDP leadership and the Y. H. Incident in 1979 that the grand pro-democracy coalition between civil society and political society was finally formed. In May 1979, Kim Young Sam, who would later become president of Korea (1993–1998), defeated Yi Ch'ŏl Sŭng, who had been accommodating to the Park regime, and regained the leadership of the NDP.. Kim Young Sam's victory signified the emergence of a genuine, hardline opposition in Korean politics. After the successful party election, Kim pledged to fight the Park regime both inside and outside the National Assembly. By "outside" the National Assembly Kim clearly meant that he would cooperate more closely with national *chaeya* movement organizations, such as the National Coalition for Democracy and the National Coalition for Democracy and Reunification.

The Y. H. Incident, the Pusan-Masan Uprising, and the Demise of the Park Regime

A labor dispute in August 1979 provided crucial momentum for facilitating the coalition between civil society groups and the opposition party. On August 9, 1979, more than 190 female former laborers of the Y. H. Industrial Company, a textile-apparel manufacturing plant, decided to stage a sit-in hunger strike at the NDP headquarters office, protesting the closure of their factory. The strikers chose the NDP office because, considering the leadership change of the NDP and its pledge to amplify its anti-Park campaign, they believed that the NDP would be able to help and would be willing to support them. Also, they thought that the headquarters of the major opposition party would be a proper asylum against suppression by the authoritarian regime. The NDP legislators, as expected, responded sympathetically, holding committee meetings to deal with the issue and promising to intensify their struggle against Park's authoritarian regime. However, to the eyes of the authoritarian regime that had long since abandoned liberal democracy and decided to impose "Korean democracy," the national headquarters of the opposition party was not a sanctuary at all. The Park regime reacted to this hunger strike with brutal repression. On the third night of the sit-in, around one thousand riot policemen stormed the NDP headquarters and arrested the protesters, killing one female protestor, Kim Kyŏng Suk, and injuring almost one hundred people, including many NDP legislators and reporters. This incident served as the most vivid indication of the brutality, violence, and lack of legitimacy of the Park regime.

Kim Young Sam declared a total war against the Park regime and, with the cooperation of civil society groups, launched a massive popular movement to bring down Yusin. In response, the authoritarian regime expelled Kim Young Sam from the National Assembly. In October 1979, progovernment legislators, blocking the opposition legislators from entering the National Assembly hall, voted unanimously for a resolution to reprimand Kim Young Sam by stripping him of his National Assemblyman status. The ostensible reason for Kim's expulsion was that he had committed a series of "impudent" acts, such as condemning Park's regime as dictatorial.

In Pusan, Kim's hometown, a full-scale antigovernment uprising erupted and spread through the entire city. Joined by a large number of citizens, thousands of students marched through the streets, chanting antigovernment slogans. Demonstrators requested the expulsion of Park and the return of Kim Young Sam. Faced with the rapid spread of the popular uprising to other cities, the Park regime had to declare martial law in Pusan and to place Masan and Ch'angwŏn under garrison decree.[19]

The direct cause of the Pusan-Masan Uprising lay in the expulsion of Kim Young Sam from the National Assembly but more fundamentally, the uprising reflected ordinary citizens' anger toward an authoritarian regime that did not respect democratic rules and that arbitrarily suppressed political opponents. What was even more important, however, were the consequences of the uprising. The Pusan-Masan Uprising, and the ensuing turmoil across the country, generated a serious split within the top leadership of the authoritarian regime. Park Chung Hee and Ch'a Chi Ch'ŏl, the head of the presidential bodyguards, supported the continuation of a hardline policy whereas Kim Chae Kyu, the director of the KCIA, argued that the hardline approach of Park and Ch'a had only exacerbated the public discontent with the government and that a more flexible stance would have defused the situation. Park and Ch'a felt that Kim had been overly soft on the "rioters" and, at a dinner meeting on October 26, 1979, trenchantly criticized Kim for his inability to prevent, contain, and stop the "riots." Kim attempted to defend and justify himself to no avail. Judging that Park could not be "weaned away from his hardline approach,"[20] Kim Chae Kyu finally shot Park and Ch'a at point-blank range, killing both of them, and marking the demise of Park's nineteen-year-old authoritarian regime. As a result, the authoritarian regime imploded due to the inner splits. However, the impetus for the split between hardliners and softliners and the ultimate implosion clearly came from the intense and protracted struggles of civil society groups and the opposition party against the authoritarian regime.

Civil Society and the Politics of Democratic Transition

Struggles between Civil Society and the Military after the Sudden Authoritarian Breakdown

The explosive demise of Park's authoritarian regime did not automatically lead to a democratic transition. Instead, a series of fierce battles between civil society groups and the military occurred during the seven months between Park's assassination in October 1979 and the declaration of nationwide martial law in May 1980. Groups in civil society that had mobilized and spearheaded the anti-Yusin movement against the authoritarian regime continued their pro-democracy struggle, demanding the complete demolition of the Yusin system and an immediate transition to democracy. In contrast, the hardliners in the military preferred to restore Yusin and revert to the status quo ante, suspending the process of the democratic transition altogether. Unfortunately, what happened was not a transition to democracy but a "multi-staged coup,"[21] in which the military hardliners incrementally crippled and completely replaced the civilian government and violently suppressed the resistance from civil society. The military finally won, and a new authoritarian regime was installed under another general-turned-president, Chun Doo Hwan.

Immediately after Park Chung Hee's assassination, both civil society groups and political parties in Korea were largely at a loss. The suddenness of the authoritarian breakdown and extreme uncertainty about the future prompted major actors in Korean politics to take one step back and rethink their goals and strategies. Groups in civil society soon decided to continue and even intensify their struggle for democracy. They were well aware, from their experience in the first democratic juncture (1956–1961), that an authoritarian breakdown did not automatically spell a democratic transition. The possibility of an authoritarian regression by either reactionary politicians or the military always lingered, as they learned from the reactionary policies of the Hŏ interim government in 1960 and the military coup in May 1961. Therefore, civil society groups focused their energy primarily on pushing the caretaker government of Ch'oe Kyu Ha to destroy completely the remnants of the authoritarian Yusin system and to implement democratic reforms. On November 12, 1979, the National Coalition for Democracy and Reunification (*Kungmin hoeŭi*), a national *chaeya* association that had united and represented the democratic coalition against the Yusin dictatorship, issued a manifesto demanding, among other things, the abolition of martial law and adoption of a new democratic constitution replacing the Yusin Constitution. In support of the manifesto, on November 24 hundreds of people in Seoul staged street demonstrations, defying the martial law prohibiting unauthorized public assembly.

Initially, the Ch'oe Kyu Ha's government responded positively to the popular demand for democratic transition by carrying out a set of liberalizing policies. Most of all, the Ch'oe government promised to amend the Yusin Constitution and hold general elections according to the new constitution. On December 4, 1979, the National Assembly established a bipartisan special committee on constitutional revision. This committee would take the critical job of revising, if not repealing altogether, the Yusin Constitution and drafting a new democratic constitution. Furthermore, Ch'oe removed certain repressive measures bequeathed from Park's authoritarian regime. For instance, the Ch'oe government released former president Yun Po Sŏn, a political rival of Park Chung Hee from the 1960s and a renowned patron and leader of the anti-Yusin resistance in the 1970s, from home arrest. Ch'oe also revoked the notorious Presidential Emergency Measure No. 9, which had been declared and strictly enforced by the Park regime in 1975 to prohibit any activities requesting, inciting, or propagating the negation, distortion, criticism, revision, or repeal of the Yusin Constitution. As the Presidential Emergency Measure No. 9 was abrogated, several hundred individuals who had served prison terms for the violation of the decree were set free. The country appeared to be on its way to democracy, and the long struggles of civil society groups seemed to be rewarded at last.

However, the situation changed dramatically after a military putsch in December 1979. On December 12 hardliners in the military, led by Chun Doo Hwan (who was in charge of the Army Security Command and the investigation into Park's assassination), arrested Army Chief of Staff and Martial Law Commander Chŏng Sŭng Hwa. Chŏng had long favored civilian control of the military and supported a transition to civilian rule based on a new constitution in place of the authoritarian Yusin Constitution. The military hardliners suspected that he had been involved in Park's assassination. Other military officials allied with Chŏng were also arrested. After this revolt, the military hardliners gradually but systematically augmented their power. In proportion, the power and authority of the Ch'oe government collapsed precipitously. In contrast to the determined military hardliners, who intended to restore or revert to the status quo ante of the Yusin system, Ch'oe was neither able nor willing to support and implement his democratic reforms. The Ch'oe government was gradually reduced to being a puppet regime of the military hardliners. In April 1980 Chun illegally assumed control of the KCIA without resigning from his military posts. His appointment touched off a wave of violent student demonstrations calling for his resignation, the lifting of martial law, and a more rapid abolition of the Yusin system.

Resurgence of Civil Society's Activism and the Military Coup

Early in 1980, similar to the period immediately following the April Uprising in 1960, university students concentrated on struggles for intracampus democratization. But when it became obvious by Chun's illegal assumption of the KCIA directorship that the military hardliners were incrementally undermining and in fact displacing the Ch'oe government, student groups returned to and amplified their political protests. Characterizing the Ch'oe regime as a mere extension of Yusin dictatorship, student groups asked the government to lift martial law immediately, to sweep out the remnants of the Yusin system, and to accelerate democratic transition. Street demonstrations resumed in April 1980, and starting with gatherings at Seoul National University and Korea University on May 2, student groups at most of the nation's colleges and universities intensified their antigovernment protests. On May 14, 1980, one hundred thousand students from thirty-four universities across the country waged street demonstrations, calling for the removal of Chun Doo Hwan from all public posts. Student demonstrations culminated on May 15, when seventy thousand to one hundred thousand students from thirty-five universities waged intense antigovernment demonstrations in the heart of Seoul.[22]

Meanwhile, labor activism also increased dramatically. New labor unions were vigorously organized, and they spearheaded a series of labor struggles. During the first five months of 1980, the number of labor disputes was nine hundred, which was almost the same as the number of disputes that occurred during the entire Yusin period (1973–1979).[23] Labor disputes intensified and spread to major industrial areas of the country, including Kyŏnggi-Inch'ŏn, Pusan, Masan-Ch'angwŏn, and Kwangju. Labor unions centered their demands around the issues of wage increase and improvement of labor conditions. Labor movement, severely repressed throughout the Yusin period, often became explosive and violent. In particular, two labor disputes in April 1980 were marked by widespread violence: one at the coal mining town of Sabuk in Kangwŏn province, and the other at the Tongguk Steel Mill in Pusan. In Sabuk, miners blocked the approach of the police and paralyzed the whole town for four days. The state as well as the union leadership lost control of the situation.

The resurgence of antigovernment protests by student groups, in addition to an unprecedented explosion of labor activism, shocked government officials and business leaders and increased the nervousness of the military. The military hardliners, who had been incrementally usurping state power since the military putsch in December 1979, were just waiting for the right moment to shove themselves to the forefront. They finally gained that chance on May 15, 1980, when a large number of students waged intense antigovernment protests in Seoul.[24] On May 16, badgered by the military hardliners who pointed to the threat to national security by violent student protests, the government held a special night meeting and decided to extend the existing martial law to the whole country starting May 17. On May 18, the martial commander prohibited all political activities, closed universities, and arrested renowned politicians, including Kim Dae Jung. The extension of the martial law on May 17 was timed to take most of the threatening nature of the student demonstrations on May

15 and to preempt the end of the martial law, which would have been discussed in the National Assembly scheduled to meet on May 20, 1980, to vote on a resolution to end the existing martial law.

The Kwangju Uprising

The decision to extend martial law to the entire country was meant to be the finale of the multistaged coup that started with the military revolt in December 1979. However, civil society groups did not surrender easily. The last and most violent confrontation between the coup leaders and pro-democracy forces in Korean civil society was the Kwangju Uprising in 1980. On May 18 in Kwangju, Kim Dae Jung's political home ground, students from Chonnam University began violent street protests demanding Kim Dae Jung's release and an end to the martial law. Various civil society groups that had led the anti-Yusin movement—university student groups, religious organizations, youth groups, labor and peasant unions—followed suit and launched massive pro-democracy demonstrations. In reaction, the regime sent in paratroopers who, informed by their superiors that Kwangju was being plundered by communists, brutally attacked both demonstrators and spectators, outraging the citizens of Kwangju. On May 21, antigovernment demonstrations spread to adjacent cities including Mokp'o, Haenam, Kangjin, Changhŭng, Muan, Yŏngam, Naju, Hwasun, and Hamp'yŏng. These demonstrations developed into full-scale insurrections, forcing the paratroopers to retreat. Demonstrators attacked police stations, armed themselves, occupied broadcasting companies, and captured the provincial hall. After a series of attempts by the demonstrators to negotiate a truce with the army failed, regular troops invaded the city on May 27, 1980, and reimposed martial law, killing 17 people and arresting 295. Overall, according to the official account, 174 people died and 389 were injured in these confrontations. Other sources claim a much higher number, around 2,000.[25] The Kwangju uprising symbolized the last and the most fierce battle between those civil society groups that advocated democratic transition and the military hardliners who preferred a reversion to the status quo ante.

The brutal suppression of the Kwangju Uprising marked the climax of the multistaged coup by Chun Doo Hwan and his clique. During the turmoil of the uprising, Chun pressured the civilian cabinet to resign, and then handpicked new cabinet members. In late May 1980, the military replaced the cabinet and legislature with the Special Committee for National Security Measures (*Kukpowi*). This committee carried out a massive social "purification" campaign, forcing newspapers to fire antigovernment reporters and canceling the registration of 172 weeklies and monthlies, including well-known dissident magazines. In August, the Martial Law Command arrested nearly 17,000 "hooligans" as part of its crackdown on "social evils," terrorizing the entire society. After his election as president by a national electoral college in August, Chun disbanded the National Assembly, political parties, and many social organizations. Throughout November and December 1980, the Legislative Council for National Security (*Ippŏp hoeŭi*) enacted various authoritarian legislations, such as the Political Climate Renovation Law, the Basic Press Law (*Ŏllon kibonbŏp*), and the laws regarding assembly and demonstration, which seriously restricted basic democratic freedoms. Thus, civil society in Korea was forced to endure another winter.

In retrospect, as Haggard and Kaufman point out, the Korean political scene in 1980 "seemed to have many of the elements that were conducive to a democratic transition: a growing economic crisis, widespread social mobilization, and a divided military apparatus."[26] However, a democratic transition did not occur, and the military and its allied institutions successfully and expeditiously reasserted their control. Several explanations for this are in order. As will be analyzed in the next section, the weak nature of the pro-democracy coalition of civil society and political society at the time was obviously one reason. The pro-democracy coalition was not extensive enough to incorporate adequately the triple solidarity of students, laborers, and churches that was evolving at the time and therefore was not able to mobilize mass power to prevent an authoritarian regression. In addition, the United States largely acquiesced in the declaration of martial law, in the release of troops to repress the Kwangju Uprising, and in Chun's rapid evolution from martial law commander to president. Also, the hardliners in the military became quickly united under Chun Doo Hwan and determined to restore the status quo ante under Yusin.[27]

Analysis of the Second Democratic Juncture

Actors

The military coup in 1961 suspended the democratic transition in progress during the first democratic juncture but did not completely terminate the growth of civil society that had been occurring during the preceding period. Throughout the 1960s, under the authoritarian government of Park Chung Hee, students and intellectuals continued their antigovernment protests, challenging the legitimacy of the government and criticizing the government's policies. Besides students and intellectuals, however, not many elements in Korean civil society participated in the antigovernment protest. Progressive parties, which had proliferated in the brief democratic intermission in 1960–1961, largely became extinct.

The Park government's success in economic development undermined popular support for students' antigovernment activism.[28] The Park regime was quite successful in converting economic development into political popularity. From today's vantage point, it may be difficult to understand why the Korean people in general, except for students and intellectuals, preferred economic development over political democracy at the time. But this is because we fall into the fallacy of "presentism," that is, assuming that "the motives and perceptions of the past are the same as those of the present."[29] In the mid-1960s, the Park regime's economic performance came as a pleasant surprise to the Korean people as a whole. Placed especially in good contrast with dismal economic records of the previous regimes, the new regime's emphasis on economic development and "removal of the rampant poverty" strongly appealed to the populace. "Development first and democracy later" was not just an empty slogan imposed by the government; it was to some degree a reflection and representation of the general will of most Koreans, who had been subject to abject poverty since the end of the Korean War. The "democracy" supported by students and intellectuals was viewed as a luxury.

Meanwhile, Park Chung Hee's authoritarian regime employed the KCIA to threaten, tame, and terrorize civil society with numerous espionage scandals and anticommunist campaigns. The regime also revived and broadly reused various rightist state-corporatist organizations to reinforce its anticommunist campaigns. Anticommunism was still influential in suppressing civil society's activism. Through state institutions and intermittent nationwide campaigns, the authoritarian regime monitored and controlled the whole civil society. In this respect, the Korean state during the Park years was a type of "garrison state,"[30] or an "army" with Park as the supreme commander.[31]

At the same time, rapid economic development in the 1960s created favorable demographic and structural conditions for an active labor movement. The export-oriented industrialization strategy was firmly in place by the mid-1960s, bringing many new workers from rural areas to booming export industries in the cities. Industrialization changed the class structure in Korea: the agricultural labor force declined precipitously while the labor class increased steadily (table 4.4). The majority of the young labor force derived from agriculture was absorbed into the manufacturing sector. When a crisis of export-oriented industrialization occurred around the early 1970s, mostly caused by serious balance-of-payments problems and widespread business failures in foreign-invested firms, it directly and severely hit the emerging labor class. Massive layoffs, a wage freeze, and delayed payments brought about labor protests in the export sector. Labor emerged as a major antigovernment force. The deepening process of industrialization, in this regard, meant a double-edged blade for the authoritarian regime: on the one hand, it provided the political legitimacy Park desperately needed, but on the other hand, it also increased the number of workers, strengthened labor solidarity, and consequently fostered the student-labor alliance.

Students played an important role in raising workers' collective consciousness in this democratic juncture through "night schools" they set up near factory towns. Workers' night schools began to appear in the early 1970s, just after Chŏn T'ae Il's self-immolation. Initially, they were established in response to young workers' aspirations for higher education. Gradually, however, the emphasis shifted from routine curricula to consciousness-raising programs tailored to workers. These night school classes provided an important arena where workers learned to articulate their daily work experiences using a new

TABLE 4.4
Changes in the Class Structure, 1960–1980
(In thousands; percentages in parentheses)

	1960	1970	1975	1980
Capitalist Class	34 (0.4)	59 (0.5)	105 (0.9)	139 (1.1)
Wage-earning middle class/intelligentsia	227 (2.9)	397 (3.7)	536 (4.5)	744 (5.8)
Self-employed	5,069 (64.9)	6,643 (61.4)	6,389 (54.0)	6,264 (48.5)
Labor class	2,477 (31.7)	3,725 (34.4)	4,811 (40.6)	5,769 (44.7)
Economically active population	7,807 (100)	10,823 (100)	11,840 (100)	12,916 (100)
Total Employed	7,207	10,369	11,330	12,167
(excluding agriculture, forestry, & fishing)	2,301 (29.5)	4,916 (45.4)	6,387 (53.9)	7,912 (61.3)

Source: Sŏ, "Han'guk sahoe kyegŭp kusŭngŭi sahoe t'onggyejŏk yŏn'gu," 92–95.

political language and where they could develop close links with student groups.[32]

Together with such student-labor solidarity, a church-labor alliance also developed. Religious organizations, enraged by the violation of basic human rights and motivated to develop alliances with the poor, actively focused on training, educating, and organizing workers.[33] Because religious organizations had already begun protecting and sponsoring full-time student activists, these three separate linkages gradually constituted a grand triple solidarity among students, laborers, and churches.[34]

Several national movement associations called *chaeya* led pro-democracy struggles against the Park Chung Hee regime in the 1970s. However, compared with the third democratic juncture, one of the serious limitations of the national movement organizations during this period was that they generally failed to reflect and incorporate the triple solidarity of students, laborers, and churches that was evolving at the time. *Chaeya* associations included religious organizations, but they to a large extent failed to encompass student groups and labor unions. Based on individual networks and commitments, their membership primarily consisted of former and current politicians, pastors and priests, intellectuals, and professionals such as lawyers, professors, and writers. These people were largely from the upper strata and lacked any real grassroots base. In some respect, they came from the same circles and ideological background as members of the ruling group.[35]

Interactions

In terms of civil society-state relations, confrontation and conflict continued to characterize this period. The degree of antagonism was higher as compared with the previous democratic juncture. Similar to the previous period, the political landscape was sharply divided between the authoritarian regime, the ruling party, and their state-corporatist organizations on one side, and pro-democracy movement associations in civil society and the opposition party in political society on the other.

The level of state repression dramatically increased after the establishment of the Yusin system. Unlike the previous regimes, the Park regime, implemented by a successful military coup, was fully supported by and in solid control of the military. The collapse of the Rhee regime was partially due to the betrayal of the military. During the Chang regime, the civilian government was not in full control of the military, unable to detect or prevent the military coup in 1961. In contrast, the Park Chung Hee regime frequently mobilized the military to discipline and repress civil society.[36] Not only did the Park regime mobilize soldiers to suppress civil society, but also the government itself was largely run by soldiers-in-mufti. The Park regime, in this respect, was a quasi-civilianized government.[37] For example, most of the powerful positions in the Park government were filled with soldiers-in-mufti. Throughout the Park regime, soldiers-in-mufti occupied almost 30 percent of the ministerial positions and were 16 percent of the National Assemblypersons (table 4.5 and table 4.6). With a strong military tone in the leadership, Park's semi-military government harshly muzzled civil society through numerous martial laws, garrison decrees, and presidential emergency measures. Of the nine martial laws throughout Korean history, five were declared during Park's reign (1961–1979).[38] In opposition to such severe repression, civil society waged demonstrations, launched signature collection campaigns, and announced pro-democracy declarations. As a result, civil society-state relations continued to be hostile and conflictual.

TABLE 4.5
Civilians and Soldiers-in-mufti in the Executive, 1948–1993
(In percentages)

Regimes	Rhee (1948–1960)	Chang (1960–1961)	Park (1963–1972)	Park's Yusin (1972–1979)	Chun (1980–1988)	Roh (1988–1993)
Civilians	93.0	97.0	70.8	73.0	79.2	81.5
Soldiers-in-mufti	7.0	3.0	29.2	27.0	20.8	18.5

Ministerial Level
Source: Ho Chin Kim, *Han'guk chŏngch'i ch'ejeron*, 271.

TABLE 4.6
Civilians and Soldiers-in-mufti in the Legislature, 1948–1993, by Regime
(In percentages)

	Rhee (1948–1960)	Chang (1960–1961)	Park (1963–1972)	Park's Yusin (1972–1979)	Chun (1980–1988)	Roh (1988–1993)
Civilians	100.0	96.0	84.0	84.0	91.3	95.0
Soldiers-in-mufti	0.0	4.0	16.2	16.0	8.7	5.0

Source: Ho Chin Kim, *Han'guk chŏngch'i ch'ejeron*, 271.

The relationship between civil society and political society during the second democratic juncture was a cooperative one. *Chaeya* leaders in civil society collaborated with politicians in various antigovernment statement campaigns. The political society at the time was sharply polarized between the ruling party and the opposition party. Unlike during the first democratic juncture, in which there was no strong opposition party available to align with civil society groups, during this juncture there was the New Democratic Party, the main opposition to the ruling Democratic Republican Party.

The cooperation and alignment between civil society and political society was not through institutionalized channels such as joint organizations. It was aligned instead through individual connections and commitments. Furthermore, the main cooperation occurred between religious leaders and opposition party politicians. The triple solidarity emerging at the time was not reflected in the civil society–political society coalition. Student groups and labor unions, two key elements of the triple solidarity, did not maintain any close links with the opposition party. This division between opposition party politicians united with *chaeya* religious leaders and the union of students and laborers lasted into the third democratic juncture and engendered an important fissure in the conception of democracy entertained by Korean civil society, as will be discussed in chapter 5. The former camp—opposition politicians and religious leaders—supported a moderate, procedural conception of democracy, while the latter camp—student groups and labor unions—advanced a radical, substantive version of democracy. This division also ultimately affected the dynamics of the politics of democratic consolidation, as I will discuss in chapter 6. Although loosely united in the anti-Park struggle through the 1970s in the second democratic juncture, different elements in Korean civil society already had seeds of division.

Issues

During the second democratic juncture, *chaeya* movement groups in Korean civil society almost exclusively focused on liberal democracy conceptualized heavily in procedural terms. The contents of major antigovernment declarations emphasized the abolition of the Presidential Emergency Measures; release and amnesty of imprisoned politicians and movement activists; guarantee of freedoms of the press, publication, and assembly; normalization of the legislature; and independence of the judiciary. All of these items are basic elements of a liberal democracy. Unlike during the third democratic juncture, the concept of substantive democracy was not advocated. Due to the harsh and ever-increasing state suppression and anticommunist tactics of the authoritarian regime, it was extremely risky for *chaeya* movement groups to put forth a radical notion of democracy.

The demand of civil society groups was especially focused on exposing the gap between the reality of political authoritarianism and the ideal of liberal democracy stipulated in the laws. All procedural components of democracy (elections, constitution, parties, civil liberties and human rights) existed in Korea at the time— but only in writing. Few of them were in practice observed or respected. *Chaeya* movement groups mainly underscored this huge gap between the realities of "Korean democracy" and the vision of liberal democracy. In other words, the pro-democracy movement by civil society consisted of "confrontation over the legitimacy of the ruling regime on the basis of democratic norms versus authoritarian practice."[39]

The reunification issue continued to be important. However, actively raising it at the time involved considerable risks. The Park regime, a semi-military regime solidly supported by the armed forces, frequently used anticommunist campaigns and measures to suppress political opposition. Discussing reunification in terms other than according to the official proposals of the government was tantamount to inviting harsh anticommunist suppression of the authoritarian state. In numerous pro-democracy statements and in the titles of various *chaeya* organizations, the theme of reunification continued to serve as a powerful symbol. But in practice the reality of the Yusin system was so harsh that civil society movement groups were barely able to concentrate on the goal of liberal democracy. To the groups in Korean civil society, national reunification always seemed to be the only fundamental cure for the dictatorship because the authoritarian regimes were so shrewd in using anticommunism as a pretext for suppressing civil society and procrastinating democratic reform. For the same reason, however, it was very risky to raise the reunification issue because it was sure to cause ruthless ideological attacks from the ruling regime. Therefore, the groups in civil society did not focus on the reunification issue but rather concentrated on human rights, the workers' situation, and political democratization during the second democratic juncture.

Summary and Conclusions

In this chapter, I analyzed the role of civil society groups in bringing down the authoritarian regime of Park Chung Hee and in promoting democratic transition during the 1973–1980 period. I first compared the internal configuration of Korean civil society in the 1960s with that in the 1950s. Student groups and dissident intellectuals, since the April Uprising in 1960, were continually active in challenging the authority and legitimacy of the Park regime. However, other sectors of civil society were largely dormant, partly due to the impressive economic development achieved by the Park regime and partly due to the extensive surveillance and suppression of civil society by the KCIA. As the 1970s approached, however, the mesmerizing effect of rapid economic development gradually subsided due to diverse economic problems. Labor unions, along with various other elements in civil society, emerged as a major antigovernment force.

I then examined how the pro-democracy movement against Park Chung Hee in the mid-1970s contributed to the demise of his authoritarian regime. A number of *chaeya* associations organized civil society groups and waged extensive moral and non-violent antigovernment struggles against a highly authoritarian political system called Yusin. Although they did not adequately reflect the triple solidarity of labor, church, and students that was developing and expanding at the time, their coalition with the opposition party generated a serious internal split within the ruling elite and ultimately caused an implosion of the authoritarian regime.

Next I reviewed the role of civil society in the aftermath of the sudden demise of Park's authoritarian regime. After the implosion of this regime, civil society groups compelled the caretaker government of Ch'oe Kyu Ha to implement democratic reforms. Student groups and religious organizations continued their pro-democracy struggles, and labor movements expanded explosively. The military hardliners under Chun Doo Hwan, taking advantage of the continued activism of pro-democracy groups and the rapid spread and radicalization of labor movements, staged a multiphased coup that undermined and ultimately usurped the power of the civilian government. The confrontation between pro-democracy groups in civil society and the military hardliners culminated violently in the Kwangju Uprising.

I also analyzed this democratic juncture in terms of its actors, interactions, and issues. The triple solidarity of students, laborers, and churches gradually developed although it was not fully reflected in the pro-democracy movement against the authoritarian regime. Civil society–state interactions remained consistently hostile and antagonistic, particularly due to the semimilitary nature of the Park regime, which was largely run by soldiers-in-mufti. The interactions between civil society and political society were collaborative but failed to include the emergent triple solidarity in civil society. Issues raised by civil society were mostly related to liberal democracy as defined in procedural terms.

In the next chapter, I will analyze how civil society groups contributed to Korean democratization in the third democratic juncture between 1984 and 1987. Unlike the previous two democratic junctures, the transition this time was not aborted in the middle and therefore reached democratic consolidation. I will focus on the crosstemporal changes in the configuration of civil society and also how civil society groups succeeded in developing a grand democratic coalition with political society against the authoritarian regime.

C H A P T E R **5**

Civil Society in the Third Democratic Juncture, 1984–1987

We resolve to mobilize all peaceful means to establish a genuinely democratic constitution and a genuinely democratic government.

NATIONAL MOVEMENT HEADQUARTERS FOR DEMOCRATIC
CONSTITUTION, 1987

We would like to live in a world where there is no torture. We would like to live in a democratized country.

CATHOLIC PRIESTS' ASSOCIATION FOR JUSTICE, 1987

"We Will Never Let Them Take You Away"
(pac chong) ch'ol,
. . .
And we will tell
Standing up, holding you tight,
Gathering today's anger, building on today's hatred
This exploitation on this land,
This never-ending repression,
These contradictions that strangle everything alive,
All those remnants,
Now we will end them.
Now we will finish them.

ANONYMOUS, 1987

I N this chapter, I turn to the third democratic juncture in Korea, between 1984 and 1987. Unlike the previous two democratic junctures, the transition in this juncture was not aborted in the middle and therefore eventually led to democratic consolidation. In section 1, I briefly describe the conditions to which Korean civil society was subject under the authoritarian regime of Chun

Doo Hwan. In section 2, I examine the role of civil society in the authoritarian breakdown of the Chun regime from 1984 to 1987. I analyze why the authoritarian regime decided to initiate a "phase of political relaxation" (*Yuhwa kungmyŏn*) that led to the rapid "resurrection of civil society." I explore the processes through which the resurrected civil society groups created a strong and inclusive pro-democracy alliance and later expanded it to the opposition party. I argue that such a grand democratic alliance was a key factor forcing the authoritarian regime to relinquish its "method of appointive, or anointed, succession"[1] and instead agree on democratic reforms. In section 3, I look into the transitional politics in the latter half of 1987. I show how labor unions, through the Great Labor Struggle (*Nodongja taet'ujaeng*) in July and August 1987, pushed the exiting authoritarian regime to go beyond procedural democracy and address "substantive" democratization. As well, I investigate how civil society groups, confronted with a serious split developing within political society, tried to remedy disunity and come up with a single opposition presidential candidate. In section 4, I analyze this democratic juncture according to my analytical framework.

Configuration of Korean Civil Society, 1980–1983

"Pacification" of Civil Society by the Authoritarian Regime

Severe state repression of civil society characterized the period between 1980 and 1983. Following the violent suppression of the pro-democracy movement in Kwangju in May 1980 and the subsequent consolidation of its power, the military regime designed and carried out a series of massive and coercive campaigns to "cleanse" (*Chŏnghwa*) the entire civil society. In June 1980, the government ordered a thorough search for and immediate arrest of 329 politicians, professors, pastors, journalists, and students on various charges of corruption, instigation and organization of antigovernment demonstrations, insurrection attempts, and so forth. In July 1980, the military regime "purged" thousands of public officials, employees of public corporations, employees of agricultural and fisheries cooperatives, and teachers and other educators, blaming the purging on their incompetence, corruption, and ideological problems. Simultaneously, the Chun regime also forced newspaper and broadcasting companies to single out and expel those journalists who were "deficient in anticommunism." Last, in August 1980, the authorities arrested 16,599 "hooligans and gangsters" and sent them to military courts, "education" (*Sunhwa*) camps, or labor camps. Included in this luckless category of "hooligans and gangsters" were numerous university students and labor activists who had participated in the antigovernment demonstrations against Yusin from 1973 to 1979 and against the military government in 1979 and 1980. Such extensive and violent "purge" campaigns by the military regime to a great extent effectively terrorized and muted civil society as a whole.

State repression continued and even intensified following the inauguration of Chun Doo Hwan as Korean president on September 1, 1980. It not only intensified but also became systematically institutionalized through various laws enacted by a legislature *pro tempore*. On October 27, 1980, Chun dissolved the National Assembly and all political parties and instead installed the Legislative Council for National Security (LCNS, *Kukka powi ippŏp hoeŭi*). On November 3, 1980, the LCNS passed the Political Climate Renovation Law (*Chŏngch'i p'ungt'o soesinbŏp*), which banned from politics anyone "responsible for causing political and social corruption or fomenting confusion."[2] Subsequently, a Political Renovation Committee (whose members were directly appointed by Chun Doo Hwan himself) issued "blacklists" disqualifying 567 politicians and intellectuals from engaging in politics. Included in these "blacklists" were the two renowned opposition leaders at the time, Kim Dae Jung and Kim Young Sam.

Antidemocratic Legislations

While the Political Climate Renovation Law was intended to intimidate and petrify political society, the LCNS also passed a series of other antidemocratic laws specifically targeting civil society. On November 29, 1980, it passed bills "regulating" assembly and demonstration, seriously restricting basic democratic freedoms. On December 26, 1980, the LCNS adopted the nefarious Basic Press Law (*Ŏllon kibonbŏp*), which was in essence an elaborate system of press censorship. The Basic Press Law stipulated that the Minister of Culture and Information had the authority to cancel the registration of publications and to suspend them for several reasons, one of which was "when they repeatedly and flagrantly violate the law in encouraging or praising violence or other illegal acts disrupting public order."[3] "Press guidelines" were distributed daily to the news media, specifically directing the press, for example, to label antigovernment protesters as " procommunist."[4]

Moreover, the new labor-related laws prohibited "third party intervention," denying the right not only of church-sponsored dissident labor groups, such as the Urban Industrial Mission or the Catholic Justice and Peace Mission, which had been active in helping workers organize labor movements in the 1970s, but also of the official Federation of Korean Trade Unions and industry-level union federations to intervene in local disputes.[5] The organization of autonomous unions and collective action by rank-and-file workers was harshly suppressed, and workers were forced to join company-controlled "labor-management councils." The LCNS, during its short lifetime of five and a half months, passed more than two hundred bills affecting virtually every segment of society.[6] The bills passed by the LCNS served as the legal and institutional basis of Chun's authoritarian regime. In addition to the existing National Security Law, the authoritarian regime could frequently resort to these new laws in containing, suppressing, and punishing the activities by the antigovernment groups in civil society. This explains why the revision and repeal of these laws often emerged as one of the most important issues later in the politics of democratic transition and consolidation.

In summary, through these "social cleansing" campaigns and antidemocratic legislations, the Chun regime basically brought the political order and social environment of Korea to the status quo ante under the Yusin system of Park Chung Hee. In this respect, Chun's multistage coup in 1979–1980 was a process of "reproducing" a military dictatorship.[7]

Civil Society and the Politics of Authoritarian Breakdown

Political Liberalization

Starting in late 1983, however, Chun's suppression of civil society gradually but significantly abated. In December 1983, the regime allowed those professors who had been dismissed from their jobs because of their involvement in the antigovernment activities during the late 1970s to return to their previous positions. Also, it permitted 1,363 college and university students to return to their schools. Most of these students had been expelled because of their anti-Yusin and, later, anti-Chun demonstrations. The authoritarian regime decided to withdraw the military police from university campuses as well. Meanwhile, in regard to political society, the regime pardoned or rehabilitated about three hundred political prisoners or "public peace breakers" (*Kongan sabŏm*). Furthermore, in February 1984, the regime lifted the ban on political activities for 202 former politicians.

Why did the authoritarian regime decide to implement such conciliatory measures for civil society and political society? In essence, it was due to the misperceptions of the regime about the status quo at the time and also due to the existence of certain critical external factors.

The authoritarian regime had considerable confidence in the institutional and legal "security valves" designed to detect, prevent, check, and control societal resistance.[8] As already noted, Chun started his term with a series of state-led social campaigns and antidemocratic laws that changed the nation's political atmosphere. Besides the existing NSL, various laws intended to monitor and suppress political society and civil society were installed. The regime expected and strongly believed that the Political Climate Renovation Law, the Basic Press Law, the laws regarding assembly and demonstration, and various labor-related laws enacted by the LCNS during 1980 and 1981 would effectively block and stem any "undesirable" or "unnecessary" developments in both civil society and political society.

In addition, the Chun regime succeeded not only in restoring the political order and social environment of the status quo ante but also in resuming the "economic miracle" of Korea. As table 5.1 indicates, the economy started to recover after the inauguration of the Chun regime. The economic crisis following the political crisis of 1979—namely, Park Chung Hee's assassination—was over. The growth rate turned from −3.7 percent in 1980 to 12.6 percent in 1983 and the unemployment rate steadily declined. Also, the inflation rate dropped from 28.7 percent in 1980 to 3.4 percent in 1983.[9] Significantly encouraged by such impressive economic success, Chun Doo Hwan, like his predecessor Park Chung Hee, concluded that economic development would secure him political legitimacy and popularity.

More specifically, on the basis of the political stability and economic development achieved during the 1980–1983 period, the Chun regime (mis)perceived that the ruling Democratic Justice Party (DJP, *Minjŏngdang*) would be electorally competitive in the upcoming National Assembly elections, sched-

TABLE 5.1
GNP Growth Rates, 1980–1983

	1980	1981	1982	1983
Growth rate (%)	−3.7	5.9	7.2	12.6
Unemployment rate (%)	5.2	4.5	4.4	4.1

Source: KITA, *Han'guk kyŏngjeŭi chuyo chip'yo*, 115.

uled for early 1985. A series of liberalizing policies aimed at "national unity" and "grand reconciliation," the regime predicted and expected, would not damage the popularity of the regime and the ruling DJP. Rather, a phase of political relaxation might improve the terrifying image of the authoritarian rule by rescinding, in part if not entirely, the "original sin" of the Chun regime—the violent suppression of the pro-democracy movement and the massive killings in Kwangju in May 1980. In summary, the authoritarian crisis in Korea at this juncture was not engendered by political or economic failure but rather was triggered by unexpected success.[10] The origins of the authoritarian crisis in the third democratic juncture of Korea, therefore, consisted in the overconfidence or even hubris on the part of the authoritarian regime about the stability and durability of the status quo.

Certain crucial external factors affected the Chun regime's decision too. Korea was scheduled to play host to two big international athletic games: the Asian Games in 1986 and the Olympics in 1988. The Chun regime needed to make the most of these two occasions to demonstrate and publicize to an international audience that Korea was a legitimate and stable democracy. In order to do this, it was essential to allow and encourage a certain degree of free political contestation and participation. In particular, the authoritarian regime gauged that it would not lose much by partially liberalizing the political system, because pardoning and rehabilitating former opposition politicians and dissident activists would most likely contribute to further fragmentation and factionalization of the opposition.[11]

Resurrection of Civil Society

The consequences of the political relaxation, however, were quite different from what the authoritarian regime had originally intended and expected. Various groups in Korean civil society—particularly pro-democracy movement groups that had been decimated and pacified by the authoritarian regime's severe repression between 1980 and 1983—were rapidly resuscitated. In particular, the phase of political relaxation in late 1983 marked the end of the externally imposed hibernation of the triple solidarity of students, workers, and churches in Korean civil society.

First, in February and March of 1984, the students who had just returned to their campuses restored and reorganized antigovernment student groups and associations. Initially, student groups did not focus on political objectives. They demanded the independence of universities from state control and intervention. But student groups gradually realized that the democratization of universities was inseparable from democratization of the entire society. In November 1984, students from forty-two universities and colleges organized the National Student Coalition for Democracy Struggle (*Chŏnhangnyŏn*). This was the first nationwide student organization since the April Uprising in 1960. Under the leadership of this organization, students began to criticize and challenge the authoritarian regime.

In addition, the Youth Coalition for Democracy Movement (YCDM, *Minch'ŏngnyŏn*) was established in September 1983. This organization, primarily composed of former student activists who were now engaged in labor and social movements, served as a crucial forum to connect and unite the older and younger generations of student activists.[12] It also connected student activists to professors, journalists, and other sympathetic intellectuals and professionals. Through regular publications, such as *Path to Democratization*, the YCDM facilitated discussions and debates on various theories of democratization and contributed to the development of strategies of pro-democracy movement.[13]

With respect to labor movement, the Korean Council for Labor Welfare (*Han'guk nohyŏp*) was organized in March 1984. Composed of various labor unions that had spearheaded anti-Yusin pro-democracy struggles in the 1970s, this organization tried to restore and strengthen unity and solidarity among labor movement groups. In April 1984, the Ch'ŏnggye apparel labor union, which had been prominent in the labor movement in the 1970s but was dissolved by the military regime in 1981, was fully restored. Emphasizing that the so-called phase of political relaxation applied to and benefited only students, professors, and journalists, labor unions focused their efforts on exposing the limited and hypocritical nature of the regime's political liberalization. The Korean Council for Labor Welfare and Ch'ŏnggye jointly launched a massive campaign against the arbitrary labor laws enacted by the LCNS during the formative years of Chun's authoritarian regime.[14] Students actively supported and cooperated with the restored labor unions. Church groups such as the Catholic Priests' Association for Justice (CPAJ, *K'at'ollik chŏngŭi kuhyŏn chŏn'guk sajedan*) assisted the labor movement as well, waging a signature campaign for the revision of objectionable labor laws.

Most important, the resurrected student groups, youth organizations, labor unions, religious organizations, and other groups in civil society became tightly united and effectively coordinated under the leadership of national umbrella organizations. Initially, there were two different national peak associations. In June 1984, the Council of Movement for People and Democracy

(CMPD, *Minminhyŏp*) was established; five months later, the National Congress for Democracy and Reunification (NCDR, *Kungmin hoeŭi*) was created under the leadership of Reverend Mun Ik Hwan. The NCDR was a successor to the National Coalition for Democracy and Reunification of 1979, which spearheaded the anti-Yusin struggle. It consisted of intellectuals and religious leaders who were politically moderate and supportive of liberal democracy. Meanwhile, the CMPD, composed of various sectoral movement groups, stressed the "mass line" and class-based struggle. It pledged to pursue independent national economy, social justice, increased political consciousness of the masses, and peaceful national reunification. The CMPD clearly marked a break with the 1970s, when labor activists individually participated in loosely organized national movement associations, such as the National Coalition for Democracy or the National Coalition for Democracy and Reunification. Now labor groups finally began to form their own independent national organizations, differentiating themselves from the movement associations of the 1970s that had been loosely based on the individual commitments of notable dissident leaders.[15] Unlike the *chaeya* movement in the 1970s, which had primarily been based on personal networks and individual commitments, the people's movement (*Minjung undong*) in the 1980s, represented by organizations such as the CMPD and the NCDR, began to have solid organizational support and clearer plans for socioeconomic reform.

Emergence of a Genuine Opposition in Political Society

Whereas various people's movement groups (*Minjung undong tanch'e*) were resurrected in civil society, a genuine opposition reemerged in political society. Between 1980 and 1983, there was no real opposition in Korean politics. Opposition parties like the Democratic Korea Party (*Minhandang*) and the Korean Nationalist Party (*Kungmindang*), created, sponsored, and controlled by the authoritarian regime, had been unable and unwilling to question and challenge the political legitimacy of the regime. What the authoritarian regime had in mind in implementing a series of liberalizing measures in 1983 and 1984 was further fragmentation and enervation of the opposition. Contrary to the regime's intention, however, the "phase of political relaxation" resulted rather in the dramatic resuscitation and expansion of a real opposition in political society. As part of the relaxation measures, in November 1984 Chun Doo Hwan lifted the ban on political activities for eighty-four persons who had been on his "blacklist." Many of these newly reinstated opposition politicians later formed the New Korea Democratic Party (NKDP, *Sinhan minjudang*) in January 1985, immediately before the National Assembly elections in February 1985. Kim Young Sam and Kim Dae Jung, veteran opposition politicians still banned from political life, were the de facto leaders of the NKDP.

The politics of authoritarian breakdown began in earnest with the formation of the NKDP and its electoral alignment with the pro-democracy movement groups in civil society. Although there were some radical groups in civil society—for example, some student groups—that attempted to boycott the National Assembly elections altogether, the majority of the people's movement groups decided to participate in the elections, raising the issues of democracy, direct presidential election, and local autonomy. Furthermore, they decided to support the newly created opposition NKDP. In January 1985, the YCDM publicly announced it would back the NKDP. Many student groups vigorously campaigned for the NKDP too. It was the first time since the early 1960s that university students supported a particular political party.

Voters were thrilled at various pro-democracy slogans by movement groups and also enthusiastic about the possibility of having a real opposition party. They were tired of the indirect "gymnasium elections" in which the members of "national electoral college" gathered in a huge gymnasium and, irrespective of the genuine popular will, unconditionally supported and elected a president. Therefore, Korean voters were particularly excited about NKDP's proposal of direct presidential election. The turnout in the National Assembly elections on February 12, 1985, was 84.6 percent, the highest since the 1950s. As table 5.2 shows, the NKDP emerged as the leading opposition, unexpectedly winning 29.26 percent of the votes, compared to 35.25 percent for the ruling DJP. After the elections, the strategy of the people's movement groups and the NKDP was to make the legitimacy question the only and the most important

TABLE 5.2
Results of National Assembly Elections, 1985

	DJP	NKDP	DKP	KNP	Others	Total
Seats	148	67	35	19	7	276
Votes (%)	35.25	29.26	19.68	9.15	6.66	100.00

Note: DJP: Democratic Justice Party; NKDP: New Korea Democratic Party; DKP: Democratic Korea Party; KNP: Korean Nationalist Party
Source: NEC, *Che 12 dae kukhoe ŭiwŏn sŏn'gŏ ch'ongnam.*

political issue.[16] The alignment between the people's movement groups and the opposition NKDP outlived the National Assembly elections and later developed into a grand pro-democracy coalition against the authoritarian regime.

The NKDP emerged as a formidable opposition through the 1985 National Assembly elections. The "new party tornado" (*Sindang tolp'ung*) swept the entire country, shocking not only the authoritarian regime and the ruling DJP but also the NKDP itself. Furthermore, in early April 1985, twenty-nine of the thirty-five newly elected legislators belonging to the Democratic Korea Party—a weak, if not unauthentic, opposition party operating between 1980 and 1985—switched their allegiance to the NKDP. With additional defections from another minority party, the Korea Nationalist Party, the NKDP increased its representation to 102 seats in the 276-member National Assembly.

Boosted by the election results and the defections of many legislators from other opposition parties, the NKDP vigorously pressed the ruling DJP for revision of the constitution—particularly for the adoption of a direct presidential election system that had been the focus of NKDP's campaign pledge during the National Assembly elections. Because the existing law provided for indirect election of the president, it was almost certain that a person hand-picked by Chun Doo Hwan would succeed him. However, the motions of NKDP legislators to deal with the issue of constitutional revision inside the National Assembly were only met by the categorical rejection of the DJP. The ruling DJP adamantly opposed the idea, and political society consequently suffered an impasse.

Emergence of a Grand Pro-democracy Alliance in Civil Society

Meanwhile, pro-democracy groups in civil society were steadily moving toward a greater unity. As noted earlier, the liberalization, or the phase of political relaxation in 1983 and 1984, brought about the emergence of two different national organizations of civil society groups—the radical CMPD and the relatively moderate NCDR. These two organizations agreed to unite themselves in their struggle against the authoritarian regime. In March 1985, the CMPD and the NCDR merged into the People's Movement Coalition for Democracy and Reunification (PMCDR, *Mint'ongnyŏn*). The PMCDR encompassed not only urban labor, landless peasants, and leading intellectuals, but also most of the country's Buddhist, Protestant, and Roman Catholic clergy and lay groups.[17] It was a nationwide umbrella organization comprised of twenty-four groups and organizations, including various intermediate groups (writers, journalists, religious activists, and intellectuals) and labor and peasant organizations, such as the Seoul Labor Movement Coalition (*Sŏnoryŏn*), the Korean Council for Labor Welfare, the Protestant Peasant Association (*Kinong*), and Catholic Peasant Association (*K'anong*).[18] Unlike numerous *chaeya* national movement associations during the 1970s, this organization was not just a group of dissident dignitaries but was truly reflective of the triple solidarity of students, laborers, and religious leaders. The people's movement groups finally stood united under the leadership of the PMCDR. On November 20, 1985, the PMCDR created the Committee for Attaining Democratic Constitution (*Minju hŏnbŏp chaengch'wi wiwŏnhoe*) and launched in earnest its push for constitutional revision and democratization.

Formation of a Grand Pro-democracy Coalition and the Movement for Constitutional Revision

Immediately after the 1985 National Assembly elections, as the NKDP began to focus more on the politics within the legislature, the coalition between the NKDP and the people's movement groups became peripheral. However, this was only a temporary phenomenon. Repeatedly frustrated by the recalcitrance of the DJP on the issue of constitutional revision, the NKDP decided to return to and rely on its old coalition with the people's movement groups in civil society. In late 1985, the NKDP finally left the National Assembly, reactivated its coalition with the people's movement groups, and started a massive democratization campaign outside the legislature against the authoritarian regime.[19]

The pro-democracy struggle for constitutional revision (*Kaehŏn t'ujaeng*) in 1986 took three different forms. The first was a series of public statements and declarations by various people's movement groups in civil society—especially religious organizations and intellectuals—chastising the authoritarian regime. The second was the signature collection campaign by the opposition NKDP. The third was a number of huge mass rallies organized and mobilized by a grand pro-democracy coalition between the people's movement groups in civil society and the opposition party.

Starting in early 1986, religious activists issued a series of declarations and statements reprimanding the authoritarian regime and demanding an immediate constitutional revision. For instance, protestant pastors argued, in a statement in March 1986, that a new constitution that would include a direct presidential election system and address basic human rights and economic equality should be drafted immediately, and the next government should be elected according to the new constitution. The Korean YMCA released a similar statement in April 1986. Cardinal Kim Su Hwan, one of the most prestigious and respected religious leaders in Korea, declared in early March 1986 that "democratization is the best way to make peace with God. The sooner the constitutional revision, the better."[20]

Religious organizations not only denounced the authoritarian regime but also defended the pro-democracy movement by the people's movement groups. On May 7 the National Council of Protestant Pastors for Justice and Peace (*Mokhyŏp*) declared that "anti-Americanism is not necessarily pro-communism," defending the radicalism displayed in some of the antigovernment demonstrations by the people's movement groups.[21] On May 6 the CPAJ, in a statement entitled "Proclaiming the Good News of Democratization and Humanization," supported labor groups and PMCDR that had been depicted by the regime as "pro-communist radical leftists."[22]

Meanwhile, starting with a statement by professors at Korea University on March 28, 1986, 783 professors at 29 colleges and universities nationwide publicly announced "statements on the current situation" (*Siguk sŏnŏn*).[23] This was an organized and peaceful nonconfidence campaign against the authoritarian regime. Most of the participants were young professors who had experienced the high tide of the student movement during the 1960s and 1970s.

Deeply frustrated by the ruling DJP's rigid stance on the issue of constitutional revision, the NKDP finally moved out of the National Assembly and launched a popular campaign to collect ten million signatures nationwide in support of constitutional revision. This number was almost half of the electorate and a quarter of the entire population of Korea at the time. The campaign started on February 12, 1986, the first anniversary of the 1985 National Assembly elections, and rapidly spread across the country. The "size and ferocity" of the signature drive astonished the authoritarian regime.[24] The police carried out a series of harsh crackdowns on the signature campaign by raiding the NKDP headquarters and the offices of people's movement groups and by arresting numerous campaign activists. But the regime could not stem the tide of the campaign.

Concurrently with the signature campaign, the NKDP reactivated its coalition with the people's movement groups in civil society and held a number of mass rallies in support of democratization. The opposition party, the NKDP, and the people's movement organization, the PMCDR, jointly set up the National Coalition for Democracy Movement (*Min'gungnyŏn*) and coordinated, organized, mobilized, and led mass rallies in major cities of the country—Kwangju on March 30, Taegu on April 5, Taejŏn on April 19, Ch'ŏngju on April 26, Inch'ŏn on May 3, Masan on May 10, and Chŏnju on May 31. In total, 500,000 to 700,000 people attended these mass rallies.[25] The people's movement groups and the opposition party were particularly encouraged and inspired at the time by the February Revolution in the Philippines, in which the Marcos regime was at last ousted by the "people's power." Such a level of mass mobilization, except during election campaigns, was the highest since the April Uprising in 1960. The grand pro-democracy coalition of the people's movement groups and the opposition party succeeded in mobilizing Koreans from all walks of life—students, workers, peasants, urban service industry employees, religious leaders, and other citizens—under the banner of "Down with the Military Authoritarian Regime and Up with a Democratic Government."

Breakdown of the Pro-democracy Coalition

However, this coalition between the people's movement groups and the opposition NKDP did not last very long. The coalition was particularly fragile in face of the authoritarian regime's tactic to split the opposition. In April 1986, the authoritarian regime took a step back and agreed to create a Special Committee on Constitutional Revision (*Kaehŏn t'ŭgwi*) in the National Assembly. The NKDP decided to accept the offer, participating in the Special Committee. The people's movement groups fiercely protested. Characterizing the NKDP's decision as conciliatory and opportunistic, the PMCDR left the National Coalition for Democracy Movement, the joint organization of the people's movement groups and the opposition party, on May 1, 1986. The rift between the people's movement groups and the NKDP was most glaring in the Inch'ŏn Mass Rally on May 3, 1986.[26] At the rally, the NKDP insisted on self-restraint and deceleration of the pro-democracy struggle, emphasizing "legal" and " intrasystemic" methods. The PMCDR opposed the move and caustically denounced both the Chun regime *and* the opposition NKDP, supporting the continuation of massive popular movement outside the National Assembly. Particularly, the Inch'ŏn Labor Federation (*Innoryŏn*), organized in February 1986, harshly criticized the conservative NKDP for having too narrow a definition of democracy by equating it with a direct presidential election. The Inch'ŏn Labor Federation and many people's movement groups put forward a broader interpretation of democracy, emphasizing the "three *mins*"—*minjung, minju,* and *minjok.* The three min's meant an autonomous economy to stop the exploitation of the people (*minjung haebang*), a democratic constitution (*minju hŏnbŏp*), and national reunification (*minjok t'ongil*). At the Inch'ŏn Rally, the Inch'ŏn Labor Federation and many people's movement groups in civil society, through violent antigovernment demonstrations, demanded the establishment of the "three min" constitution, withdrawal of the military authoritarian regime, and the awakening of the "conservative" NKDP.[27]

The opposition NKDP, despite the harsh criticism and protest by the people's movement groups in civil society, decided to participate in the Special Committee on Constitutional Revision in the National Assembly. However, little progress was made in this forum. The major participants in the Committee differed from the outset on the fundamentals of the new constitution. Nor were the authoritarian regime or the ruling DJP prepared to resolve the issue, as the opposition suggested, by putting the question to a national referendum. Rather, the ruling party was adamantly signaling that it would accept democratization only on terms chosen by and advantageous to the authoritarian regime. The NKDP was stuck in a serious deadlock in dealing with the ruling DJP and the authoritarian regime.

Restoration of the Grand Pro-democracy Coalition and Pro-democracy Movement

In early 1987, the coalition between the people's movement groups and the opposition NKDP was restored. It was this grand pro-democracy coalition that directly caused the authoritarian breakdown in June 1987. Three factors facilitated the restoration of the coalition between the people's movement groups and the opposition party.

First, the authoritarian regime attempted to coopt the NKDP and make it drop its demand for direct presidential election. In the early months of 1987, Yi Min U, the nominal leader of the NKDP, indicated to the ruling DJP that he would abandon his insistence on direct presidential election and would instead consider the DJP's formula of parliamentarianism in exchange for the guarantee of seven basic democratic reforms, including the release of political prisoners and freedom of the press. However, the de facto leaders of the NKDP—Kim Young Sam and Kim Dae Jung—and other hardliners, who had been unwavering in their insistence on direct presidential election and who constituted the mainstream faction of the party, harshly criticized Yi's view as opportunistic. Kim Young Sam and Kim Dae Jung bolted the NKDP, taking with them sixty-six of the ninety NKDP lawmakers. The two Kims formed, in March 1987, a hardline opposition party, the Reunification Democratic Party (RDP, *T'ongil minjudang*). The more radical RDP tried to reactivate and remobilize the coalition with the people's movement groups in civil society.

Then, having realized that its attempt to coopt the opposition had only led to the emergence of an even more radical opposition, the regime suddenly suspended a year-long debate on how to revise the constitution. Chun Doo Hwan declared on April 13, 1987, that he could no longer "tolerate" "wasteful" discussions on constitutional revision. This unilateral decision to terminate the public discussions on constitutional revision caused massive protests by the people's movement groups in civil society.

Starting with a public statement criticizing and opposing Chun's decision by Korea University professors on April 22, 1,475 professors from 48 universities joined the statement campaign by May 19. Artists, novelists, writers, and actors followed suit. Religious leaders and priests waged a series of hunger strikes. Cardinal Kim Su Hwan and many religious organizations, including the CPAJ, the National Council of Protestant Pastors for Justice and Peace, and the Korean National Christian Church Council (*Han'guk kidokkyo kyohoe hyŏbŭihoe*), also expressed their strong opposition to the decision.[28] Violent antigovernment protests by students, labor unions, and other people's movement groups spread across the country, and tens of thousands of Koreans in major cities demonstrated against the decision.

By contrast, many state-corporatist interest groups expressed their enthusiastic endorsement of the April 13 decision by Chun. For example, capitalist organizations such as the Federation of Korean Industries (*Chŏn'gyŏngnyŏn*), the Korea Chamber of Commerce and Industry (*Taehan sanggong hoeŭiso*), the Korea International Trade Association (*Han'guk muyŏk hyŏphoe*), the Korea Association of Employers (*Kyŏngch'ong*), and the Korea Federation of Small and Medium Enterprise Associations (*Chungso kiŏp hyŏptong chohap chunganghoe*) all issued announcements in support of the authoritarian decision.[29]

Then, at the dawning of 1987, Pak Chong Ch'ŏl, a Seoul National University student, was tortured to death during a police interrogation. The police initially announced that Pak died from a heart attack, not torture. On May 18, however, the CPAJ disclosed that Pak died from police torture and that the police and the regime had attempted to conceal the truth.

Pak Chong Ch'ŏl's torture death and the revelation of the regime's conspiracy to cover up the crime put the authoritarian regime and the ruling party on the defensive. On the other hand, it dramatically augmented the position and power of the pro-democracy coalition. In May 1987, the people's movement groups established the National Movement Headquarters for Democratic

Constitution (NMHDC, *Kungmin undong ponbu*). This organization, consisting of the PMCDR and twenty-five other people's movement groups, covered all major sectoral groups and geographical areas. Specifically, the inaugural membership included: (1) sectoral representatives—253 Catholic priests, 270 Protestant pastors, 160 Buddhist monks, 35 people from the PMCDR, 213 opposition politicians, 162 women's movement leaders, 308 from the Council for the Promotion of Democracy Movement (*Minch'uhyŏp*), 171 peasant activists, 39 labor activists, 18 urban poor activists, 43 publishers and journalists, 43 authors and writers, 66 artists, 55 educators, 12 youth movement leaders, and 74 lawyers; (2) regional representatives—11 from Kyŏnggi province, 73 from Kangwŏn province, 29 from Ch'ungnam province, 54 from Chŏnbuk province, 40 from Chŏnnam province, 56 from Pusan, and 89 from Kyŏngbuk province.[30] The NMHDC brought together civil society and political society under a unified leadership, resolving differences among people's movement groups and also between civil society groups and the opposition party.[31]

Organizing and coordinating local branches throughout the country, the NMHDC mobilized a series of massive pro-democracy demonstrations against the authoritarian regime in June 1987. The mobilization escalated particularly after Yi Han Yŏl, a Yonsei University student, was hit by tear gas bomb fragments on June 9 and injured critically. On June 10, the NMHDC organized the Uprising Rally to Defeat the April 13 Decision and to End Dictatorship. On June 26, it held the Peace Parade, in which one million people participated nationwide. Not only the people's movement groups but also many middle-class citizens participated in these mass rallies.[32] Pak Chong Ch'ŏl s death by torture and Yi Han Yŏl s injury (and later death) particularly angered middle-class citizens because these two incidents most vividly demonstrated the immoral, illegitimate, violent, and repressive nature of the authoritarian regime.[33] Just like the death of a high school student, Kim Chu Yŏl, in the first democratic juncture and the death of a female labor striker, Kim Kyŏng Suk, in the second democratic juncture, the deaths of Pak Chong Ch'ŏl and Yi Han Yŏl brought to the minds of ordinary citizens the image of democratic martyrdom. The grand pro-democracy coalition between civil society and political society, through reminding ordinary citizens of the many democratic martyrs in the checkered history of Korean democratization, was able to effectively mobilize the support of the middle class.

Cornered by the unprecedented mobilization of the people's movement groups in civil society and their coalition with the opposition party, the authoritarian regime finally announced dramatic and unexpected concessions to the demands of the people's movement groups on June 29, 1987, adopting a direct presidential election system.[34]

Civil Society and the Politics of Democratic Transition

The Great Labor Struggle

The June 29 declaration finally put an end to the protracted and intense confrontations between the authoritarian regime and the grand pro-democracy coalition of civil society and political society in Korea. Concomitantly, it also ushered Korean politics into a new stage: democratic transition.

As during the previous democratic junctures, the authoritarian breakdown in June 1987 was also followed by a civil society explosion, particularly a dramatic increase in labor activism. Immediately after the June 29 declaration, the labor movement erupted and engulfed all of Korea in July and August 1987. Workers in nearly all industrial sectors took collective action to express their repressed interests, demanding wage increases, better working conditions, and the right to create democratic unions. The number and intensity of labor strikes were unprecedented. During July and August 1987, 3,337 strikes occurred, more than 12 times the number of strikes in the entire year of 1986 (table 5.3). It was also quadruple the number of strikes in 1980 (848), immediately after the authoritarian breakdown of the Park Chung Hee regime.[35] In addition, 1,278 new unions were created during the same period, which amounted to one third of the total number of unions in existence at the end of 1987.[36]

The massive and violent labor movement in the summer of 1987—the Great Labor Struggle—began with the organization of new labor unions in one of the most powerful business conglomerates (*Chaebŏl*) in Korea, Hyundai Group. In early July 1987, labor unions were created, and disputes erupted in

TABLE 5.3
Trade Unions and Labor Disputes, 1983–1987

	1983	1984	1985	1986	1987
Unions	3,083	2,868	2,884	3,004	4,086
Strikes	98	113	265	276	3,749

Sources: EPB, *Han'guk t'onggye wŏlbo*; KLI, *Pun'gibyŏl nodong tonghyang punsŏk*; FKTU, *Saŏp pogo*

Hyundai Engine in Ulsan city and Hyundai Shipbuilding in Mip'o city. Strikes quickly spread to other Hyundai companies and reached other industrial areas in August 1987, affecting all the major industrial cities in Korea in mid-August. As compared with other labor explosions during the previous democratic junctures, the Great Labor Struggle of 1987 had two distinctive characteristics.

First of all, the demands raised during the struggle were not limited to economic issues such as the guarantee of a minimum wage, overtime pay, paid vacation, or improvement of labor conditions. Rather, the struggle focused on the democratization of the workplace—in particular, the complete liquidation of the existing state-corporatist unions and the establishment of democratic unions in their place.[37] The democratic unions organized during this period later led the movement for a democratic national peak association of trade unions (Korean Confederation of Trade Unions, *Minju noch'ong*), replacing the existing FKTU.

Secondly, there was no central organization that could lead or coordinate the struggle. Instead, strikes spontaneously erupted from below by ordinary laborers.[38] The official FKTU neither supported nor helped the establishment of democratic labor unions. Rather, the FKTU obstructed the struggle by declaring that it would fight to the death any attempt to disrupt and undermine its authority and leadership. FKTU's anachronistic sabotage and the lack of coordination among scattered labor movements prompted many labor activists to vigorously push for the establishment of a new democratic labor federation against the state-corporatist FKTU.

Until early August 1987, the ruling regime tolerated and stayed away from the labor explosion that had been sweeping across the entire nation. Most of all, the exiting authoritarian regime did not want to tarnish its newly acquired democratic image by resuming the cycle of suppression and resistance. However, the regime at last yielded to the repeated appeals and requests from various capitalist associations. Starting with the statement by the Federation of Korean Industries on August 11, capitalist associations, such as the Korea Association of Employers, the Korea Chamber of Commerce and Industry, and the Korea Federation of Small and Medium Enterprise Associations, vehemently assailed labor activism, characterizing the so-called Great Labor Struggle as violent, destructive, illegal, and communist-sponsored. They repeatedly called for state intervention to stop social turmoil and restore stability. On August 20, the regime finally responded to their requests by setting up a special investigative agency for uprooting the "leftists" masterminding the "labor unrest." The government suppression of labor movement culminated in the violent repression of Hyundai heavy industry and Daewoo Auto on September 4, 1987.[39]

The Great Labor Struggle in July and August, 1987, was both a continuation and a break with the previous pro-democracy movement by the people's movement groups. The continuity lay in the fact that the struggle pushed further the democratic reforms. Whereas most of the other people's movement groups were confused about how to respond to the sudden surrender of the authoritarian regime, labor activists continued their struggle for democracy by calling for the demise of the state-corporatist unions and the establishment of autonomous and democratic labor unions. As already noted, workers during the Great Labor Struggle focused their demands on the democratization of the workplace and the organization of new labor unions that would be more democratic and more accountable to members.

Meanwhile, the break occurred because different interpretations of democracy emerged and evolved. The June 29 declaration by the authoritarian regime did not mention such issues as economic (in)equality or social (in)justice.[40] The statement primarily concerned basic human rights, political freedom, and the electoral system. Whereas students, intellectuals, religious leaders, and the middle class felt that the June 29 democratization package had, to a considerable degree, contained their major demands and their ideals of democracy, laborers did not concur.[41] In other words, labor groups could not "satisfice," while most other people's movement groups did. Most of all, without addressing socioeconomic inequality and injustice, democracy sounded rather empty to labor activists. While the other groups defined democracy primarily in procedural terms, labor groups defined it in "substantive" terms. The Great Labor Struggle, in this respect, revealed the split between two different pro-democracy movements: one by those who could be contented with "procedural democracy"; and the other by those who wanted to achieve "substantive democracy."[42]

Marginalization of Civil Society and Defeat of the Opposition in the Presidential Election

During the pro-democracy struggle and up until the authoritarian breakdown in June 1987, civil society groups had always been effecting political changes in Korea. Particularly, the resurrection, reactivation, and remobilization of the people's movement groups played a leading role in facilitating the authoritarian breakdown. The people's movement groups formed a formidable pro-democracy alliance and challenged the authority and legitimacy of the ruling regime. They also took the initiative in forging and developing a grand pro-democracy coalition with the opposition party. In short, civil society groups had largely exercised hegemony over political parties. However, after the authoritarian regime agreed to carry out a set of democratic reforms, including a direct presidential election, the hegemony of civil society over political society started to erode. The focus of the transitional politics was placed on the founding elections—the presidential election in December 1987 and the National Assembly elections in April 1988. As the founding elections were approaching, Korean politics gravitated and revolved more and more toward party politics and electoral competitions in political society. People's movement groups in civil society became incrementally marginalized.

The NMHDC and other people's movement groups in civil society, such as the PMCDR and the YCDM, continued demanding more democratic reforms, including the release of all political prisoners and the complete termination of torture. Also, they kept fighting for the repeal of antidemocratic laws enacted by the LCNS in the early 1980s, like the Basic Press Law, the laws regarding assembly and demonstration, and various labor-related laws. Overall, however, the people's movement groups were relatively inactive after the authoritarian breakdown.

Meanwhile, a serious split emerged within political society. Friction developed between the two most powerful leaders of the opposition RDP—Kim Young Sam and Kim Dae Jung—over who should be the party's candidate in the upcoming presidential election. During the pro-democracy struggle, the two Kims had presented a united front most of the time, resisting government efforts to undermine their alignment. However, the united front, at best a political marriage of convenience, began to fall apart after the June 29 declaration and the adoption of direct presidential election.[43] On September 29, 1987, the negotiation between the two Kims failed. Announcing that he would also enter the presidential race, Kim Dae Jung seceded from the RDP and established a new party—the Party for Peace and Democracy (P'yŏnghwa minjudang).

The breakdown of the unity between Kim Young Sam and Kim Dae Jung profoundly disappointed the people's movement groups in civil society that had been expecting a single candidate to run against the ruling DJP's candidate Roh Tae Woo. The people's movement groups feared and predicted that the split between the two prominent opposition leaders would enable Roh to win the election in December 1987. To remedy the internal fragmentation of political society and to save their hard-fought pro-democracy struggle, the people's movement groups in civil society launched a campaign to reunite the two Kims.

However, although the people's movement groups widely agreed that they should have a unified single opposition candidate to win the presidential election, they did not have a consensus on whom to support. The people's movement groups were split into three different camps. The first camp argued that they should "critically support" (*Pip'anjŏk chiji*) Kim Dae Jung, who was "relatively progressive." The PMCDR, many student organizations, and the YCDM took this position. The second camp called for the resumption of talks between the two Kims and insisted that a single candidate should arise through negotiations. This camp argued that the important issue was not the progressiveness but the "electability" of a candidate. Various student groups and the Seoul Labor Movement Coalition belonged to this camp. The third camp, composed of many labor unions and radical student groups, deeply distrusted political society and proposed to have an independent "people's candidate." This camp argued that it was now time for the people's movement groups to organize themselves as a meaningful political force. Later, the second and the third camps merged and pushed for a grand compromise between the two Kims on who would run as a single opposition candidate.[44]

Despite the efforts of the people's movement groups, however, neither Kim Young Sam nor Kim Dae Jung changed his mind, and they finally ran separately in the elections. The election returns showed that DJP candidate Roh Tae Woo won the race by receiving 35.9 percent of the popular vote. Kim Young Sam finished second with 27.5 percent, trailed by Kim Dae Jung, who garnered 26.5 percent. The two Kims together received 54 percent of the vote. As widely predicted by most people's movement groups in civil society, a single opposition candidate would have won the election. Observers were all but unanimous in believing that the primary reason for the defeat of the opposition was the almost even split of the 54 percent of the vote between the two Kims.[45]

Analysis of the Third Democratic Juncture

Actors

During the first few years of the Chun Doo Hwan regime, due to harsh state suppression, civil society remained largely silent. Various institutional and legislative measures by the authoritarian regime succeeded in suppressing and muting civil society as a whole. At the same time, the authoritarian regime was also in full control of the political society at the time, which was composed of the ruling DJP and pseudo-opposition parties. Both civil society and political society were fully pacified, depoliticized, and atomized by the authoritarian state. Ironically, owing to this tight and putatively "perfect" control of civil society, the ruling bloc in late 1983 dared to relax its social control and to liberalize the political system.

The reason why the ruling regime decided to open the political process was not because of the fatal split between hardliners and softliners in the leadership. Rather, it was primarily owing to the hubris of the authoritarian regime. Unlike some of the classic cases of democratic transition in Southern Europe and Latin America, where the beginning of democratic transitions was the consequence of "important divisions within the authoritarian regime itself, principally along the fluctuating cleavage between hardliners and softliners,"[46] there were no present or potential cleavages within the ruling bloc. The ruling bloc in Korea at the time was considerably homogeneous and unified. The ruling bloc was united not only *before* the liberalization, but also *after* the liberalization into the democratic transition.[47] Instead, the political liberalization was due to the misperceptions of the regime and international pressure. Overconfidence in the social control mechanisms and institutions introduced in the formative years of the authoritarian regime precipitated the unraveling of the authoritarian system itself.

Although Korea differs from Southern Europe and Latin America in that the initial momentum of authoritarian breakdown did not originate from a division between hardliners and softliners in the ruling bloc, it is similar to the other two geographic areas in terms of the consequence of political liberalization. What is called the "resurrection of civil society" ensued. As O'Donnell and Schmitter point out, "Once the first steps toward liberalization are made, the whole texture, density, and content of intellectually authoritative discourse changes, giving an enormous impulse to the demise of authoritarian rule." The culmination of the resurrection of civil society, "popular upsurge," performed the "crucial role of pushing the transition further."[48] Civil society groups, which had been silent in the initial years of the Chun regime, became rapidly resurrected. They quickly organized national associations and began questioning the legitimacy and authority of the authoritarian regime. By late 1984, the triple solidarity of students, workers, and churches, which had been in the making during the anti-Park struggle in the 1970s, was fully restored and reinforced under various national people's movement organizations.

What is particularly notable during this third democratic juncture is the role of the middle class. Although the middle class did not have its own organizations, it actively supported students, workers, and churches during the pro-democracy movement in 1987. Mainstream members of the middle class actively participated in the democratization struggles not necessarily because of their inherent democratic impulse against authoritarian rule. Rather, the "cumulative effects of numerous political struggles of students, intellectuals, and workers, as well as a series of revelations about the regime's brutality, aroused moral anger among the middle class."[49] As a result, by June 1987, the differences between the mainstream middle class and the more radical dissidents seemed to have largely disappeared in face of the common enemy—namely, Chun Doo Hwan's authoritarian regime.

Throughout the 1970s, the middle class was not a politically significant force in Korean civil society. As the economic development exceeded a certain level, however, the middle class became more and more impatient and exasperated with its postponed political rights and mortgaged civil liberties. The classical Lipsetian thesis seems to hold true in the case of Korea: "Increased wealth . . . affects the political role of the middle class by changing the shape of the stratification structure."[50] Not only did the economic development change the stratification structure of Korean society, but it also changed the attitude, political culture, and *Weltanschauung* of the middle class.[51]

Interactions

During the third juncture, civil society–state relations continued to be antagonistic and conflictual. Many civil society groups felt Chun Doo Hwan's authoritarian regime had to be opposed, resisted, and eventually overthrown. The political battle, as it had been during the previous junctures, was between the pro-democracy forces in civil society and the authoritarian regime with its state-corporatist allies.

What was significantly different during this juncture, as compared with the earlier two democratic junctures, was the power, breadth, and unity of the pro-democracy alliance of civil society groups. Unlike the first democratic juncture, students were not alone in the protests against the authoritarian regime, and unlike the second democratic juncture, the triple solidarity was not left unreflected in the national associations. Several powerful and effective national people's movement organizations coordinated civil society groups. Furthermore, as opposed to the occurrences during the previous two democratic junctures, the pro-democracy struggles of people's movement groups were supported and joined by the middle class, the ordinary citizens. The sheer number of people participating in the antigovernment gatherings and the mobilizational power of the democratic alliance of civil society groups intimidated the authoritarian regime.

During the previous two democratic junctures the state easily used the military to suppress the protest, but this time it became extremely difficult for the ruling regime to control and suppress the political opposition without generating serious domestic and—more important—international repercussions. The World Olympic Games, scheduled for 1988, were quickly approaching, and harsh suppression of the pro-democracy alliance of civil society groups would irrevocably tarnish the reputation and prestige of Korean democracy and degrade the status of Korea internationally.

In summary, although conflict continually characterized the civil society–state relations during this period, the content, quality, and degree of the conflict were quite different. During the third juncture, the protest politics of civil society was so intensive and extensive that the ruling authoritarian regime did not actually enjoy the option of ignoring or simply suppressing it. Some kind of compromise, solution, and negotiation seemed necessary and inevitable to avoid a massive, disastrous, and internationally disgraceful tragedy.

In terms of the civil society–political society relationship, the third democratic juncture shared both similarities and differences with the second democratic juncture. During the third juncture, as in the second democratic juncture civil society groups were able to form alignments with a strong, hardline opposition party, unlike in the first democratic period. Just as during the previous democratic juncture, it was exactly when the opposition party removed the moderate component in the party—which was suspected to have been coopted by the ruling regime—and proclaimed a shift to a hardline struggle against the authoritarian regime that the real pro-democracy coalition between civil society and political society was made possible. This happened in the second democratic juncture when Kim Young Sam returned to the leadership of the opposition New Democratic Party. In the third democratic juncture this occurred when Kim Young Sam and Kim Dae Jung rejected Yi Min U's moderate position and created a new party, the RDP.

However, the cooperation between civil society and political society became much more organized and systematic in the third democratic period. During the previous juncture, the cooperation was mainly between individual opposition politicians and individual religious leaders. Through individual networks, they made commitments to the pro-democracy movement and jointly released a series of statements and declarations to castigate the Park regime. Important elements in civil society, such as student groups and labor unions, were left out of the coalition between civil society and political society. The two camps—that is, student and labor movements on the one hand and religious leaders and party politicians on the other—tended to go separate ways. But during the third democratic juncture civil society organizations, as noted earlier, were truly reflective and representative of the triple solidarity resurrected and reactivated in the aftermath of political liberalization in the 1983–1984 period, and these strong organizations aligned with the main opposition party. This time, civil society and political society collaborated not only through joint statements and declarations, but also through a common, unified, coherent organizational entity, such as the NMHDC and the National Coalition for Democracy Movement. The cooperation and alignment between civil society and political society became significantly organized, systematized, and institutionalized through these common political entities.

Issues

Democracy continued to be the first priority for civil society groups. However, different conceptions of democracy emerged during the third democratic juncture: one procedural and the other substantive. This divergence of different segments of civil society on the definition of democracy had already been adumbrated during the second democratic juncture, when many national *chaeya* associations failed to reflect student and labor components in civil society. While students and laborers supported a more radical definition of democracy, including socioeconomic equalities ignored and sacrificed in the process of the rapid, export-oriented industrialization in the 1960s and 1970s, conservative politicians and religious leaders had a relatively moderate, procedural definition of democracy. In the third democratic juncture, this division initially became manifested in the establishment of the two different—and, in some respect, competing—national organizations of civil society groups in 1984.

The severity and urgency of forming and sustaining a unified front against the repressive authoritarian regime, however, substantially suppressed such a disagreement on the definition and contents of democracy. The merger of the two organizations, the CMPD and the NCDR, appeared to remedy the division. The national associations effectively reflected the triple solidarity and united the people's movement groups. However, as expressed in the Inch'ŏn Mass Rally, the division between the two segments in civil society was not completely contained. Different groups widely agreed that the authoritarian regime should exit, but they did not have any explicit, clear consensus on what kind of democracy should be installed in its place. The suppression of this crucial division was only temporary. Immediately after the authoritarian breakdown, the division became obvious in the Great Labor Struggle in July–August 1987. The democracy supported and promoted by laborers and students, substantive democracy, was broader and addressed the issue of socioeconomic equalities, while the democracy supported by other segments of civil society and party politicians, procedural democracy, was narrower and focused on institutional reforms in the political arena. These two conceptions of democracy would continue to compete and conflict with each other into the democratic consolidation stage, as I will discuss in chapter 6.

The reunification issue reemerged in the third democratic juncture. Although it was viewed as largely secondary to the more urgent goal of political democratization, it was actively raised and promoted by civil society groups. As a result, in the democratization drama of 1987, the issues raised by civil society in its struggle against Chun's authoritarian regime were a mixture of democratization, national reunification, and anti-imperialism (or anti-Americanism). This combination was quite similar to the group of issues raised during the first democratic juncture. As already pointed out, democracy, reunification, and self-assertive foreign relations were seen as inseparably linked during the first democratic juncture. In the third democratic juncture reunification, namely the overcoming of the national division, was also considered to be the key to genuine democratization. Furthermore, national reunification was viewed as the first step to achieving true national independence and to terminating the Korea's lateral dependence on the United States.

However, the reemergence of the reunification issue signified the realization of civil society leaders that the Korean people would no longer buy the unconvincing anticommunist argument of the government, especially considering the ever-widening economic and demographic disparity between North and South Korea. The anticommunist ideology and offensive had already been overused by the preceding authoritarian regimes and the Chun regime. Movement activists in civil society and opposition politicians in political society still faced severe legal sanctions and the ignominious label of "pro-communists" when they participated in pro-democracy movements. But the effectiveness of anticommunist attacks, as compared with the previous two democratic junctures, was considerably impaired. Just like the young shepherd in one of Aesop's fables who repeatedly lies, only to his own disadvantage, the authoritarian regimes in Korea had used anticommunist tactics too many times and thus rendered them largely useless.

Summary and Conclusions

In this chapter, I examined the role of civil society in the authoritarian breakdown and democratic transition in Korea from 1984 to 1987. I began by reviewing the overall configuration of Korean civil society in the early 1980s. Chun Doo Hwan's authoritarian regime, through a series of "social purification campaigns" and antidemocratic legislations, pacified and depoliticized civil society as a whole. Because of the state's tight control, civil society remained silent from 1980 to 1983. However, exactly because of such "successful" control of civil society, the authoritarian regime decided to relax and liberalize the political system in late 1984, which only led to an extensive and rapid "resurrection of civil society."

I then analyzed the role of civil society in the authoritarian breakdown. It was primarily the people's movement groups in civil society—the triple solidarity of student groups, labor unions, and religious organizations—and their pro-democracy coalition with the opposition party that contributed to the authoritarian breakdown between 1984 and 1987. As compared with the previous two democratic junctures, the scope and power of the pro-democracy coalition had considerably increased. The pro-democracy coalition included not only the triple solidarity, but also many middle-class citizens. Furthermore, the coalition was headed by influential national associations. These central organizations tightly coordinated and effectively mobilized various sectoral and regional groups in their antiregime campaigns and demonstrations. Such a grand pro-democracy coalition was the real cause for the authoritarian breakdown in 1987.

The role of civil society during the democratic transition was discussed next, as I highlighted how the focus of the transitional politics quickly moved from civil society to political society following the June Uprising in 1987. Civil society, in a sense, delegated the politics of democratic transition to political society and became gradually marginalized. However, political society suffered a severe internal fragmentation—specifically between Kim Young Sam and Kim Dae Jung—and eventually failed to achieve a genuine alternation of power. Civil society groups belatedly tried to remedy the split and produce a unified opposition presidential candidate, to no avail. In short, civil society's premature delegation of the transitional politics to political society prevented a more fundamental transition. Presumably, the split between the two opposition leaders was inevitable. But if the people's movement groups had retained their hegemony over political society a little longer after the authoritarian breakdown the mode and character of Korean transition could have been different.

Finally, I analyzed the third democratic juncture in terms of its actors, interactions, and issues. No specific class or classes contributed to Korean democratization; rather, the pro-democracy coalition basically consisted of diverse *Stände* groups. The philosophy of "no bourgeoisie, no democracy"[52] has little relevance to Korea because most capitalist associations avidly supported the continuation, if not perpetuation, of the tenure of the authoritarian regime. The Korean bourgeoisie, created and nurtured by the strong developmental state, had always been a loyal, subsidiary partner to the authoritarian regimes. As far as Korea was concerned, the reigning sentiment was "bourgeoisie, no democracy." Meanwhile, "no working class, no democracy"[53] is at best applicable to Korea only partially because it was not the working class alone that promoted democratization but rather many intermediate groups of students, intellectuals, religious people, and dissident politicians also supported the cause. Civil society and the state were continually in a conflictual relationship. Meanwhile, under the leadership of joint organizations, the pro-democracy alliance in civil society succeeded in forging and solidifying a grand coalition with the opposition party. The democratic coalition of civil society and political society was the greatest and strongest in the history of Korea, posing a considerable threat to the authoritarian regime. Two different conceptions of democracy, which had already been hinted at during the second democratic juncture, became fully developed and articulated during the third democratic juncture. During the authoritarian breakdown, different elements in civil society, despite their disagreement on the definition of democracy, cooperated in a unified struggle against the authoritarian regime. As soon as the democratic transition began, however, the division between the two different camps in civil society became obvious. Different camps in civil society started to pursue their own versions of democratization. This division was to affect and determine largely the politics of democratic consolidation in Korea, as we will see in chapter 6. Therefore, in the following chapter, I will explain what happened to Korean civil society after the democratic transition and how civil society groups have affected democratic consolidation since 1988.

C H A P T E R 6

Civil Society in Democratic Consolidation, 1988–Present

The reason we pursue this movement in a nonviolent, peaceful, popular, and legal fashion is to make ordinary citizens feel comfortable about joining our movement. The reason we avoid abstract, theoretical discussions and instead seek specific alternatives is because ordinary citizens will respond only if they are presented with concrete, realistic, and practical alternatives.

CITIZENS' COALITION FOR ECONOMIC JUSTICE, 1989

Koreans from all walks of life need to participate in the political process, propose constructive and detailed social policies, and put them into law. We want to build a democratic society in which liberty, justice, human rights, and human welfare are protected and promoted by participating citizens.

PEOPLE'S SOLIDARITY FOR PARTICIPATORY DEMOCRACY, 1994

IN this chapter, I explore the latest phase of Korean democratization—consolidation of democracy. Focusing on the posttransitional settings, I analyze how civil society groups have been affecting and shaping the politics of democratic consolidation in Korea. In section 1, I examine the changes in the internal composition of Korean civil society since 1988. In section 2, selecting several prominent themes and issues in the politics of democratic consolidation, I investigate how various groups in civil society have interacted with each other to influence political processes. In section 3, I briefly consider the impact of the recent economic crisis in Korea on civil society and democratic consolidation. In section 4, I review this latest phase of Korean democratization according to my analytical framework.

Configuration of Korean Civil Society, 1988–Present

Two different but closely interrelated trends have characterized Korean civil society since the democratic transition in 1987. The first is the emergence and expansion of new social movement groups called "citizens' movement groups." The second is the transformation and adjustment of the existing people's movement groups.

Citizens' Movement Groups

One of the most notable trends in Korean civil society since 1988 has been the proliferation of new movement groups called citizens' movement groups (Simin undong tanch'e). Coordinated under the Korea Council of Citizens' Movements (KCCM, Siminhyŏp), prominent examples of citizens' movement groups include the Citizens' Coalition for Economic Justice (CCEJ, Kyŏngsillyŏn) and the Korea Federation for Environmental Movement (KFEM, Hwan'gyŏngnyŏn). The KCCM was created on September 12, 1994, by thirty-eight citizens' movement groups. The initial membership encompassed a wide variety of social groups, such as religious groups (for example, Buddhist, Protestant, Tonghak, Wŏn Buddhist groups), environmental organizations (for example, the KFEM, church-environmental institutes, green movement associations), women's groups, consumer movement groups, reunification movement organizations, the movement for educational reform, and organizations of the handicapped. In its inaugural declaration, the KCCM proclaimed that its supreme goal was to make civil society more active and strengthen solidarity and cooperation among civil society groups with a view to achieving social development. It put special emphasis on: (1) the autonomy and consolidation of citizens' movement groups; (2) internationalization of citizen movements; (3) reinforcement of solidarity among citizens' movement groups; and (4) augmentation of the power of civil society and maximization of participatory democracy. Some leading members of the KCCM, particularly the CCEJ and the KFEM, had consistently emphasized that they would lead a new generation of social movement in Korea, different from the class-based and confrontational movement of the past. The formation of the KCCM symbolized that they had at last officially proclaimed the dawn of such a new era.

In a number of respects, the citizens' movement groups are different from the existing people's movement groups, which played important roles in the authoritarian breakdowns and democratic transitions in the third democratic juncture.[1] In terms of movement participants, the citizens' movement groups principally include middle-class citizens such as white-collar workers, professionals, religious leaders, and intellectuals. By contrast, the people's movement groups were and still are primarily composed of blue-collar laborers, peasants, the urban poor, students, and other local residents. As far as movement goals are concerned, the citizens' movement groups emphasize gradual institutional reforms. They do not oppose the capitalist system *per se*; instead, they only underscore and try to correct the distorted and unjust aspects of its socioeconomic consequences. Meanwhile, the people's movement groups pursue fundamental and structural reforms that are intended to address and eventually overcome economic inequality and political suppression. In relation to movement style, the citizens' movement groups rely mostly on legal and nonviolent methods such as publicity campaigns, lectures, and the distribution of pamphlets. The people's movement groups, however, do not strictly comply with legal and peaceful methods of protest. They often resort to illegal and violent measures like strikes, demonstrations, and sit-ins. In regard to issues, the citizens' movement groups focus on a range of social issues, including fair elections, consumers' rights, the fight against corruption, the environment, and gender inequality. By contrast, the people's movement groups place their priority on overcoming various forms of political and economic inequalities— particularly the inequalities between the elite and the masses and between capitalists and laborers. According to the people's movement groups, rectifying such inequalities is crucial in consolidating and deepening Korean democracy.

Although the citizens' movement groups differ from the people's movement groups in numerous ways, the two camps share some similarities too. Above all, they significantly differ from the "new social movements" in Western Europe and other industrial and postindustrial societies. In Western Europe, the new social movements emerged as both a challenge and an alternative to the "conservative" labor movement, raising new issues like peace (the antinuclear stance), the environment (environmental safety, the preservation of the environment), and women (feminism, gender equality). The new social movements, emphasizing grassroots democracy, tried to transcend materialism and the distinction between left and right. They relied as well on unconventional and radical movement strategies. The new movement groups in Korea are similar to those movements in addressing various postindustrial issues. However, the goals of the citizens' movement groups in Korea are still materialistic (such as consumers' rights, economic justice, and economic equality). Also, as already noted, their movement methods are largely moderate and reformist.

Most of all, the labor class in Korea, unlike its counterparts in some Western societies, is not yet so conservative as to prompt the radicalization of other social movements.[2]

The citizens' movement groups have proliferated in an unprecedented fashion after the democratic transition in 1987. A survey study shows that of sixty-nine major citizens' movement groups existing in 1993, forty-seven were created after 1988 (table 6.1). Such associational explosion of the citizens' movement groups has been particularly salient in social, women's, and youth organizations (table 6.2).

People's Movement Groups

The people's movement groups (*Minjung undong tanch'e*), which played a crucial role in facilitating the authoritarian breakdown and democratic transition in 1987, have been striving to find their new identity and role in the politics of democratic consolidation. Immediately after the transition, between 1988 and 1990, the people's movement groups were reorganized into several new national associations. For example, in 1987 the National Council of University Student Representatives (*Chŏndaehyŏp*) was established as a national organization of student groups. In January 1989, the Korea Coalition for National Democracy Movement (*Chŏnmillyŏn*) was formed, succeeding the People's

TABLE 6.1
Citizens' Movement Groups, 1945–1993

Period	Number	%
1944	4	5.8
1945–1959	2	2.9
1960–1964	1	1.4
1965–1969	3	4.3
1970–1974	2	2.9
1975–1979	2	2.9
1980–1984	1	1.4
1985–1987	7	10.1
1988–1990	25	36.2
1991–1993	22	31.9
Total	69	100.0

Source: IDD, *Simin undong tanch'e hwalsŏnghwa pangane taehan yŏn'gu*, 7.

Movement Coalition for Democracy and Reunification (PMCDR) during the democratic transition. Also in 1989, the Korean Peasant Movement Coalition (*Chŏnnong*) and the Korean Teachers' and Educational Workers' Union (KTEWU, *Chŏn'gyojo*) were formed. In January 1990, the Korea Trade Union Council (*Chŏnnohyŏp*) was established. These three national organizations— the Korean Peasant Movement Coalition, the KTEWU, and the Korea Trade Union Council—led movements against the existing state-corporatist groups such as various official agricultural cooperatives, the Korea Federation of Teachers' Associations (*Kyoch'ong*), and the Federation of Korean Trade Unions (FKTU). As mentioned in the preceding chapters, these progovernment groups had been supportive of the authoritarian regimes in the past. For instance, the Korea Federation of Teachers' Associations supported the Legislative Council for National Security (LCNS) in 1980, and its president at the time served as a member of the LCNS. Also, as pointed out in the previous sections, the FKTU released numerous progovernment declarations and promoted antidemocratic activities throughout the authoritarian periods.

However, compared to the PMCDR (which played such a crucial role in the authoritarian breakdown and democratic transition in 1987), both the Korea Coalition for National Democracy Movement in 1989 and its successor, the National Alliance for Democracy and Unification of Korea (NADUK, *Chŏn'guk yŏnhap*) in 1992, have been far less visible and influential in Korean politics. During Roh Tae Woo's term (1988–1993), the people's movement groups focused on exposing the continuity between Roh's "pseudo" democracy and Chun's authoritarian regime, pejoratively characterizing Roh as Chun with a wig (Chun was bald). But after the inauguration of the Kim Young Sam gov-

TABLE 6.2
Social, Women's, and Youth Groups, 1980–1993

	Social Groups	Women's Groups	Youth Groups	Total
1980	13	36	24	73
1984	12	36	31	79
1988	51	38	31	120
1990	55	43	28	126
1992	58	54	30	142
1993	61	78	28	167

Source: *Tonga yŏn'gam*, 1980–1993.

ernment (1993–1998), the people's movement groups experienced a serious setback. This situation did not change much during the Kim Dae Jung government (1998–present). Kim Young Sam, immediately after his inauguration, stunned civil society as a whole, preempting the opposition of the people's movement groups in particular by carrying out a series of reforms that had been unimaginable during the previous authoritarian regimes. Under the slogan of "moral restoration" and "new Korea," Kim publicly disclosed his private assets, encouraged public officials and politicians to follow suit, ordered the investigation of wrongdoings perpetrated by former political and military leaders, and drastically implemented the "real-name bank account system" to cut the close association between business and politics.[3] Shocked by the pace at which the Kim regime implemented democratic reforms, the people's movement groups underwent a crucial identity crisis.[4] Although people's movement groups recovered relatively quickly from this identity crisis and regained solidarity, mainly owing to the failure of economic and political reforms during the later years of the Kim Young Sam government, most people's movement groups are still trying to adjust to the political dynamics of democratic consolidation.[5]

Some people's movement groups decided to distance themselves from their old images, in which they almost reflexively and instinctively castigated the ruling regime and criticized the status quo. Groups such as the Korea Trade Union Council, the KTEWU, and the Korean Peasant Movement Coalition, whose leaders spearheaded the pro-democracy movement in 1987, announced that they would abandon the militant style of their past movements and adopt a "softer" style, promoting and sponsoring public policy debates and waging peaceful campaigns instead of violent demonstrations. On the other hand, some other groups are leaving the people's movement camp, trying to repackage themselves as part of citizens' movement camp.[6]

Student groups, which were extremely instrumental in all of the previous authoritarian breakdowns and democratic transitions, have also experienced a crisis. In March 1993 the National Council of University Student Representatives officially announced its disintegration. Although it was succeeded by another national organization, the National Coalition of University Student Councils (NCUSC, *Hanch'ongnyŏn*) in 1993, more and more student leaders deplore that they can no longer organize and mobilize students in massive demonstrations as they did in the past. New students do not care much about such broad issues as political democracy, economic equality, or national reunification. Instead, they are becoming more and more interested in intracampus and practical issues. For instance, students are far more concerned about sky-rocketing tuition, expensive books, poor service at campus restaurants, inaccessible computer facilities, and crowded soccer fields. Whether and how to cope with these changing concerns of students has been a source of heated debate inside the NCUSC.[7] It declared in 1993 that it would avoid radical and violent demonstrations and would stick to a nonviolent, peaceful movement style. In 1995, the NCUSC pledged that it would faithfully respond to the concerns of "ordinary" students.[8] These public pledges notwithstanding, student groups in general continue to be the most radical segment of Korean civil society. In August 1996, NCUSC students, while staging a massive antigovernment protest at Yonsei University in Seoul, engaged in a violent confrontation with police.

The continued violence and radicalism of student groups make them more and more isolated from the main social movements in civil society today. Even Cardinal Kim Su Hwan, one of the most consistent and strongest supporters of the student movement throughout the previous democratic junctures, stated in an interview in 1997, "I regret that student movement, because it is so distant from what the ordinary citizens think, is more and more isolated and disregarded by Koreans."[9] As is the case with the NADUK, some of the local university student councils are deserting the NCUSC, criticizing the association's radicalism and pursuing more practical movement goals.

Meanwhile, intellectuals who had previously been engaged in the *praxis* of pro-democracy movement are now shifting to *theory* in trying to understand the tumultuous years of political transformation in the 1980s and to provide predictions and prescriptions for the future of Korean democracy. Leading scholars and intellectuals, who had been members of the people's movement groups during the authoritarian periods, established the Korea Council of Academic Groups (*Haktanhyŏp*) in November 1988. This organization includes various academic groups in literature, arts, law, history, geography, education, economics, journalism, sociology, gender studies, political science, and philosophy. The purpose of the council is to facilitate scientific research on Korean society and to contribute to democratization and reunification through academic research. Also, the council aims to help the expansion and further the activation of the people's movement groups, or what they call the "progressive" or "democratic" camp. The Korea Council of Academic Groups has held annual symposia on various topics, such as the state of the humanities and the social sciences in Korea; Korean society and the ruling structure in the 1980s; socialist reform and the Korean peninsula; the capitalist world system and Korean society; the democratic transformation of Korea and policy alternatives; the current tasks for Korean democracy; social, economic, and political systems of a reunified Korea; the economic crisis; and the Kwangju Uprising.[10]

Civil Society and the Politics of Democratic Consolidation

In chapter 2, I defined democratic consolidation as the process in which "democracy becomes so broadly and profoundly legitimate among its citizens that it is very unlikely to break down."[11] What is central to this definition of democratic consolidation is legitimacy, which is not merely an abstract but rather a shared normative and behavioral commitment to democracy. As Linz and Stepan underscore, a consolidated democracy is a political situation in which democracy has become "the only game in town."[12] For democracy to be "the only game in town" and to be "broadly and profoundly legitimate" a new democratic regime must deal with a number of critical challenges. Some of the challenges inherent in democratic consolidation include, for example, greater executive and military accountability to the law and the public; more effective protection for the political and civil rights of all citizens; enhancement of political participation of the traditionally marginalized social groups in the populace; reduction of political corruption; a clear break with the authoritarian past; and higher institutionalization of the representation of various societal interests.[13] By overcoming these challenges of democratic consolidation, the procedural minimum of democracy is firmly established, and an authoritarian regression becomes extremely unlikely, if not impossible. In Korea, civil society groups have been playing significant roles in the politics of democratic consolidation by pressuring the governments since 1988 to meet many of these important challenges of democratic consolidation.

Settling the Old Scores

The liquidation of the authoritarian past is one of the most critical issues in the politics of democratic consolidation. Without a reasonably clean separation from the previous authoritarian regimes it is almost impossible for a new democratic regime to establish and broaden its legitimacy.[14] Investigating and punishing the past wrongdoings and corruption are essential in increasing legitimacy and consolidating the fledgling democracy. As I pointed out in my analysis of the first democratic juncture, the Chang Myŏn's "democratic" regime (1960–1961) failed miserably to achieve a clean break with Syngman

Rhee's authoritarian regime, generating frustration among civil society groups and eventually precipitating a democratic breakdown.

During the first two years (1988–1989) of his term, Roh Tae Woo, another general-turned-president elected in the 1987 presidential election, made efforts to settle some of the old scores bequeathed by the Chun Doo Hwan regime. For instance, the chief justice, Kim Yong Ch'öl, who participated in the trial of Kim Dae Jung in connection with the Kwangju Uprising in 1980, resigned after a petition demanding his removal received the support of a number of members of the judiciary. Chun Kyŏng Hwan, Chun Doo Hwan's younger brother, was arrested and sentenced to a seven-year prison term for embezzlement and corruption. Other family members, in-laws, and associates of Chun Doo Hwan were also investigated, prosecuted, and imprisoned. Eventually, Chun Doo Hwan himself, faced with multiple allegations of malfeasance, was forced to testify before the National Assembly, offer a public apology, return his wealth to the state, and go into exile in a distant Buddhist temple for two years.[15]

At the time, the impetus for a clean break with the previous authoritarian regimes came primarily from political society. As table 6.3 shows, in the National Assembly elections in February 1988 the ruling Democratic Justice Party was deprived of majority control of the National Assembly. This *yŏso yadae* (small ruling party versus large opposition parties) composition of the National Assembly empowered the opposition to push for investigations into irregularities of past governments. Because Roh himself was the greatest beneficiary of the past authoritarian regime and the successor to Chun Doo Hwan, however, there were certain limits to what he could do regarding the liquidation of the authoritarian past.

More serious efforts to break with the authoritarian past began in 1993

TABLE 6.3
Results of National Assembly Elections, 1988

	DJP	PPD	RDP	NDRP	Others	Total
Seats	125	71	59	35	9	299
Votes	33.9	19.2	23.8	15.5	7.6	100.0

Note: DJP: Democratic Justice Party; PPD: Party for Peace and Democracy (Kim Dae Jung); RDP: Reunification Democratic Party (Kim Young Sam); NDRP: New Democratic Republican Party (Kim Jong Pil)
Source: NEC, *Che 13 dae kukhoe ŭiwŏn sŏn'gŏ ch'ongnam.*

with the installation of the Kim Young Sam regime. Immediately following his inauguration, Kim reshuffled the top command of the military by removing nineteen generals and admirals who had been involved either in a previous coup or in corruption. The Board of Audit and Inspection, under the leadership of a former Supreme Court judge, Yi Hoe Ch'ang (who is currently the leader of the main opposition party in Korea), began to rigorously investigate illegal acts or misconduct committed by public officials in the past. The board even asked Chun Doo Hwan and Roh Tae Woo to answer questionnaires on their roles in past decisions. Chun was asked to clarify his role in the construction of a multimillion-dollar "peace dam" against possible flood attacks from North Korea before the 1988 Olympics in Seoul. Roh was asked to explain his role in the 1991 decision to buy 120 F-16 fighters from the General Dynamics Corporation instead of the F-18s from McDonnell-Douglas that had previously been decided on.

Most important, the Kim government characterized Chun's takeover of power on December 12, 1979, as "a coup-like event" and promised further investigations into the military putsch as well as the Kwangju massacre in 1980. After a year-long investigation, the government prosecutor's office announced in October 1994 that Chun and Roh had engineered a military revolt. To the chagrin of many Koreans, however, the government said that it would not prosecute them because it wanted to avoid any damage to "national unity." Fearing that prosecution might cause serious political unrest, the Kim government urged the nation to "let history judge" the December coup of 1979. In July 1995, pointing to the statute of limitations, the government announced its final decision not to pursue insurrection charges against Chun Doo Hwan and Roh Tae Woo.

This government announcement was followed by a series of protests by many civil society groups, which ultimately led to a national crisis. College and university professors took the initiative. On August 14, 1995, the Korea Council of Professors for Democratization (Min'gyohyŏp) released a statement criticizing the government's decision and demanding a special law for prosecuting the coup leaders. About 150 professors waged protest sit-ins. They also submitted a legal petition that the statute of limitations not apply to those involved in the May 18 massacre.

In addition, 221 Seoul National University professors released a statement calling for the enactment of a special law and an immediate reinvestigation of the May 18 insurrection in 1980. This was the third time that Seoul National University professors released antigovernment statements—the first was during the April Uprising in 1960, and the second was during the June Uprising in 1987. The number of professors who signed the statement exceeded the number that had signed in the campaign of 1987. Many deans and senior professors also joined this time. As of August 29, 1995, 3,912 professors from 80 universities had participated in the signature campaign calling for the punishment of Chun and Roh.[16]

On September 29, 1995, under the leadership of the NCUSC, students at many universities, including Seoul National University, Pusan University, and Chonnam University, boycotted classes in protest. Some professors cooperated by canceling classes in advance. This was the first nationwide class boycott since the inauguration of the Kim Young Sam regime. On September 30, the streets of 13 major cities across the country were filled with students, workers, and ordinary citizens who held massive meetings and demonstrations calling for a special law to prosecute and punish those involved in the May 18 Kwangju massacre in 1980.

Lawyers also participated in the antigovernment campaigns. Notably, it was not only the members of Lawyers' Association for a Democratic Society (*Minbyŏn*) that joined the movement. The group had been an active element in the people's movement camp. The Korean Bar Association (*Pyŏnhyŏp*), which had been one of the progovernment groups under the past authoritarian regimes, also refuted the government decision and appealed for the participation of all lawyers in the campaign to enact a special law for dealing with the May 18 massacre.[17] Also, on October 16, 1995, 111 law professors at 39 universities submitted to the Constitutional Court an "opinion statement" on the government decision not to prosecute those involved in the May 18 coup and massacre in 1980. In the statement, law professors countered the government's argument by maintaining that there should be no statute of limitations for the prosecution and punishment of crimes such as insurrections or massive killings. If it is applicable, they argued, the statute of limitations should exclude the period in which the criminals were in political power.[18]

The disclosure of Roh Tae Woo's corruption scandal by an opposition National Assemblyman in October 1995 dramatically escalated the campaign for the prosecution of Chun and Roh. On November 1, 1995, three hundred members of the Preparatory Committee for the Korean Confederation of Trade Unions (*Minnojun*) staged demonstrations in Seoul. The NADUK, which was the official umbrella organization of the people's movement groups, also staged sit-ins at its office. The All-Nation Emergency Committee on Enacting a Special Law for Punishing the Perpetrators of the May 18 massacre was established by 297 people's and citizens' movement groups, including the NADUK, the Lawyers' Association for a Democratic Society, the CCEJ, the People's Solidarity for Participatory Democracy, the Korea Women's Associations United (*Yŏyŏn*), the CPAJ, and the Preparatory Committee for the Korean Confederation of Trade Unions. This committee waged signature campaigns and street protests. In the signature campaign, 1,000,000 people participated. It held the People's Action Day to call for the imprisonment of Roh Tae Woo, which ten thousand citizens and students attended.[19] After the rally, thousands of students, workers, activists, and citizens waged street demonstrations throughout the main streets of Seoul. Just as in the June Uprising of 1987, ordinary citizens, drivers, and pedestrians all cheered the demonstrators with support and sympathy. There were also similar gatherings in Pusan, Kwangju, Taegu, Inch'ŏn, Suwŏn, Sŏngnam, Anyang, and Ch'unch'ŏn.[20]

In November 1995, street demonstrations by students and public statements by professors rocked the whole country. On November 3, Students' Day in Korea, the NCUSC called for the immediate imprisonment of Roh Tae Woo and enactment of a special law for punishing those involved in the May 18 massacre at a gathering of three thousand students at Sungkyunkwan University.[21] Throughout November 1995, thousands of university students waged street demonstrations in Kwangju, Pusan, Cheju, and other major cities of the country. By November 25, 1995, 6,549 professors at 89 colleges and universities had participated in the signature campaign that had been originally launched by some Korea University professors. This number was far greater than that of participants in the June Uprising in 1987.[22]

Yielding to the popular pressure that had engulfed the whole nation for several months, the Kim Young Sam government jailed Roh Tae Woo in mid-November 1995 on bribery charges, making him the first Korean president to face legal action for misdeeds in office. State prosecutors grilled thirty-six business leaders about how Roh collected the $650 million secret fund he had admitted maintaining when he was president from 1988 to 1993. Moreover, on November 24, 1995, the ruling party finally decided to enact a special law that would punish retroactively those involved in the violent suppression of the Kwangju Uprising in 1980. Kim Young Sam himself ordered the ruling party to draft the law, admitting that the military crackdown on the Kwangju Uprising had tarnished the honor of the country and its people and had immensely damaged the nation's pride. He also emphasized that a special law was necessary to deal with the people responsible for causing suffering and sorrow of the people by staging a coup. Consequently, as of late February 1996, a total of eleven former generals, including Chun and Roh, had been arrested in connection with the crackdown. Chun and Roh were prosecuted and imprisoned on multiple charges of bribery, insurrection, and treason.

Chun Doo Hwan and Roh Tae Woo were eventually amnestied and released in December 1997, actions that were harshly criticized and protested by many civil society groups. The arrests and imprisonments of the two former presidents on various charges of insurrection and corruption, however, served to establish a clear demarcation between the democratic present and the authoritarian past. The prosecution of former dictators, unimaginable in many other fledgling democracies in the world, unambiguously symbolized the end of authoritarian rule and officially proclaimed the beginning of a new era in which democracy had become "the only game in town." In making this transition, civil society groups played an extremely crucial role in democratic consolidation. As a result, an authoritarian regression has become extremely unlikely, if not unimaginable, in Korea today.

Institutionalizing and Expanding Democracy

The "liquidation" of authoritarian legacy has been one of the most important issues in the politics of democratic consolidation in Korea. But it is not the *only* item on the agenda. Since 1988, civil society groups in Korea have continued their pro-democracy movement for ensuring and enhancing the "democraticness" of Korean polity. Through such pro-democracy movement, civil society has played an important role in protecting, institutionalizing, expanding, and deepening the nascent democracy in Korea.

As already analyzed in the previous chapter, civil society was significantly marginalized and seriously fragmented during and in the aftermath of the presidential election of December 1987. After the inauguration of the Roh Tae Woo government in early 1988, however, civil society groups in Korea, particularly the people's movement groups that had led the pro-democracy coalition in the June Uprising in 1987, quickly remobilized themselves and resumed their pro-democracy campaign with a vigor comparable to or stronger than that during the democratic transition.

One of the most important reasons why civil society groups could regain their solidarity and influence relatively expeditiously lay in the continuity the Roh regime maintained with the previous authoritarian regime. Roh himself was not an effective symbol of a clear break with the past. Although he was popularly elected, he was just another general-turned-president, exactly like

Park Chung Hee and Chun Doo Hwan. Roh had been a close friend of Chun Doo Hwan, having been deeply involved in the multistaged military coup of 1979 and 1980 and the subsequent consolidation of the authoritarian political system. He had been groomed and eventually anointed as the official successor to Chun until the last minute, when the ruling bloc decided to yield to popular pressure, proclaiming the June 29 democratization package. Roh was the greatest beneficiary of the past authoritarian regime and, therefore, was extremely constrained in terms of what he could do regarding the liquidation of the authoritarian past. To most of the civil society groups that had led the June Uprising in 1987, the Roh regime was regarded as a mere extension of authoritarian rule. At best, Roh's regime was a *dictablanda* (liberalized authoritarianism), and hence the need to continue the pro-democracy struggle appeared vital.[23]

Furthermore, the grand party merger and the establishment of the Democratic Liberal Party (*Minju chayudang*) in 1990 served as glaring evidence that the Roh Tae Woo regime was indeed just a continuation of the past authoritarianism. In early 1990, Roh, who had been seriously concerned about his political vulnerability in the National Assembly since his inauguration because of the *yŏso yadae* configuration, succeeded in merging with two opposition parties. In accomplishing this party merger, Roh of course did not consult the Korean people—it had occurred primarily through clandestine elite negotiations and compromises. The two opposition parties were the Reunification Democratic Party (led by Kim Young Sam) and the New Democratic Republican Party (led by Kim Jong Pil). This was similar to *trasformismo* in Italy, where in 1876 Agostino de Pretis, the new prime minister, invited the opposition Destra Party to shift to the government majority in exchange for personal benefits, access to state patronage, and the right to local rule. The opposition parties, finding themselves marginalized from power and state spoils, agreed and "transformed" themselves from the opposition into a stable part of the governing majority.[24] A Korean-style *trasformismo* was viewed by most civil society groups as a frontal attack on the consolidation of democracy in their country—civil society groups in this regard had no choice but to continue and intensify their pro-democracy movement during the Roh regime.

Kim Young Sam, after a series of intraparty struggles, was nominated as the ruling Democratic Liberal Party candidate for the 1992 presidential election. He won the election and was sworn in as the new Korean president in 1993. Because Kim had betrayed and deserted the pro-democracy coalition through a transformistic merger with the ruling party in 1990, however, his regime had a "birth defect" from its very beginning.[25] The Korean people in general, and pro-democracy groups in civil society in particular, entertained a profound suspicion and confusion about the kind of democracy Kim Young Sam would pursue.

Initially, when Kim Young Sam joined the ruling bloc, civil society groups were sharply divided in their assessment of Kim's transformism. Some criticized him as a traitor and judged his career as a pro-democracy leader as over, whereas some others hopefully predicted that Kim could prove himself to be a "Trojan horse" who would emerge as a reformer within the ruling bloc, implementing progressive reforms. A series of unprecedented political and economic reforms in the beginning years of Kim Young Sam's term, namely in 1993–1994, in fact appeared to support the Trojan horse theory. Even Kim's strongest critics were taken aback by the wide breadth, rapid pace, and profound significance of his initial social reforms, as already indicated in the previous section on the people's movement groups. Over time, however, Kim Young Sam became outnumbered and overruled by conservatives in the ruling bloc. Most of his initial reforms failed to get institutionalized and materialized owing to various structural factors and his leadership styles.[26] In response, civil society groups, particularly in the last two years of Kim Young Sam's tenure (1996–1997), intensified their pro-democracy struggle.

The current Kim Dae Jung government in Korea, since its inauguration in February 1998, has dedicated its entire energy to overcoming the present economic crisis in the country. In response, as we will see in the next section, civil society groups have also in large measure focused on the movement for economic reforms. At the same time, however, civil society groups continue their pro-democracy movement for political reforms and other outstanding issues in democratic consolidation. Civil society's activism continues to be critical in the politics of democratic consolidation in Korea, particularly because the Kim Dae Jung government is not entirely free of a "birth defect"—Kim Dae Jung forged an electoral alignment with ultraconservative Kim Jong Pil to win the 1997 presidential election and maintained a de facto coalitional government with Kim Jong Pil and his party in 1998 and 1999. As seen in chapter 4, Kim Jong Pil was one of the principal engineers of the military coup in May 1961 that toppled the democratically-elected civilian government of Chang Myŏn; he was the founder of the Korean Central Intelligence Agency, which had been repeatedly misused and abused by the authoritarian governments to suppress political opposition; and he served as a prime minister under Park Chung Hee's authoritarian regime. Kim Jong Pil, who had been one of the archenemies and oppressors of civil society groups throughout the 1960s and 1970s, served as the first prime minister of the Kim Dae Jung government and is still active as one of the influential political figures in Korea today.

Throughout the politics of democratic consolidation in Korea since 1988, pro-democracy movement by civil society groups has focused on two themes in particular. The first issue, addressed mainly by the citizens' movement groups, is to carry out various institutional reforms in the political process. The second theme, pursued primarily by the people's movement groups, is to expand civil liberties and promote human rights.

Civil society groups have been trying to transform the "election climate" (*Sŏn'gŏ p'ungt'o*) of Korea. Many citizens' movement groups have joined their efforts to monitor the election process and increase political participation. The most notable in this regard are the formation and activities of the Citizens' Council for Fair Elections (CCFE, *Kongsŏnhyŏp*). The CCFE was created in 1991 by seven civil society groups—the CCEJ, the FKTU, Hŭngsadan, the Federation of Women Voters, the Congress of 300 Free Intellectuals, the Christian Coalition for Fair Elections, and the Buddhist Citizens' Coalition for Fair Elections. Vowing to terminate Korea's corrupt election practices through concerted citizen action, the CCFE has demanded the revision of unfair election laws, run report centers for unethical conduct, held hearings, sponsored policy debates, published reports comparing public promises of the candidates, distributed "selection criteria" for choosing the right candidate, disseminated information, and developed solidarity with the people's movement groups in enhancing voter participation.[27] Through a number of local, National Assembly, and presidential elections since 1991, it has now grown into a prestigious nationwide organization in the movement for fair elections, encompassing all religious denominations—Protestant, Buddhist, Catholic, Wŏn Buddhist, and Confucian—and all classes.

Particularly, in the National Assembly elections in April 2000 various civil society organizations formed Citizens' Solidarity for the National Assembly Elections (*Ch'ongsŏn yŏndae*) and engaged in a nationwide campaign for rejecting "unfit" candidates. The Citizens' Solidarity reviewed the backgrounds of all candidates and selected eighty-six who had been involved in antidemocratic acts, corruption, tax evasion, draft dodge, and other illegal and immoral activities. After disclosing the list to the public, civil society groups waged a vigorous mass campaign for voting out these "inappropriate" candidates. As a result, almost 70 percent of those listed by the Citizens' Solidarity failed to be elected.[28]

Fair election is just one element of civil society groups' broader campaign for political reform. Citizens' movement groups, such as Citizens' Solidarity for

Political Reform (*Chŏnggaeryŏn*) and Korea Citizens' Council for Social Development (*Hansilhyŏp*), have focused on making legislative process in the National Assembly more transparent to citizens, achieving democratization within political parties, promoting and institutionalizing civil society groups' political participation, and decreasing political corruption and regionalism.[29] Particularly because most political parties and politicians have been reluctant to design and implement serious political reforms, citizens' groups have argued that the momentum and pressure for political reform should emanate from civil society. Political reform has been one of the central themes in the politics of democratic consolidation in Korea since 1988.[30]

Meanwhile, many other civil society groups, particularly the people's movement groups have continually paid greater attention to increasing the inclusiveness of Korean democracy. For example, the Association of Families of Political Prisoners (AFPP, *Min'gahyŏp*), together with other people's movement groups like the NADUK and religious organizations, waged a campaign for the release of long-term political prisoners and organized the Investigative Committee on the Fabrication of Spy Stories by the National Security Planning Agency. This committee severely criticized the National Security Planning Agency (formerly Korea Central Intelligence Agency, currently National Intelligence Service) and the Kim Young Sam regime for suppressing the opposition and civil society groups by exaggerating or fabricating spy stories prior to almost every election, just as the preceding authoritarian regimes had done. Many people's movement groups have emphasized that the power and influence of the intelligence agency should be decreased so as not to allow, for example, domestic surveillance of opposition politicians and civil society activists.

The AFPP was founded on December 12, 1985, under Chun Doo Hwan's dictatorship. It could not hold an opening ceremony, however, because its members were arrested by the police. The members of the AFPP—mostly mothers and sisters of political prisoners—played a critical role in facilitating the June Uprising in 1987, staging street demonstrations in front of police headquarters in protest of the torture death of Pak Chong Ch'ŏl with purple hemp cloth head bands on their heads. Since then, the AFPP has been known to the outside world as one of the most famous human rights organizations in Korea. Owing in large measure to the persistent struggle of the AFPP, Kim Sŏn Myŏng, who had spent forty-five years in prison, was released on August 15, 1995, and U Yong Kak, who had spent forty-one years in prison, was released on March 1, 1999.[31] Particularly since the inauguration of the current Kim Dae

Jung government, numerous political prisoners and prisoners of conscience have been amnestied and released, thanks to the movement of the people's movement groups such as the AFPP.

At the same time, many people's movement groups, including the NADUK, have been persistently demanding the repeal of the National Security Law (NSL), not only during the Kim Young Sam regime but also into the current Kim Dae Jung regime. For example, on February 6, 1999, the NADUK held a meeting of its members and university students in the heart of Seoul to demand the repeal of the National Security Law and the release of political prisoners.[32] To most people's movement groups, which had been the most frequent subject of harsh application of the NSL, Korean democracy is at best "pseudo" and is highly hypocritical without substantially increasing the level of tolerance to different political ideologies, ideas, and opinions. In this regard, the repeal of the NSL, which had been abused so frequently by the preceding authoritarian regimes, is an essential step toward democratic consolidation. Unlike many previous regimes, the current Kim Dae Jung government in Korea has responded positively to this proposal of the people's movement groups and has been working on a revision of the NSL.

The most recent tide of pro-democracy mobilization of people's movement groups came in late 1996. On December 26, the ruling New Korea Party (*Sinhan'guktang*; originally the Democratic Liberal Party, currently the Grand National Party) passed several labor-related bills and a reform bill regarding the Agency for National Security Planning. These bills had been intensely debated and contested among Koreans. Labor unions had opposed the proposed labor reform bills because, if legislated, they would weaken labor unions and facilitate massive layoffs. People's movement groups in civil society had disputed the proposed Agency for National Security Planning reform bill because the bill would expand the investigative power of the already powerful state agency, contrary to the strong demand of the civil society groups. Despite these concerns and criticisms from labor unions, people's movement groups, and the opposition parties, the ruling party resolved to force the bills through the National Assembly at 6 AM on December 26 clandestinely without opposition legislators.

This railroading of the controversial bills profoundly outraged civil society groups and led to a series of antigovernment protests. Lawyers and university professors waged sit-ins and street demonstrations, demanding the immediate nullification of the bills passed. Student organizations, comparing the passage of the bills to the notorious legislation of two antidemocratic laws during the

Chang Myŏn government in 1961 (discussed in chapter 3 of this volume), launched nationwide demonstrations. Labor unions characterized the Kim Young Sam government as a civilian dictatorship and led a series of strikes, including a successful general strike in January 1997 for the first time since the birth of the Korean state in 1948. Catholic churches and groups, including the CPAJ, supported the student demonstrations and labor strikes. Buddhist and protestant organizations also joined the support.[33] Well into mid-March 1997 massive demonstrations and signature collection campaigns by civil society groups and labor strikes destabilized the whole country. Most of the citizens' movement groups, including the CCEJ, remained conspicuously absent throughout this pro-democracy struggle, which clearly indicates that the citizens' movement groups were primarily concerned with the establishment and consolidation of a narrower version of democracy that does not involve any substantive dimension.

The Kim Young Sam government remained uncompromising, yielding nothing to the pressure engendered by such popular mobilization. Nevertheless, the Kim regime lost the battle because these antigovernment protests greatly tarnished the regime's previous democratic image and drastically diminished Kim's popularity. After the onset of the economic crisis in late 1997, Kim Young Sam's government degenerated into the worst—and most unpopular—government in Korean history.

Diversifying Issue Areas

As already pointed out, the addition of new movement groups, called the citizens' movement groups, has transformed the overall landscape of Korean civil society. One of the most significant implications of the emergence and expansion of the citizens' movement groups for Korean politics has been the fact that more diverse issues are now being addressed by civil society groups. Under the authoritarian regimes, civil society groups focused their energy chiefly on political democracy. Civil society, encapsulated by the pro-democracy alliance of people's movement groups, demanded the restoration, if not installation, of democracy. Either explicitly or implicitly, other issues were considered marginal or "petty" and subject to the greater cause of political democratization. Since the democratic transition in 1987, however, such issue hegemony of political democracy has been incrementally eroded. Groups in civil society have raised a variety of new issues, particularly those issues neglected and underrepresented in the past.

Of the newly created movement groups in Korean civil society, the most salient are the environmental organizations.[34] Table 6.4 summarizes the dramatic increase of environmental groups in Korea since the mid-1980s. Although the environmental movement existed even during the 1960s and the 1970s, it was spontaneous, transient, and local in nature. Moreover, the environmental movement at the time was considered marginal and luxurious not only by the developmental state but also by many people's movement groups in civil society. Most groups in civil society concentrated on the "more urgent" issues of human rights, labor conditions, or political democratization. It was not until the democratic transition in the mid-1980s that the environmental movement finally began to gain influence.

The history of the environmental movement in Korea is inseparable from the establishment and expansion of the Korean Anti-Pollution Movement Association (KAPMA, *Kongch'uryŏn*). The KAPMA was established in 1988 by merging two existing environmental organizations—the Korean Antipollution Citizen Movement Council (*Konghae pandae simin undong hyŏbŭihoe*) and the Korean Antipollution Movement Youth Council (*Konghae ch'ubang undong ch'ŏngnyŏn hyŏbŭihoe*).

Since its inauguration, the KAPMA concentrated on diverse antipollution and antinuclear activities. It organized numerous conferences, round-the-country slide shows, and picture exhibitions, pressuring the business community to spend more on pollution control as well as raising awareness in the general public. Also, especially alarmed by the Chernobyl disaster in 1986, the leaders of the KAPMA actively joined the debate on nuclear issues and launched a major campaign against the construction of nuclear plants in

TABLE 6.4
Environmental Groups, 1960–1993

Period	Number
1960–1969	7
1970–1979	9
1980–1985	9
1986–1990	54
1991–1993	58

Source: CCEJ-*Chosŏn ilbo, Hwan'gyŏngŭl chik'inŭn hangugŭi min'gan tanch'e.*

Korea, organizing mass rallies and collecting signatures. It published monthly newsletters, such as "Survival and Peace" and "Against Nuclear Plants," to create a national consensus against nuclear power plants and to consolidate the existing local environmental movements.[35] Moreover, by participating in the Rio Conference in 1992, the KAPMA played a leading role in building solidarity with international environmental organizations to bring to international attention the enormity of the environmental problems in Korea.

On April 2, 1993, with other local environmental organizations—such as Pusan Antipollution Citizen Movement Council, Kwangju Citizens' Alliance for Environmental Movement, Mokp'o Green Study Group, Masan-Ch'angwŏn Antipollution Citizen Movement Council, Taegu Antipollution Movement Council, Ulsan Antipollution Movement Association, and Chinju Citizens' Group for Protecting the River Nam—the KAPMA created the Korea Federation for Environmental Movement. This organization is the largest environmental movement group in Korean history. In its inaugural address, the KFEM put forward the following goals: (1) environmental movement as a daily practice; (2) environmentally sound business practices; (3) development of feasible policy alternatives; (4) consistent support for an antinuclear position; and (5) strengthened solidarity with environmental groups abroad to cope with environmental problems on a global scale. It currently consists of the central headquarters and thirty-two regional offices. As of December 1998, the KFEM had fifty thousand dues-paying members, including many working journalists, lawyers, professors, religious leaders, medical doctors, nurses, social workers, artists, businesspersons, farmers, workers, students, and ordinary citizens. The leadership positions of the KFEM are filled with the new urban middle class. The cadres or activists who carry out everyday duties of the organization are also highly educated and reform-oriented.

Since its establishment, the KFEM has concentrated on a number of "focal projects" each year. These projects have included, for example, preserving clean water; reducing air pollution; increasing international solidarity with the antinuclear movement; expanding the membership and local organizations of the KFEM; enhancing environmental education; computerizing environmental information; waste reduction; diversification of energy sources; environment-friendly local politics; and child education programs centered around environmentalism.

Another issue area that has been vigorously explored and developed by the citizens' movement groups is economic justice. The Citizens' Coalition for Economic Justice was founded in July 1989 by about five hundred academics, lawyers, and church activists. The educational backgrounds of the inaugural membership were quite impressive—63 percent of the total membership were college graduates or postgraduates. High levels of education were also reflected in the occupational distribution, with 27 percent employed in white-collar occupations, 26 percent in professional occupations, nearly 10 percent in small and medium business or self-employment; 15.5 percent were college students. Blue-collar workers constituted only 1.7 percent. Also, in terms of age, the membership was strikingly young, with 73 percent under 40 years old and 41 percent under 30.[36] In its inaugural statement, the CCEJ emphasized that the most important socioeconomic issues in Korea were unearned income, land speculation, misdistribution of income, and the tax system. These economic injustices, according to the statement, could not be changed by the government or politicians alone, but ultimately must be "solved by the organized power of the civil society."[37] It also proclaimed that the strategy of the CCEJ to achieve its goals would be: (1) to organize the ordinary citizens; (2) to make its demands in peaceful, nonviolent, and legitimate ways; (3) to seek concrete and workable alternatives; and (4) to mobilize civil society on a non–class-struggle principle.

The CCEJ has now grown into a national organization of twenty-five dues-paying members.[38] Under the banner of "economic justice through the power of committed citizens," it has supported the independence of the central bank from government control, revision of tax laws to discourage land speculation, and regulation of the rental system in favor of the poor. Some of its major programs, including the Economic Injustice Complaint Center, Legislature Watch, and Research Institute for Economic Justice, have received wide public attention.[39] It is publishing a bimonthly English newsletter, *Civil Society*, and a Korean monthly magazine, *Wŏlgan kyŏngsillyŏn* [CCEJ Monthly], in which academic and journalistic writings on issues related to economic reform are being published. Conducting research into dozens of policy sectors covering practically all aspects of social, economic, and political life, the CCEJ has assumed a commanding position as the voice of all middle-class reformists in Korea.[40]

Economic Crisis and Civil Society

In 1997, beginning with the collapse of one of the *chaebŏl* groups, *Hanbo*, several big business conglomerates in Korea became insolvent and fell into court receivership. Foreign banks and investors pulled their funds out of Korea, leading to a foreign exchange crisis. In spite of efforts by both the government and the Bank of Korea, the exchange rate and stock market plummeted, putting Korea virtually on the brink of defaulting on its foreign debt obligations. On December 3, 1997, the International Monetary Fund agreed to give a $57 bil- lion package to Korea, which was the largest loan in IMF's history. Various con- ditions were attached to the loans, including requiring that Korea implement stringent macroeconomic policies, restructure the financial and corporate sec- tors, and pursue rapid capital and trade liberalization.

Since the IMF bailout, Korea has been going through a grave economic crisis and a comprehensive structural adjustment. The impact of the crisis has permeated all sectors of Korean society. To a country that had boasted high growth rates since the 1960s and to a people who had reveled in virtual lifetime employment, the recent economic crisis came as a shock, a puzzle, a disgrace, and a daunting challenge.

What effects has the recent economic crisis in Korea had on civil society and its activism? One of the most notable ones has been that some of the out- standing civil society groups' activities have begun to revolve around and grav- itate toward economic issues. Many civil society groups have insisted upon the investigation into the causes of the economic crisis and the punishment of the policymakers involved. On September 26, 1998, forty people's movement groups, including the NADUK and the Korean Confederation of Trade Unions (KCTU, *Minju noch'ong*), launched a nationwide signature collection cam- paign for the guarantee of jobs for workers and for the punishment of those businesspersons and politicians responsible for the economic crisis.[41] They also held a massive popular rally in November 1998 on the punishment issue. At the meeting, attended by about thirty thousand people, the NADUK, the KCTU, the KTEWU, and other people's movement groups also called for political re- forms and protection for the laborers from arbitrary layoffs.[42] Partly in re- sponse to such public clamor, a National Assembly hearing on the economic crisis was held in January 1999. During the hearing, people's movement groups also organized numerous committees to monitor and evaluate critically the process of the National Assembly hearing.[43]

In addition, many civil society groups have been calling strongly for eco- nomic reforms, particularly reforms of the *chaebŏl*. Both Korean analysts and foreign observers have broadly agreed that what is at the center of the current economic crisis in Korea is the moral hazard of the *chaebŏl*. Thanks to the pro- tection and preference of the developmental state, the *chaebŏl* successfully ex- panded throughout the 1960s, 1970s, and 1980s. In the 1990s, particularly under the Kim Young Sam government, the *chaebŏl* could continue with their disastrous management practices because the state pursued a policy of intentional indifference, making the *chaebŏl* more powerful and autonomous.[44] *Chaebŏl* reform was also one of the top national agendas during the previous Kim Young Sam government, but it dismally failed to maintain and carry out the well-intended reforms it pursued in 1993–1994.[45] There is currently an extensive consensus in and outside of Korea that the economic crisis could have been avoided had Kim Young Sam's *chaebŏl* reform been successfully carried out. In this regard, many civil society groups consider it to be vital to pressure the current Kim Dae Jung government to sustain and strengthen its *chaebŏl* reforms.

In the movement for *chaebŏl* reform, one of the civil society groups that has consistently received much public attention since the economic crisis is the People's Solidarity for Participatory Democracy (PSPD, *Ch'amyŏ yŏndae*). The PSPD was established on September 10, 1994, by approximately two hundred young professionals such as professors, lawyers, and doctors. This group, under the slogan of "progressive citizens' movement," has been trying to combine the new citizens' movement and the existing people's movement, putting the two movement groups in a unified framework.[46] Since its inauguration, the PSPD has consistently tried to remedy the bifurcation of Korean civil society into two different, and to some degree competing, camps. Partly owing to the efforts of the PSPD, the citizens' movement groups and the people's movement groups cooperated, for example, in the movement for the prosecution and imprisonment of the two former presidents.

The PSPD, together with people's movement groups like the NADUK and the KCTU, was an integral part of the movement for the holding of national assembly hearings on the economic crisis and the punishment of those responsible for it. In 1998, the PSPD proposed an initiative to protect and encourage the rights of minority shareholders in supervising and monitoring *chaebŏl* companies. To achieve this, the PSPD is waging a campaign to encourage every Korean citizen to buy ten stocks in a major *chaebŏl* company. Chang Ha Sŏng, a Korea University economics professor and a leading member of the PSPD, has filed class action suits against several *chaebŏl* on behalf of minority shareholders, charging the companies with mismanagement and abuse of power. The PSPD is tenaciously leading a movement to hold economically powerful actors in Korea more accountable to the law and to the general public.[47] Other civil society groups, including the CCEJ, are also joining the movement for *chaebŏl* reforms.

In summary, the recent economic crisis in Korea made civil society groups shift their focus to economic issues. Civil society groups have demanded a thorough investigation into the crisis and comprehensive economic reforms, including fundamental restructuring of the *chaebŏl* system. Koreans in general approach their economic crisis in a holistic manner, comprehensively reviewing their past experiences with industrialization while trying simultaneously to generate a new blueprint for future development. Civil society groups—particularly people's movement groups—are facilitating such a critical assessment of the past development and industrialization. In the process, they raise various issues related to socioeconomic inequalities that have been largely ignored during the process of democratization so far. In this respect, the current economic crisis might be a blessing in disguise or a crisis cum opportunity for the consolidation of Korean democracy.[48]

Analysis of the Democratic Consolidation

Actors

One of the most prominent changes in Korean civil society since the democratic transition in 1987 has been the bifurcation of civil society groups into two different camps, namely citizens' movement groups and people's movement groups. What explains this bifurcation? In other words, what explains the emergence and expansion of the citizens' movement groups and the eclipse and weakening of the people's movement groups?

First of all, the dramatic expansion of the citizens' movement groups was primarily due to two factors. As analyzed in chapter 5, what provided the final push for the authoritarian breakdown and democratic transition in 1987 was the support of the urban middle class. Middle-class citizens poured onto the streets of Seoul and actively joined students, blue-collar workers, and other people's movement groups to criticize the authoritarian regime and demand democratization. Immediately following the authoritarian breakdown, however, particularly during the Great Labor Struggle in July and August 1987, these ordinary citizens realized how different their perceptions and ideas of democracy were from those entertained by laborers and the people's movement groups. Therefore, they felt it was imperative to organize and mobilize themselves as a separate political force, distinct from the "radical" movement of the people's movement groups. This is why the new citizens' movement groups from the very beginning have persistently emphasized the differences between themselves and the existing people's movement groups, using nonviolent, peaceful, and legal movement styles and specific policy alternatives. In this respect, the emergence of the citizens' movement groups was to a great extent a reaction to the perceived dominance of the "old, radical" social movement groups in Korean civil society.

Secondly, what facilitated this voluntary organization and mobilization of ordinary citizens was the divide-and-rule strategy of different governments since 1988. The Roh Tae Woo and Kim Young Sam governments used a two-pronged strategy in dealing with the different movement camps in civil society. They promoted and supported moderate citizens' movement groups while suppressing the "radical" people's movement groups. The conservative mass media assisted the government's divide-and-rule tactic by extensively—and most of the time favorably—covering the activities of citizens' movement groups while disapproving of, if not entirely ignoring, the activities of people's movement groups.

On the other hand, the retreat of the people's movement groups was, in part, also due to the Roh Tae Woo and Kim Young Sam governments' divide-and-rule strategy assisted by the conservative mass media. More important, however, the collapse of socialism in the late 1980s seriously weakened the people's movement groups in Korean civil society. Either implicitly or explicitly, many people's movement groups during the previous democratic junctures had idealized and pursued a socialist transformation of Korean society. The demise of the communist bloc and the resultant disappearance of a realistic alternative to capitalism and liberal democracy profoundly disconcerted people's movement groups.[49] "The end of history" also seemed to mean the end of people's movement groups in Korea.[50]

At the same time, albeit temporarily, the dramatic political and socioeconomic reforms in the beginning of the Kim Young Sam government also substantially undermined the people's movement groups. Because of the fundamentalist nature of people's movement groups' criticism of the government, the appeal of these groups to a large extent hinges on the success or failure of the government's reform initiatives. In the long run, therefore, the people's movement groups must find a way to invigorate their power and influence, independent of the success or failure of the government's policies.

In the relationship between the citizens' movement camp and the people's movement camp there has been some degree of cooperation and a loose prore-form alliance. But unlike during the transition, where different elements in civil society were tightly united under the banner of pro-democracy struggle, actors in Korean civil society during the 1990s, except for some nationwide campaigns, have been mostly in competition. There has been an implicit division of labor between different camps of civil society groups. As analyzed above, citizens' movement groups and people's movement groups have focused on different issue areas in the politics of democratic consolidation.

Interactions

Unlike during the three democratic junctures analyzed in the preceding chapters, civil society–state relations in this period began to vary depending on the elements in civil society. In the pretransition period, nearly all components in Korean civil society, except for the state-corporatist groups that had been consistently in collusion with the authoritarian regimes, had constant and violent confrontations and conflicts with the state, characterized by an endless cycle of repression and resistance. The political arena was acutely dichotomized and therefore uncomplicated: it consisted of the authoritarian state and its state-corporatist allies on one side versus the grand pro-democracy coalition of civil society groups and opposition parties on the other. For many civil society groups, the state was always something to challenge, reject, combat, and overthrow. Because of the changes in the internal constitution and configuration of civil society since 1988, however, this is no longer the case. The state has incrementally become something different—something to engage, accept, affect, restrain, and control.

In particular, the new citizens' movement groups have varied their relations with the state. Basically acknowledging and consenting to the legitimacy of the democratic governments, the citizens' movement groups have tried to diversify their relations with the state. Depending on specific policy issues, they sometimes cooperate with and sometimes oppose the state, which is no longer the target of unconditional and absolute rejection. The people's movement groups, on the other hand, have largely maintained their hostile relations with the state. However, even the people's movement groups have been exploring different modes of civil society–state relations other than conflictual engagement. Groups in Korean civil society slowly but steadily are learning how to forge and maintain different kinds of relationships with the state depending on the specific issues and policies at hand.

At the same time, however, the incremental disappearance of the conflictual civil society–state relationship also means that civil society is becoming vulnerable to the attempt of the state to incorporate and "statize" civil society. The depopulation or depletion of civil society has been a pivotal issue in the politics of democratic consolidation in Korea. During the Kim Young Sam government, several prominent leaders of the CCEJ joined the government, which jeopardized the existence and activities of this organization.[51] During the current Kim Dae Jung government, to the surprise of many observers, one of the corepresentatives of the KFEM was appointed as the Minister of Environment in May 1999. Moreover, the Kim Dae Jung government's Second Nation-Building Campaign, despite the government's repeated assurance that the movement would be entirely civilian, voluntary, and bottom-up, is becoming more and more state-centered and top-down. It has been widely reported that this national campaign is an attempt by the Kim government to incorporate and statize as many civil society groups as possible to expand the mass base of the ruling party and therefore improve on the precarious status of the semicoalitional government surrounded by the conservatives.[52]

Such continued statization of civil society groups is likely to pose a serious threat to the consolidation of Korean democracy. As Dryzek (1996) emphasizes, "If a group leaves the oppositional sphere to enter the state, then dominant classes and public officials have less to fear. There may be some democratic gain in this entry, but there is almost democratic loss in terms of a less vital civil society."[53] Unless the state inclusion is "benign"—that is to say, the defining interest of the grouping can be related quite directly to a state imperative—inclusion is virtually synonymous with cooptation or defection.[54] Therefore, it is imperative that civil society groups in Korea develop clear criteria about the issue of state inclusion. In determining whether state inclusion is benign, Korean civil society groups should consider first whether the group gains real influence through the entry and, more important, whether the group's entry into the state leaves behind a flourishing civil society.[55]

The relationship between civil society and political society is also undergoing fundamental changes. During the authoritarian period, the relationship between civil society and political society largely involved a united coalition formed to resist authoritarian regimes. But in the politics of democratic consolidation since 1988, the civil society–political society relationship has become increasingly competitive in collecting public opinion, detecting interests, formulating policies, and influencing the state.

Meanwhile, a danger similar to the issue of statization also exists in terms of civil society's relationship with political society. Current Korean laws prohibit civil society groups' political activities such as supporting a specific candidate for elections. Because of such legal restrictions, the only possible ways for a civil society group to participate effectively in politics are either to organize an independent political party or to join an existing party. This situation caused serious debates within many civil society groups and different civil society activists made different choices. Sŏ Kyŏng Sŏk, former leader of the CCEJ, joined a political party during the Kim Young Sam government, despite considerable internal criticisms. Ch'oe Yŏl, leader of the KFEM, decided not to join a political party because of harsh opposition and criticism within the organization. Meanwhile, the NADUK, the KCTU, and many people's movement groups have been working on establishing their own political parties. However, for Korean civil society to continue its distinctive functions of promoting and enhancing democracy, a massive defection to political society, or "political societization," is not advisable. Rather than leaving civil society and plunging into partisan politics, leaders of civil society groups need first to struggle against those legal restrictions prohibiting political activities and then to explore, establish, develop, and institutionalize various links and channels with political society.

Issues

Civil society groups broadly agree on the need to continue movement for sustaining various political and socioeconomic reforms. However, in terms of the specific contents of those reforms, civil society groups diverge. Unlike during the democratic transition, when different elements of civil society were united under the slogan of political democracy, currently different groups raise and pursue different issues. The people's movement groups, which had spearheaded the pro-democracy alliance during the democratic transition, are focusing on the substantive dimension of democracy. The citizens' movement groups, which emerged after the transition, are concentrating on the procedural aspect of democracy. Together these two different camps of civil society groups are continually contributing to the consolidation of Korean democracy. At the same time, the citizens' movement groups have successfully explored issue areas that had been largely ignored in the previous democratic junctures, such as the environment, economic justice, consumers' rights, and gender equality. Unlike during the democratization, when political democracy and democratization received utmost attention, such issue hegemony no longer prevails in Korean civil society today.

In terms of movement strategies, the two camps differ. While the people's movement groups still rely on "traditional" methods that do not eschew violence, the citizens' movement groups adopt strategies and methods focused on nonviolent and legal methods. Whereas the people's movement groups continue their pro-democracy protest, the citizens' movement groups focus steadily on developing policy alternatives.

Reunification is still an important issue for civil society groups in Korea. However, as compared with the three previous democratic junctures, where reunification was viewed as an essential component of movement, the importance of reunification has been considerably decreased. During the Roh Tae Woo regime and the first few years of the Kim Young Sam regime, civil society groups vigorously raised and supported the reunification issue. In the second half of the Kim Young Sam regime and during the current Kim Dae Jung regime, however, reunification has virtually ceased as a pivotal issue for the civil society groups in Korea.

One reason the reunification issue is no longer current is because the serious food and economic crisis in North Korea in recent years has prompted civil society groups in South Korea to shift the focus of their movement to humanitarian aid to North Korea. Because an immediate integration with an economically bankrupt North Korea would only have negative, if not disastrous, effects on the economic development and democratic consolidation of South Korea (and of Korea as a whole), civil society groups are trying to help North Korea stabilize its economy and political system before undertaking any serious discussion of a possible reunification. Since the onset of the economic crisis in South Korea in 1997 the issue of reunification has been considerably overshadowed by the issue of economic recovery and structural reform.

Meanwhile, the current Kim Dae Jung government's softline reunification policy ("sunshine policy"), intended to facilitate and encourage the economic reform and opening of North Korea through economic and humanitarian aid, has basically preempted the reunification movement by civil society groups.[56] Conservatives, who support the idea of "benign neglect" of North Korea, are unhappy about the Kim government's softline policies. However, from the vantage point of many civil society groups, the Kim government's reunification policy is the most progressive one in the history of Korea and contrasts greatly with the conservative and reactionary reunification policies of the preceding authoritarian regimes. Civil society groups find the Kim Dae Jung government's reunification policy largely agreeable. For these reasons the issue of reunification, unlike in the previous democratic junctures, is not likely to occupy center stage in civil society's activism in the near future.

Summary and Conclusions

In this chapter, I analyzed how various groups in civil society have influenced the politics of democratic consolidation in Korea since 1988. I reviewed some important changes in the internal composition of Korean civil society and examined the role of civil society in consolidating the nascent democracy in

Korea. I began by reviewing the changed internal configuration of civil society in the aftermath of the democratic transition. The dynamics of interactions among different groups in civil society have significantly changed compared to the previous periods of authoritarian breakdown and democratic transition. In the past the conflict and confrontation between the people's movement groups and the repressive state and its state-corporatist allies was principally important. After the democratic transition in 1987, however, new movement organizations (called citizens' movement groups) emerged and evolved, which altered to a great extent the overall configuration of Korean civil society. The citizens' movement groups, distancing themselves from the existing people's movement groups, are now exploring new issues, movement styles, and methods.

Next I assessed some of the outstanding themes civil society groups have raised and pursued in the politics of democratic consolidation. Civil society groups in Korea, both the new citizens' movement groups and the old people's movement groups, have contributed significantly to the stages of democratic consolidation. Various civil society groups have focused on the different challenges of democratic consolidation. Whereas the citizens' movement groups focus on issues such as fair elections, political reform, and anticorruption, the people's movement groups concentrate on issues such as ideological tolerance and socioeconomic equalities. But the two camps of civil society groups also often unite for common causes—for example, for the liquidation of the authoritarian past and for humanitarian support for North Korea. Overall, the interactions and shifting alliances in different civil society groups have greatly affected the political dynamics of democratic consolidation. In the literature on democratic transition and consolidation, scholars have emphasized that the choices made by the elite predominate during the consolidation phase although the opinions of the mass public and its interaction with the elite do count during the earlier stages of democratization.[57] In Korea, however, this is not the case because civil society continues to play an important role in consolidating Korean democracy.

Subsequently, the impact of the recent economic crisis in Korea on civil society's activism was considered as I discussed how the economic crisis prompted civil society groups to switch their focus and emphasis to economic reforms. Various groups in civil society have demanded a thorough review of Korea's past experiences with industrialization and have asked for the establishment of a more sustainable development strategy for the future. They particularly call for a serious *chaebŏl* reform to restructure the economy and remove the deep-rooted state-business collusion. Finally, I analyzed the democratic consolidation in Korea in terms of its actors, interactions, and issues. The bifurcation of civil society actors occurred mostly because of the organization of the middle class, the regimes' divide-and-rule strategy, and the collapse of the communist bloc. Civil society–state relations are still partially conflictual but slowly show some variations. However, civil society–political society relations are becoming competitive. In both civil society–state relations and civil society–political society relations one important issue is how to prevent a possible incorporation of civil society by either the state (statization) or political society (political societization). Civil society should protect its independence so that it can continue with its distinct contributions to democratization.

C H A P T E R **7**

Conclusion
From Protest to Advocacy

Democracy requires the construction of a vibrant, vigorous and pluralistic civil society.

LARRY DIAMOND, 1992

At all stages of the democratization process, a lively and independent civil society is invaluable.

JUAN J. LINZ AND ALFRED STEPAN, 1996

Civil society is not, however, an unmitigated blessing for democracy.

PHILIPPE C. SCHMITTER, 1997

I N this book, I have argued that civil society groups consistently commenced and forwarded various stages of Korean democratization. Diverse groups in civil society—particularly student groups, labor unions, and religious organizations—contributed to authoritarian breakdown and democratic transition in different periods. In addition, unlike in some cases in other regions of the world, where civil society was rapidly demobilized and depoliticized after the transition from authoritarian rule, civil society in Korea continues to play a significant role in the politics of democratic consolidation.

In the first democratic juncture (1956–1961), primarily students and urban intellectuals revolted against the repression and corruption of Syngman Rhee's authoritarian regime. Subsequently, during the phase of democratic transition under Chang Myŏn, student groups aligned and cooperated with progressive opposition parties in their campaigns for democracy, self-assertive diplomacy, and reunification. Compared with later democratic junctures, however, the coalition between civil society groups and political parties was temporary and tenuous.

In the second democratic juncture (1973–1980), numerous national associations of dissident intellectuals, journalists, professionals, and religious leaders played an important role in galvanizing the anti-Yusin movement against Park Chung Hee's authoritarian regime. These national associations, called *chaeya*, formed and developed a pro-democracy coalition with the opposition New Democratic Party and waged intense pro-democracy struggles. These struggles ultimately generated a fatal split between hardliners and softliners in the ruling bloc and finally brought about an implosion of the authoritarian regime. Although the pro-democracy coalition during this period was broader and stronger compared with the first democratic juncture, national movement associations of civil society groups were in large part limited, especially because they did not adequately encompass the crucial triple solidarity of student groups, labor unions, and religious organizations that was emerging and evolving at the time. In addition, the coalition between civil society and political society, principally predicated on individual commitments and connections, was not very systematic or stable.

The pro-democracy alliance of civil society in the third democratic juncture (1984–1987) incorporated the triple solidarity of students, workers, and churches and also encompassed the middle class. Civil society groups were effectively united and led by national associations that consisted of numerous sectoral and regional organizations. Moreover, groups in civil society closely cooperated and coordinated with the opposition party through numerous joint organizations. The concerted efforts of civil society groups and the opposition party pressured the ruling authoritarian regime to accede to the popular demand for democratization. Even in the politics of democratic consolidation (1988–present), civil society groups in Korea continue to play important roles. Different civil society groups have played a crucial role in compelling Korean governments since 1988 to launch and carry out various political and socioeconomic reforms.

Tables 7.1 and 7.2 incorporate my analysis of the Korean case as presented in chapters 3–6. The first table presents a chronological summary of the major events and incidents in the three democratic junctures and in the current period, while table 7.2 provides an analytical synopsis of the three democratic junctures in terms of their actors, interactions, and issues.

One important conclusion that emerges from my comparative-historical analysis of the different democratic junctures in Korea is that the major momentum for democratic changes in Korea almost invariably came from the politics of protest by multiple civil society groups and their coalitions with political society. Diverse elements in civil society—particularly student groups, labor unions, and religious organizations— provided the impetus for greater democracy in Korea. In Korea, "[t]he momentum for greater democracy has consistently emanated from oppositional civil society, not from the state."[1] Theoretically, therefore, the Korean case firmly verifies the civil society paradigm—namely, the thesis that civil society contributes positively to democratization.

The most significant conclusion to be drawn from my analysis of Korea is that the two contending dominant paradigms—the preconditions paradigm and the contingency paradigm—of democratization could be integrated. I challenge the preconditions paradigm by showing that Korean democratization was not an automatic or mechanical product of some macrolevel workings of socioeconomic or cultural factors. At the same time, however, my analysis enriches the preconditions paradigm by probing how economic development and the concomitant cultural changes provided favorable conditions and contexts for democratization in Korea. Specifically, I highlight how structural factors such as industrialization, urbanization, and culture affected the nature, composition, and power of pro-democracy groups in civil society and how these dynamics eventually led to democratization in Korea.

This study takes issue with the contingency paradigm by demonstrating that in Korea democratization was not a result of strategic calculations, interactions, and "pacts" of individual political elites. An excessive focus on elites and their behaviors is misleading in the study of Korean democratization. At the same time, however, I expand the contingency paradigm by considering the strategic interactions between civil society and other societal spheres, such as the state and political society. Rather than focusing narrowly on individual elites and their strategic interactions, my examination suggests that we should study interactions between social groups, forces, and coalitions. Therefore, as in similar cases in Asia, Eastern Europe, and Africa, the Korean situation can potentially make a significant theoretical contribution to the establishment and development of a synthetic analytical framework, combining the two most powerful paradigms in the study of democratization.

At the same time, my study of Korea also proposes an important modification of the contingency paradigm that is most dominant in the literature. In its mode of democratization the Korean case clearly represents an example of "transition by reform," principally characterized by "mass-ascendancy."[2] Extensive popular mobilization from below forced the elite to make a compromise with the masses. Dissimilar to some of the cases in Southern Europe and Latin

TABLE 7.1
Civil Society and Democratization in Korea: Chronology

1. THE FIRST DEMOCRATIC JUNCTURE, 1956–61

State & Political Society	Civil Society
1952 Constitutional revision (to change to a direct presidential election system to allow Syngman Rhee's reelection)	Labor disputes in Pusan
1954 Constitutional revision (to abolish term limit for Syngman Rhee) State-corporatist groups: Korea People's Association, Federation of Korean Trade Unions (FKTU), Korea Women's Association, Korea Youth Organization, Federation of Peasant Unions	
1956 Presidential election (Syngman Rhee, Sin Ik Hŭi, Cho Pong Am) Progressive Party established	Labor disputes in Taegu
1958 National Assembly election Strengthening of the National Security Law	
1959 Leader of the Progressive Party Cho Pong Am executed	Shutdown of the pro-opposition newspaper Kyŏnghyang Daily Student organizations Korea Trade Union Council
1960 Presidential election (Syngman Rhee, unopposed)— massive election-rigging State-corporatist groups such as FKTU, Korea Anticommunist Youth Association deeply involved in election-rigging	
Collapse of the Rhee regime	April Uprising
Interim government of Hŏ Chŏng Socialist Mass Party, Federation of Progressive Comrades, Korea Socialist Party established General election	April Revolution Youth-Student Alliance, Federation for the Promotion of National Reunification, Association of the Wounded in the April Revolution
Inauguration of the Chang Myŏn regime State-corporatist groups: Association of Anticommunist Groups, Korea Economic Council	Youth Association for Democracy and Nationalism, Youth Association for Reunification and Democracy, Student Leagues/Fronts for National Reunification,
	Teachers' Labor Unions, white-collar unions Korea Federation of Labor Unions
1961	New labor movement Reunification campaign Anti-Korean–U.S. economic agreement struggle Anti–bad laws struggle
Military coup	

2. THE SECOND DEMOCRATIC JUNCTURE, 1973–1980

State & Political Society	Civil Society
1963 Presidential election (Park Chung Hee, Yun Po Sŏn)	
1964–65 People's Revolutionary Party incident	Student demonstrations against Korean-Japanese Normalization and Korean participation in the Vietnam War
1967 Presidential election (Park Chung Hee, Yun Po Sŏn)	Labor protests by miners' unions
1968 Reunification Revolutionary Party incident	Labor protests by railway workers' unions
1969 Constitutional revision (to allow a third term for Park Chung Hee) State-corporatist groups: National Headquarters for Reconstruction, Korea Youth Association, Korea Women's Association, 4H Clubs, Federation of Korean Industries, Korean Chamber of Commerce and Industry, Korea International Trade Association, FKTU	Student protest against the constitutional revision Labor protests by stevedores' unions
1970	Death of labor activist Chŏn T'ae Il
1971 Presidential election (Park Chung Hee, Kim Dae Jung)	
1972 Yusin	
1973 Kim Dae Jung kidnapped National Assembly election One-Million Signature Collection Campaign by New Democratic Party	Anti-Yusin student demonstrations
1974 Presidential Emergency Measures	Emergence of *chaeya* and the triple solidarity of students, laborers, and churches Catholic prayer meetings Korea Ecumenical Youth Council, Young Catholic Workers, Urban Industrial Mission, Korea Christian Academy, Catholic Priests' Association for Justice National Congress for the Restoration of Democracy
1978 National Assembly election	National Coalition for Democracy
1979 Park assassinated December 12 military putsch	National Congress for Democracy and Reunification Y.H. incident Pusan-Masan Uprising
1980 May 17 coup	Kwangju Uprising

TABLE 7.1 (continued)
Civil Society and Democratization in Korea: Chronology
3. THE THIRD DEMOCRATIC JUNCTURE, 1984–1987

State & Political Society	Civil Society
1980 Special Committee for National Security Measures Legislative Council for National Security State-corporatist groups: FKTU, Federation of Korean Industries, Korea Chamber of Commerce and Industry, Social Purification Committee	
1983 Phase of political relaxation	
1984	Youth Coalition for Democracy Movement National Student Coalition for Democracy Struggle Korea Council for Laborers' Welfare established and Chŏnggye Trade Union restored Council of Movement for People and Democracy National Congress for Reunification and Democracy
1985 New Korea Democratic Party (Kim Young Sam + Kim Dae Jung) National Assembly election	People's Movement Coalition for Democracy and Reunification
1986 National Coalition for Democracy Movement	
1987 Reunification Democratic Party (Kim Young Sam + Kim Dae Jung)	Antiregime statement struggle
April 13 statement	National Movement Headquarters for Democracy Constitution
	June uprising
June 29 statement	July–August Workers' Struggle
	National Council of University Student Representatives
Party for Peace and Democracy (Kim Dae Jung)	
Presidential election (Roh Tae Woo, Kim Young Sam, Kim Dae Jung)	

4. DEMOCRATIC CONSOLIDATION, 1988–

State & Political Society	Civil Society
1988 Presidential inauguration National Assembly election	
1989	Korea Coalition for National Democratic Movement established Korean Peasant Movement Coalition established Korean Teachers' and Educational Workers' Union established Citizens' Coalition for Economic Justice established
1990 Democratic Liberal Party (Roh Tae Woo + Kim Young Sam + Kim Jong Pil)	Korea Trade Union Council established
1991	Citizens' Coalition for Fair Elections established
1992 Presidential Election (Kim Young Sam, Kim Dae Jung, and Chŏng Chu Yŏng)	National Alliance for Democracy and Unification of Korea established
1993 Inauguration of the Kim Young Sam regime	National Coalition of University Student Councils established Korea Federation for Environmental Movement established
1994	Korea Council of Citizens' Movements established People's Solidarity for Participatory Democracy established
1995 Imprisonment of Chun and Roh	Campaign for the liquidation of the authoritarian past Korea Confederation of Trade Unions established
1996 Passage of antidemocratic laws	Protest against the passage of antidemocratic laws
1997 Economic crisis Presidential election (Kim Dae Jung, Yi Hoe Ch'ang, Yi In Che)	Movement for *chaebŏl* reform
1998 Inauguration of the Kim Dae Jung regime (Kim Dae Jung + Kim Jong Pil)	Movement for political reform
1999 Economic restructuring	Korea Confederation of Trade Unions officially recognized
2000 National Assembly election	Citizens' Solidarity for National Assembly Elections Campaign for rejecting "unfit" candidates

America, democratization in Korea did not result from an internal split between hardliners and softliners in the ruling bloc. Rather, authoritarian crises began when the ruling bloc was considerably united and eager to extend, if not to perpetuate, its tenure through whatever methods it could utilize. The Syngman Rhee regime resorted to a series of anticommunist offensives and massive election rigging. The Park Chung Hee regime staged an executive coup and installed a highly authoritarian political system of Yusin, while the Chun Doo Hwan regime initiated a phase of political relaxation to fragment the opposition and to consolidate further the authoritarian political order. But these attempts led to unexpected and unintended consequences—the resurrection, reactivation, and remobilization of civil society, which drove the reluctant and often recalcitrant ruling regime to initiate and pursue democratic reforms. Therefore, the resurrection of civil society came *before*—not during or after—the transition. In the second democratic juncture, the resurrection of civil society preceded and even *caused* the fatal split between hardliners and softliners within the ruling bloc, marking a stark contrast with the occurrences in Southern Europe and Latin America. Civil society arose *before*, not after, democracy. In this respect, the Korean case deviates from some of the representative cases in the recent "third wave" of global democratization. It is rather like some of the "classic" cases of democratization in Western Europe in which civil society, primarily composed of the bourgeois class, had existed before democracy and had promoted it.

However, the similarities between Korea and the West should not be overstated. Undoubtedly, the growth of civil society in Korea in recent decades, as in the West, has been directly related to capitalist industrialization. Capitalist development facilitated the growth of civil society in Korea by increasing the level of urbanization, by bringing workers together in factories, by improving the means of communication and transportation, and by raising the level of literacy.[3] But the evolution of civil society in Korea did not exactly follow Western precedents.[4] Most of all, unlike in Western societies, Korea's civil society did not emerge under the leadership of the bourgeoisie. Rather, it arose *in opposition* to it. Because the bourgeois class and its representative associations in Korea generally partook in the state-corporatist political arrangement and sided with the authoritarian regimes, civil society's political protest for democracy was not only against the state but also against the bourgeoisie. In Korea, "the absence of bourgeoisie hegemony was ... a cause ... of a highly politicized civil society."[5] The notable nonexistence of the bourgeois class in civil society's protracted and arduous pro-democracy struggle in Korea is in fact consistent

TABLE 7.2
Civil Society and Democratization in Korea: Analysis

	1st Democratic Juncture (1956–1961)	2nd Democratic Juncture (1973–1980)	3rd Democratic Juncture (1984–1987)	Democratic Consolidation (1988–)
Actors	Students	Triple solidarity: Students Workers Churches National associations	Triple solidarity Students Workers Churches National associations Middle Class	People's Movement Groups Citizens' Movement Groups
Interactions Civil society–state	Conflict	Conflict	Conflict	Conflict Cooperation Incorporation
Civil society–political society	Cooperation With marginal progressive parties	Cooperation With major opposition party Religious leaders + opposition politicians Joint statements Based on individual commitments and personal networks	Cooperation With major opposition party Triple solidarity + opposition party Joint organizations Based on institutionalized organizations	Competition Issue-dependent cooperation Incorporation
Issues	Procedural democracy Reunification Self-assertive foreign relations	Procedural democracy Human rights/labor rights Reunification	Procedural democracy Substantive democracy Reunification Self-assertive foreign relations (Anti-Americanism)	Expansion and deepening of democracy Socioeconomic justice New issues Political and economic reforms

with other cases in which "the classes that benefited from the status quo nearly without exception resisted democracy and the subordinate classes fought for democracy."[6] Unlike in the West, therefore, the strength of Korean civil society resides not in the "multiplicity of independent civic organizations or in the existence of powerful social classes," but in a "stubborn and resistant political culture and a latent mobilizational capacity of civil society, both the products of tumultuous political history of contemporary Korea."[7]

Placed in comparative perspective, Korean democracy, characterized by mass-ascendancy, may fare better than other fledgling democracies in Southern Europe and Latin America. In the case of Brazil, for example, "a smooth, relatively easy transition from authoritarian rule paradoxically ensured not a strong, vibrant democracy, but a perverted one skewed toward the representation of elite interests whose procedures and policies are subject to military review."[8] Similarly, the elite-ascendant, "pacted" transitions in Venezuela (in 1958) and Colombia (in 1958) undermined the notion of majority rule and institutionalized the practice of political clientelism in these countries.[9] An elite-ascendant democracy such as Brazil might be more stable than a mass-ascendant democracy such as Korea but an elite-ascendant democracy is "narrower and shallower."[10]

Despite such comparative advantage vis-à-vis elite-ascendant democracy, however, mass-ascendancy and a highly resistant civil society in Korea are by no means an "unmitigated blessing for democracy."[11] As pointed out repeatedly throughout this book, mass-ascendancy of Korean democratization has entailed conflictual engagement between civil society and the state. Even under the current Kim Dae Jung government, many of the people's movement groups in Korean civil society still maintain largely conflictual engagement with the state. Continuation of this situation between civil society and the state may have several negative effects on the further consolidation of Korean democracy.

Conflictual engagement may unduly restrict the potential role of civil society in promoting democracy. Resisting the domination of an authoritarian regime and hastening its exit from power are a crucial but not the *only* function of civil society. There are many other roles civil society can and should play in furthering and deepening democracy. Particularly, unlike in the phase of democratic transition, where opposition to an authoritarian regime is deemed essential, the phase of democratic consolidation requires various other functions of civil society, such as providing an important basis for democratic competition, supplementing the role of political parties in stimulating political participation, increasing the political efficacy of democratic citizens, promoting an appreciation of the obligations as well as rights of democratic citizenship, improving welfare at the local level, and so forth.[12] The continuation of conflictual engagement between civil society and the state causes civil society groups to be perpetually militant in preparation for a possible battle with the state, which makes it extremely difficult to support and nurture those other functions of civil society vital to sustaining and deepening democracy. If unconditional and almost reflexive criticism of and opposition to the state are considered to be the only legitimate functions of civil society, persistent political instability is very likely to result.

Institutionalization of political parties may also be hindered by conflictual engagement. As a result, the key issues of politics continue to be handled during the direct, intense, and sometimes brutal confrontation between civil society and the state. This aggravates one of the chronic problems of Korean politics—the low institutionalization and underdevelopment of political society.[13] During the direct interactions between civil society and the state, political parties are regarded as peripheral at best and irrelevant at worst. Unfortunately, it is broadly agreed upon in the literature on democratic transition and consolidation that in the stage of democratic consolidation the role of political parties becomes far more important compared to that of civil society.[14] Democratic transition is a "war of movement" determined by the actors' actions and choices. By contrast, democratic consolidation is a "war of position" determined by interactions among highly institutionalized groups and spheres as the actors "settle into the trenches."[15] It can rarely be successful without an institutionalized political society. Therefore, a continuation of conflictual engagement may be destructive to the institutionalization of political society.

Furthermore, the emergence and development of a political culture that appreciates and promotes tolerance, moderation, negotiation, consultation, bargaining, and compromise may also be prevented by conflictual engagement. Thus, it hinders the evolution of a "civic culture," known to be essential to the daily workings of a viable democracy. Instead, the continued antagonism and confrontation between civil society and the state fosters and amplifies radicalism, extremism, fundamentalism, and even violence. In the midst of intense battle between the two opposing sides, moderation and tolerance are viewed as opportunism and indecisiveness. During the democratic transition, such a clear-cut distinction between "we" and "they" significantly contributed to the unity and power of the pro-democracy alliance and coalition. But in the phase of democratic consolidation, the legacy of mass-ascendancy bequeathed from the authoritarian period only delays the development of a democratic political culture and may create a political environment in which stability and governability remain permanently elusive.[16]

This is not to argue that struggle and militancy in general are necessarily detrimental to the further development of democracy in Korea. It is still essential for civil society groups to continue their pro-democracy struggle to expand and deepen Korean democracy. Establishing a procedural democracy and eliminating the possibility of an authoritarian regression are not the end of democratization. Korea should constantly attempt to expand its democracy to guarantee civil liberties irrespective of political ideologies and to enhance socioeconomic equalities. The activities of the people's movement groups, however militant they may be, are integral to the expansion and deepening of Korean democracy. At the same time, however, the groups' clashings with the state—particularly their reflexive and almost instinctive criticism of and opposition to the state—only aggravate the dependency of civil society on the state. Without providing clear visions and specific policy alternatives, the status and power of civil society would largely depend on whether the state succeeds or fails in its proposed reform policies. In a very zero-sum fashion, the state's gain would be civil society's loss and civil society's gain would be the state's loss. Unfortunately, unlike in the dichotomous world under the authoritarian rule, such simple arithmetic can no longer capture and explain the complex dynamics of democratic consolidation. In democratic consolidation, "state-society relations need not always be confrontational but under certain circumstances may be complementary."[17]

Another important conclusion that can be drawn from my analysis of the Korean case is that the role of civil society in Korea should gradually change from protest against political authoritarianism to policy advocacy. As pointed out in chapter 6, some civil society groups in Korea are moving already in that direction. Other civil society groups in Korea, particularly the people's movement groups that spearheaded the pro-democracy struggles during the past democratic junctures, must also follow suit, developing their concrete visions of Korean democracy and suggesting specific policy alternatives to achieve those visions. The role of civil society should change. In the past, its purpose was to challenge, oppose, and even overthrow the authoritarian regimes. Now, civil society must engage, affect, monitor, check, and control the state by articulating and promoting new visions and developing and presenting new policy prescriptions.[18] The urgent task for Korean civil society now is to rethink its role in democratic development and redefine itself as a reservoir of new visions and new policy solutions, gradually moving from protest to policy advocacy. Consequently, the consolidation and persistence of Korean democracy will largely depend on whether and how civil society groups accomplish this crucial transformation.

Notes

Chapter 1. Introduction: Korean Democratization and Civil Society

1. Holding relatively free, fair, and regular elections is a central element found in numerous definitions of democracy. See Dahl, *Polyarchy*, 3; Huntington, *Third Wave*, 7; Diamond, Linz, and Lipset, *Democracy in Developing Countries*, 6.

2. For a definition of democracy that emphasizes civil liberties in particular, see Diamond, Linz, and Lipset, *Democracy in Developing Countries*, 7.

3. Schmitter and Karl, "What Democracy Is . . . and Is Not," 45.

4. Cha, "Politics and Democracy under the Kim Young Sam Government," 855–56.

5. For a good review, see Mun, "Han'gugŭi minjujuŭiroŭi ihaengrone taehan kŏmt'o," 277–94.

6. Oberdorfer, "U.S. Policy toward Korea in the 1987 Crisis Compared with Other Allies," 179–81.

7. O'Donnell and Schmitter, *Transitions from Authoritarian Rule*. 18.

8. See, for example, Hyug-Baeg Im, *Sijang, kukka, minjujuŭi*, 253–97; Cheng and Kim, "Making Democracy."

9. O'Donnell and Schmitter, *Transitions from Authoritarian Rule*, 19.

10. *Ibid.*, 48; Higley and Gunther, *Elites and Democratic Consolidation in Latin America and Southern Europe*, 3.

11. Tarrow, "Mass Mobilization and Regime Change," 205–7.

12. Sŏng, "Han'guk chŏngch'i minjuhwaŭi sahoejŏk kiwŏn," 121–23; Tae Hwa Chŏng, "Han'guk minjuhwawa chibae seryŏgŭi kyoch'e," 181; Mun, "Han'gugŭi minjujuŭiroŭi ihaengrone taehan kŏmt'o," 287.

13. Diamond, "Toward Democratic Consolidation," 5.

14. Choi, "Han'gugŭi minjuhwa"; Sŏng, "Han'guk chŏngch'i minjuhwaŭi sahoejŏk kiwŏn"; Sin, "Han'gugesŏŭi simin sahoe hyŏngsŏnggwa minjuhwa kwajŏngesŏŭi yŏkhal"; Sunhyuk Kim, "Civic Mobilization for Democratic Reform."

15. Throughout this volume, I use, for distinction, "alliance" to refer to collaboration within civil society and "coalition" to refer to collaboration between civil society and political parties. Regarding East European and African cases, see Bernhard, "Civil Society and Democratic Transition in East Central Europe"; Weigle and Butterfield, "Civil Society in Reforming Communist Regimes"; Chazan, "Africa's Democratic Challenge"; Fatton, "Democracy and Civil Society in Africa."

16. This is not to claim that civil society is the *only* determinant of Korean democratization. If expressed in a mathematical function, $y = f(w, x, z, \ldots)$, where y is democratization and $w, x, z, \ldots$ are diverse explanatory variables. However important it may be, civil society is just one of the many independent variables. I nevertheless argue in this book that civil society is the *most crucial* variable.

Chapter 2. Civil Society and Democratization:
Conceptual and Theoretical Issues

1. Huntington, *Third Wave.*

2. Diamond and Plattner, *Global Resurgence of Democracy.*

3. Diamond, *Democratic Revolution.*

4. Huntington, *Third Wave,* 21–26; Diamond, "Globalization of Democracy," 32–38.

5. For useful typologies of transition from authoritarianism, see Mainwaring, *Transitions to Democracy and Democratic Consolidation;* Karl, "Dilemmas of Democratization in Latin America"; Karl and Schmitter, "Democratization around the Globe."

6. Incidentally, it is not only comparativists who have been intrigued by the third wave of global democratization. The international relations literature has also focused on the macro level impact of global democratization. For debates on the "democratic peace" in particular, see Doyle, "Kant, Liberal Legacies, and Foreign Affairs"; Maoz and Russett, "Normative and Structural Causes of Democratic Peace"; Russett, *Grasping the Democratic Peace;* Owen, *Liberal Peace, Liberal War.*

7. Examples include O'Donnell and Schmitter, *Transitions from Authoritarian Rule;* O'-Donnell, Schmitter, and Whitehead, *Transitions from Authoritarian Rule;* Stepan, *Rethinking Military Politics;* Diamond, Linz, and Lipset, *Democracy in Developing Countries;* Lowenthal, *Exporting Democracy;* Przeworski, *Democracy and the Market;* Rueschemeyer, Stephens, and Stephens, *Capitalist Development and Democracy;* Higley and Gunther, *Elites and Democratic Consolidation in Latin America and Southern Europe;* Mainwaring, O'Donnell, and Valenzuela, *Issues in Democratic Consolidation;* Diamond and Plattner, *Global Resurgence of Democracy;* Gunther, Diamandouros, and Puhle, *Politics of Democratic Consolidation;* Haggard and Kaufman, *Political Economy of Democratic Transitions;* Linz and Stepan, *Problems of Democratic Transition and Consolidation;* Casper and Taylor, *Negotiating Democracy;* Diamond, *Developing Democracy.* For a good review of some of these works, see Shin, "On the Third Wave of Democratization"; Munck, "Democratic Transitions in Comparative Perspective."

8. For the origins and theoretical expandability of "transitology" and "consolidology," see these debates in *Slavic Review:* Schmitter and Karl, "Conceptual Travels of Transitologists and Consolidologists"; Bunce, "Should Transitologists Be Grounded"; Karl and Schmitter, "From an Iron Curtain to a Paper Curtain"; Bunce, "Paper Curtains and Paper Tigers."

9. Karl, "Dilemmas of Democratization," 2–8.

10. Lipset, *Political Man,* 51. Regarding the elaboration and verification of Lipset's thesis, see Diamond, "Economic Development and Democracy Reconsidered."

11. Almond and Verba, *Civic Culture.*

12. The most representative work is Putnam, *Making Democracy Work.*

13. The most representative work is O'Donnell and Schmitter, *Transitions from Authoritarian Rule.*

14. Karl, "Dilemmas of Democratization," 6.

15. Diamond, "Civil Society and the Development of Democracy," 3.

16. O'Donnell and Schmitter, *Transitions from Authoritarian Rule;* Stepan, *Rethinking Military Politics.*

17. Gold, "Resurgence of Civil Society in China"; Strand, "Protest in Beijing"; Ahn, "Economic Development and Democratization"; Choi, "Political Cleavages in Korea"; Ngo, "Civil Society and Political Liberalization in Taiwan"; White and Howell, *In Search of Civil*

Society; He, *Democratic Implications of Civil Society in China;* Jones, "Democratization, Civil Society, and Illiberal Middle Class Culture in Pacific Asia." Also see special issue of *Modern China* 19,2 (1993), particularly the following: Chamberlain, "On the Search for Civil Society in China"; Rowe, "Problem of 'Civil Society' in Late Imperial China"; Wakeman, "Civil Society and Public Sphere Debate."

18. Bayart, "Civil Society in Africa"; Bratton, "Beyond the State"; Fatton, "Democracy and Civil Society in Africa"; Chazan, "Africa's Democratic Challenge"; Lewis, "Political Transition and the Dilemma of Civil Society in Africa"; Gyimah-Boadi, "Associational Life, Civil Society, and Democratization in Ghana"; Bratton and Van de Walle, *Democratic Experiments in Africa.*

19. Arato, "Civil Society against the State"; Pelczynski, "Solidarity and the Rebirth of Civil Society"; Krizan, "'Civil Society'—A New Paradigm in the Yugoslav Theoretical Discussion"; Lapidus, "State and Society"; Frentzel-Zagorska, "Civil Society in Poland and Hungary"; Weigle and Butterfield, "Civil Society in Reforming Communist Regimes"; Bernhard, *Origins of Democratization in Poland;* Fish, *Democracy from Scratch;* Ekiert, *State against Society.*

20. Bellin, "Civil Society"; Schwedler, *Toward Civil Society in the Middle East?.*

21. Diamond, *Democratic Revolution,* 7–15.

22. O'Donnell and Schmitter, *Transitions from Authoritarian Rule,* 48–56.

23. Bernhard, "Civil Society and Democratic Transition in East Central Europe," 326.

24. Ngo, "Civil Society and Political Liberalization."

25. Fatton, "Democracy and Civil Society," 89; Woods, "Civil Society in Europe and Africa," 94.

26. Schmitter, "Civil Society East and West," 247; Diamond, "Toward Democratic Consolidation," 7–11.

27. O'Donnell and Schmitter, *Transitions from Authoritarian Rule,* 8.

28. Dahl, *Polyarchy,* 3.

29. Schmitter and Karl, "What Democracy Is," 42. Minimalist definitions, focused on electoral competition, originally descend from Joseph Schumpeter, who defined democracy as a system "for arriving at political decisions in which individuals acquire the power to decide by means of a competitive struggle for the people's vote." Schumpeter, *Capitalism, Socialism, and Democracy,* 269.

30. Huntington, *Third Wave,* 7; Diamond, Linz, and Lipset, *Democracy in Developing Countries,* 6–7.

31. O'Donnell and Schmitter, *Transitions from Authoritarian Rule,* 7–8.

32. Diamond, "Toward Democratic Consolidation," 15. For more elaborate definitions, see Valenzuela, "Democratic Consolidation in Post-Transitional Settings," 69; Linz and Stepan, *Problems of Democratic Transition,* 5–6. Linz and Stepan define democratic consolidation in terms of three dimensions—behavioral, attitudinal, and constitutional.

33. Regarding the historical and philosophical permutations of the concept and theory of civil society, see Keane, "Despotism and Democracy." Also see Fine and Rai, *Civil Society.*

34. Diamond, "Toward Democratic Consolidation," 4; Stepan, *Rethinking Military Politics,* 3–4; Gold, "Resurgence of Civil Society," 20; Arato, "Civil Society," 23; White, "Prospects for Civil Society in China," 65; Shils, "Virtue of Civil Society," 4; Keane, *Democracy and Civil Society,* 14.

35. Schmitter, "Civil Society East and West," 240.

36. Diamond, "Toward Democratic Consolidation," 6–7; Fish, "Russia's Fourth Transition," 41.

37. Weigle and Butterfield, "Civil Society in Reforming Communist Regimes," 3.

38. Arato, "Civil Society," 23; Keane, *Democracy and Civil Society,* 14; Ngo, "Civil Society and Political Liberalization," 3; Fatton, "Democracy and Civil Society," 84.

39. Shils, "Virtue of Civil Society," 3.

40. Regarding corporatism as compared with other systems of interest representation and intermediation (namely, pluralism, syndicalism, and monism), see Schmitter, "Still the Century of Corporatism?" 93–98. For the distinction between societal and state corporatism, see *Ibid.*, 102–5.

41. Schmitter, "Civil Society East and West," 240.

42. Diamond, "Toward Democratic Consolidation," 7.

43. Schmitter, "Civil Society East and West," 240.

44. Stepan, *Rethinking Military Politics,* 3.

45. Diamond, "Toward Democratic Consolidation," 7; Diamond, *Developing Democracy,* 223.

46. This is called "nonusurpation." See Schmitter, "Civil Society East and West," 240.

47. Diamond, "Toward Democratic Consolidation," 7.

48. However, this does not mean that the boundaries between different societal spheres are completely sealed. For example, part of civil society becomes or moves to political society when movement groups form or join a political party ("political societization"). Similarly, part of civil society changes to the state when constituents of civil society leave civil society and join the state ("statization"). The boundaries should be considered fluid rather than rigid. See chapter 6 of this book for a discussion of these issues in the case of Korea.

49. Shils, "Virtue of Civil Society," 4.

50. Diamond, "Toward Democratic Consolidation," 6–7.

51. Putnam, *Making Democracy Work,* is a detailed case study on how a set of important cultural traits and norms facilitate the formation and evolution of civil society or what Putnam calls a "civic community." Regarding how the concept of civil society differs from Putnam's "civic community," see Diamond, *Developing Democracy,* 225–27.

52. Schmitter, "Civil Society East and West," 240; Weigle and Butterfield, "Civil Society in Reforming Communist Regimes," 3; Shils, "Virtue of Civil Society," 4.

53. Keane, *Democracy and Civil Society,* 14; Diamond, "Toward Democratic Consolidation," 5.

54. Fatton, "Democracy and Civil Society," 86.

55. Collier and Collier, *Shaping the Political Arena,* 29. For their critical juncture framework, see *Ibid.*, 29–31.

56. Lewis, "Political Transition," 45.

57. Linz and Stepan, *Problems of Democratic Transition,* 5.

58. Moore, *Social Origins of Dictatorship,* 418.

59. Rueschemeyer, Stephens, and Stephens, *Capitalist Development.*

60. In this book, I will not focus on the relationship between civil society and basic units of production and reproduction (RD2 in figure 2.2). Although the relationship is an interesting and important issue, it seems to be a subject for an anthropological or a sociological inquiry unless it has direct and obvious implications for *political* change and democratization. In political science, Putnam's *Making Democracy Work* in part deals with this relationship, although his main focuses are intergroup relations and norms *within* civil society—or what he calls a "civic community."

Chapter 3. Civil Society in the First Democratic Juncture, 1956–1961

1. For the concept and theoretical framework of "conflictual engagement" between state and civil society, see Bratton, "Beyond the State." The intense confrontation between state and civil society is a perennial theme in the study of Korean democratization. For a framework of a "strong" state vs. a "contentious" civil society, see Koo, "Strong State and Contentious Society." For a framework of a "strong" state vs. a "strong" society, see Sŏng, "Han'guk chŏngch'i minjuhwaŭi sahoejŏk kiwŏn." Regarding the legacy of Japanese colonialism in Korea in general, see Cumings, "American Policy and Korean Liberation"; Cumings, "Legacy of Japanese Colonialism in Korea."

2. The colonial state in Korea was "strong" in terms of both institutional coherence and relative insulation from domestic societal forces. With regard to conceptualization and measurement of state strength, see Doner, "Limits of State Strength"; Krasner, "Approaches to the State"; Skocpol, "Bringing the State Back In." About the issue of state strength in an East Asian context, see Cotton, "Limits to Liberalization in Industrializing Asia." Regarding the traditional monarchy in precolonial Korea, see Palais, *Politics and Policy in Traditional Korea*.

3. For instance, the number of mining and industrial workers soared from 133,046 in 1930 to 937,918 in 1944. See Nak Chung Kim, *Han'guk nodong undongsa*, 49.

4. For social movements during the colonial period, see Yŏng T'ae Im, *Singminji sidae han'guk sahoewa undong*; Mangwŏn Study Group, *Han'guk kŭndae minjung undongsa*.

5. Choi, *Han'guk minjujuŭiŭi iron*, 157–58. For a thorough analysis of domestic and international political dynamics in Korea in 1945–1950, see Cumings, *Origins of the Korean War*.

6. Choi, *Han'guk minjujuŭiŭi iron*, 157–58.

7. RGKP, *Han'guk chŏngch'isa*, 133; Yŏng Myŏng Kim, *Han'guk hyŏndae chŏngch'isa*, 140–42.

8. Tong An Yang, "Hollan sogŭi kukka hyŏngsŏng," 86.

9. *Ibid.*, 84–87.

10. Choi, *Han'guk minjujuŭiŭi iron*, 157–58. In particular, regarding the role of the police under the USAMGIK, see Wang Sik Kim, "Migunjŏng kyŏngch'arŭi chŏngch'ijŏk wisang."

11. Pong Suk Son, "Cheil konghwagukkwa chayudang," 144; Su In Yi, "Chayudang chŏnggwŏnŭi yŏksajŏk sŏnggyŏk."

12. Nak Chung Kim, *Han'guk nodong undongsa*, 231.

13. Kong, "1950 nyŏndae han'guk sahoeŭi kyegŭp kusŏng," 259.

14. Eckert, Lee, Lew, Robinson, and Wagner, *Korea, Old and New*, 348.

15. Pong Suk Son, "Cheil konghwagukkwa chayudang," 138, 151.

16. Chae O Yi, *Han'guk haksaeng undongsa*, 115–16.

17. NEC, *Taehan min'guk sŏn'gŏsa*, 477–78.

18. Pong Suk Son, "Cheil konghwagukkwa chayudang," 154.

19. NEC, *Taehan min'guk sŏn'gŏsa*, 789.

20. Korean society underwent a rapid urbanization during the 1950s. Between 1945 and 1960, the proportion of Koreans living in cities of 50,000 or more almost doubled. Urbanization was stimulated and accompanied by booms in education. The literacy rate more than tripled, recording 70 percent in 1960. See Eckert, Lee, Lew, Robinson, and Wagner, *Korea, Old and New*, 353.

21. Pong Suk Son, "Cheil konghwagukkwa chayudang," 157.

22. Yŏng Myŏng Kim, *Han'guk hyŏndae chŏngch'isa*, 207.

23. Nak Chung Kim, *Han'guk nodong undongsa*, 249–50.

24. This makes a good contrast with another Korea Trade Union Council in 1990. The KTUC in 1990 was formed by activists who had been an integral part of the pro-democracy movement during the 1970s and 1980s. The Roh Tae Woo regime (1988–1993) suppressed the KTUC for its radical and "leftist" nature.

25. "Pujŏng sŏn'gŏ wŏnhyung naemubu sagŏn p'an'gyŏlmun," 67.

26. Kyŏng Tae Kim, "4 wŏl hyŏngmyŏngŭi chŏn'gae kwajŏng," 14.

27. Nak Chung Kim, *Han'guk nodong undongsa*, 239.

28. Ryu, "Han'gugŭi uik chiptan yŏn'gu," 251–52.

29. Kyŏng Tae Kim, "4 wŏl hyŏngmyŏngŭi chŏn'gae kwajŏng," 16–17.

30. *Ibid.*, 44 (n. 17).

31. *Ibid.*, 17–19.

32. RGKP, *Han'guk chŏngch'isa*, 311.

33. T'aek Hwi Yi, "Minjujuŭi t'och'akhwaŭi siryŏn," 185–96; RGKP, *Han'guk chŏngch'isa*, 314–17.

34. RGKP, *Han'guk chŏngch'isa*, 320–22.

35. Han, "Chei konghwaguk," 215.

36. For the platforms and policies of these parties, see Kwŏn, *Han'guk hyŏksin chŏngdanggwa sahoejuŭi international.*

37. RGKP, *Han'guk chŏngch'isa*, 322–24.

38. Ko, "4 wŏl hyŏngmyŏngŭi inyŏm," 167.

39. Han, "Chei konghwaguk," 218; RGKP, *Han'guk chŏngch'isa*, 332–33.

40. Nak Chung Kim, "4 wŏl hyŏngmyŏnggwa minjok t'ongil undong," 225–26.

41. Hŭi Yŏn Cho, "50, 60, 70 nyŏndae minjok minju undongŭi chŏn'gae kwajŏnge kwanhan yŏn'gu," 69–76.

42. Nak Chung Kim, *Han'guk nodong undongsa*, 277–92; RGKP, *Han'guk chŏngch'isa*, 320–22.

43. Kwang Sik Kim, "4 wŏl hyŏngmyŏnggwa hyŏksin seryŏgŭi tŭngjanggwa hwaltong," 204.

44. Regarding Chang Myŏn's leadership style, see Chŏng Hŭi Yi, "Chei konghwagugŭi chŏngch'i hwan'gyŏnggwa Chang Myŏnŭi leadership."

45. Han, *Failure of Democracy in Korea*, 182.

46. Han, "Chei konghwaguk," 222–23.

47. For the concept of the "overdeveloped state," see Alavi, "State in Post-Colonial Societies." For an application of this concept to the Korean case, see Choi, *Han'guk hyŏndae, chŏngch'iŭi kujowa pyŏnhwa*, 81–113.

48. This was by no means unique to Korea. In Japan too, MacArthur's initial experiment with popular democracy was suspended in the middle and eventually replaced by policies emphasizing security, economic development, and political stability ("reverse course"). See Nakamura, "Democratization, Peace, and Economic Development"; Ishida and Krauss, *Democracy in Japan*, 9–11. As George Kennan openly and summarily put it, "Where the concepts and traditions of popular government are too weak to absorb successfully the intensity of the Communist attacks, then we must concede that harsh government measures of repression may be the only answer." See Bethell, "From the Second World War to the Cold War," 64–65.

49. For applications of corporatism to the Korean case, see Ho Chin Kim, *Han'guk*

chŏngch'i ch'ejeron, 438–57; Choi, *Han'guk minjujuŭiŭi iron*, 263–91; Hyug-Baeg Im, *Sijang, kukka, minjujuŭi*, 335–71; Cumings, "Corporate State in North Korea."

50. Schmitter, "Still the Century of Corporatism?" 97.

51. Lewis, "Political Transition," 45.

52. Ki Yŏng Chŏng, "4 wŏl hyŏngmyŏngŭi chudo seryŏk."

53. Eckert, Lee, Lew, Robinson, and Wagner, *Korea, Old and New*, 354.

54. Some scholars claim that such remonstrance was the evidence that there existed a "Confucian civil society" during the Chosŏn period. See, for example, Hein Cho, "Historical Origin of Civil Society in Korea." For a general claim beyond Korea, see de Bary, *Asian Values and Human Rights*. However, it should be noted that such "remonstrance" was conducted consistently within the boundary of Confucian canons and Confucian scholars at the time were largely dependent on the state, constantly seeking opportunities to serve as public officials. Autonomy from the state and pluralism within civil society were critically lacking, which makes it problematic to call Confucian community a "civil society." For a criticism of the argument for "Confucian civil society," see Sunhyuk Kim, "Civil Society and Democratization in South Korea."

55. The prominence of students in civil society is not unique to Korea; such was also the case in China. As Strand observes, "In 1989, the core of students was there as it had been in 1919 and 1986, but the students now were joined by hundreds of thousands of people from all walks of life." Strand, "Protest in Beijing," 11. Regarding the Chinese case, also see He, "Dual Roles of Semi-Civil Society in Chinese Democratization," 168. For a historical survey of student movement in Korea, see Billet, "History and Role of Student Activism in the Republic of Korea."

56. Furthermore, many leading figures of the April student "revolution" later changed their course and joined the authoritarian regimes. See Chong Sŏk Yi, "4 wŏl hyŏngmyŏng chudo seryŏgŭi pyŏnch'ŏn kwajŏng."

57. For a theoretical analysis of the process of democratic breakdown in general, see Linz, *Breakdown of Democratic Regimes*.

58. This is by no means to argue that North Korea was not a military threat to South Korea. I am also not saying that the North Korean regime did not use very similar "national division" arguments and "anti-U.S. imperialism" slogans to suppress its own political opposition and to restrict civil liberties. The issues of national division and national security were used, misused, and overused by both Koreas to maintain their political authoritarianism.

Chapter 4. Civil Society in the Second Democratic Juncture, 1973–1980

1. With respect to the political crisis surrounding the Korean-Japanese Normalization in the mid-1960s, see Kwan-Bong Kim, *Korea-Japan Crisis and the Instability of the Korean Political System*.

2. Choi, "Political Cleavages in South Korea," 33.

3. In this respect, students tried to reveal and criticize the "lateral weakness" of the Korean state (toward the United States) at the time. For the concept of "lateral weakness," see Cumings, "Abortive Abertura."

4. Haggard and Moon, "State, Politics, and Economic Development in Postwar South Korea," 65.

5. Eckert, Lee, Lew, Robinson, and Wagner, *Korea, Old and New*, 361.

6. Wŏn Sun Pak, *Kukka poanbŏp yŏn'gu*, 184–206.

7. Regarding the origins and development of these economic interest associations, see

Yŏng Rae Kim, *Han'guk iik chiptan'gwa minju chŏgch'i palchŏn*. About the concept of "developmental state" and its application to developing countries, see White, "Developmental States and Socialist Industrialization in the Third World." See Eun Mee Kim, *Big Business, Strong State*, regarding the cooperation between the developmental state and business in Korea.

8. Chang, "Chesam konghwagukkwa kwŏnwijuŭijŏk kŭndaehwa," 234–35.

9. Mok Hŭi Yi, "10 wŏl Yusin'gwa minju nodong undongŭi oeroun ch'ulbal," 77.

10. *"Chaeya"* or *"chaeya* movement circle" (*chaeya undonggwŏn*) were sometimes used to refer generally to the opposition party and dissident movement together. The authoritarian regime and the ruling bloc particularly preferred such a generic usage. Of course, they often described *chaeya* as communist-instigated.

11. Choi, *Han'guk hyŏndae chŏngch'iŭi kujowa pyŏnhwa*, 191–192.

12. T'ae Kyun Pak, "Han'guk minjujuŭiŭi chudo seryŏk," 169.

13. According to Bernhard, dissidence is a form of moral suasion, chastising the authoritarian regime as to how it should act, whereas opposition is the concentration of efforts on society as the basis for resistance. Bernhard, "Civil Society and Democratic Transition," 311–14. Also see Bernhard, *Origins of Democratization*, 7–9.

14. Nam, *Korean Politics*, 73.

15. *Ibid.*

16. Choi, "Political Cleavages," 34. Also see Sohn, *Authoritarianism and Opposition in South Korea*.

17. *Chaeya* and people's movement groups are often interchangeably used, which is misleading. For example, the authoritarian regimes used the two words broadly to mean "political opposition." In this book, I differentiate the two terms: *chaeya* primarily refers to the national movement organizations in the 1970s composed of religious leaders and associations that espoused a procedural definition of democracy; people's movement mainly refers to the student organizations, labor unions, and their national organizations in the 1980s that entertained a broader, substantive definition of democracy.

18. Se Chung Kim, "10 wŏl yusin'gwa minju hoebok undong."

19. Nam, *Korean Politics*, 169; Hyŏn Ch'ae Pak, "79 nyŏn Puma sat'aeŭi yŏksajŏk paegyŏnggwa yŏksajŏk ŭiŭi."

20. Nam, *Korean Politics*, 173.

21. Ho Ch'ŏl Son, *Haebang 50 nyŏnŭi han'guk chŏngch'i*, 159–60.

22. RGKP, *Han'guk chŏngch'isa*, 373.

23. Choi, *Han'guk hyŏndae chŏngch'iŭi kujowa pyŏnhwa*, 199.

24. On the very next day, May 16, student representatives from twenty-four universities from the Kyŏnggi-Inch'ŏn area announced, upon the suggestions of opposition politicians Kim Young Sam and Kim Dae Jung, that they would stop street demonstrations lest they should provide a good excuse for a military intervention, which proved to be too late.

25. Regarding the Kwangju Uprising, see Clark, *Kwangju Uprising;* Hae Ku Chŏng, *Kwangju minju hangjaeng yŏn'gu;* Son, *Haebang 50 nyŏnŭi han'guk chŏngch'i*, chapter 5.

26. Haggard and Kaufman, *Political Economy of Democratic Transitions*, 89.

27. *Ibid.*, 90.

28. Regarding the specific dynamics involved in the politics of development during 1961–1970, see Haggard and Moon, "State, Politics, and Economic Development," 65–73.

29. Schmitter and Karl, " Conceptual Travels of Transitologists," 173.

30. Chong Kuk Paek, "Han'gugŭi kukka, simin sahoe, kŭrigo chibae yŏnhabŭi pyŏndong," 138.

31. Yong Pok Kim, "Han'guk chabonjuŭiwa kukka, kwallyo," 134.

32. Koo, "State, *Minjung*, and the Working Class in South Korea," 141.

33. KNCC, *1970 nyŏndae nodong hyŏnjanggwa chŭngŏn*, 94–122. A similar phenomenon occurred in Taiwan. Beginning in the late 1960s, the relationship between the ruling Kuomintang and the Presbyterian church deteriorated when the church increasingly showed its concern over social justice, human rights, and political freedom. The church became one of the major political opposition groups with a mass base. See Ngo, "Civil Society and Political Liberalization," 3–15.

34. To modify the term "ruling triad" that refers to the collusion among bureaucrats, politicians, and businesspeople in Japan, the triple solidarity in Korea might be called a "resisting triad."

35. Sohn, *Authoritarianism and Opposition*, 177–79.

36. Pyŏng Ki Yang, "Han'guk chŏngch'iesŏŭi min–gun kwan'gyeŭi chŏn'gaewa sŏnggyŏk."

37. Finer, *Comparative Government*, 552–53.

38. Ho Chin Kim, *Han'guk chŏngch'i ch'ejeron*, 238.

39. Choi, "Political Cleavages," 20.

Chapter 5. Civil Society in the Third Democratic Juncture, 1984–1987

1. Cumings, "Abortive Abertura," 7.

2. *Tonga ilbo*, November 3, 1980.

3. Youm, "Press Freedom under Constraints," 872.

4. Youm and Salwen, "Free Press in South Korea," 314.

5. Hyug-Baeg Im, "State, Labor and Capital in the Consolidation of Democracy," 11.

6. Nam, *Korean Politics*, 246.

7. Tae Hwa Chŏng, "Han'guk minjuhwawa chibae seryŏgŭi kyoch'e," 191.

8. Hyug-Baeg Im, *Sijang, kukka, minjujuŭi*, 269–71.

9. Sŏng, "Han'guk chŏngch'i minjuhwaŭi sahoejŏk kiwŏn," 110.

10. Hyug-Baeg Im, *Sijang, kukka, minjujuŭi*, 269.

11. Sŏng, "Han'guk chŏngch'i minjuhwaŭi sahoejŏk kiwŏn," 110–11.

12. Ch'oe, "80 nyŏndae ch'ŏngnyŏn undongŭi sŏnggyŏkkwa kŭ chŏn'gae," 250–56.

13. Choi, *Han'guk hyŏndae chŏngch'iŭi kujowa pyŏnhwa*, 214.

14. Hong, "Kwangju minjung hangjaengŭi chwajŏlgwa chinbojŏk nodong undongŭi mosaek," 122–27; Kŭm Su Kim, *Han'guk nodong undongŭi hyŏnhwanggwa kwaje*, 20–23.

15. Ch'ae and Kim, "T'ongil chŏnsŏn undongŭi chŏn'gae," 374–76.

16. Cotton, "From Authoritarianism to Democracy in Korea," 251.

17. Harrison, "Dateline from Korea," 154–75.

18. Ch'ae and Kim, "T'ongil chŏnsŏn undongŭi chŏn'gae," 376–77.

19. CISJD, *Kaehŏn'gwa minjuhwa undong*, 34–35.

20. *Ibid.*, 40.

21. *Ibid.*, 40–41.

22. *Ibid.*

23. *Ibid.*, 42.

24. Nam, *Korean Politics*, 302.

25. CISJD, *Kaehŏn'gwa minjuhwa undong*, 43.

26. Hyug-Baeg Im, *Sijang, kukka, minjujuŭi*, 278.

27. CISJD, *Kaehŏn'gwa minjuhwa undong*, 62.

28. CISJD, *6 wŏl minjuhwa taet'ujaeng*, 242–243.

29. CISJD, *7–8 wŏl nodongja taejung t'ujaeng*, 287.

30. *Ibid.*, 272; Ch'ae and Kim, "T'ongil chŏnsŏn undongŭi chŏn'gae," 377–79.

31. Sŏng, "Han'guk chŏngch'i minjuhwaŭi sahoejŏk kiwŏn," 118–19.

32. Dong, "Democratization of South Korea," 276–79.

33. Hsiao and Koo, "Middle Classes and Democratization," 316–17.

34. The following is a summary of the June 29 Declaration:

(1) The constitution should be expeditiously amended through agreement between the ruling party and the opposition to adopt a direct presidential election system. Presidential elections should be held according to the new constitution to achieve a peaceful transfer of power in February 1988;

(2) It is necessary to revise the Presidential Election Law so that fair competition is secured and the genuine verdict of the people can be given. A revised election law should guarantee the greatest fairness and justness in election management, from the campaigns to the casting, opening and counting of ballots;

(3) Antagonisms must be eradicated not only from the political community but also from all other sectors of society to accomplish national reconciliation and unity. In this respect, Kim Dae Jung should be amnestied, and his civil rights should be restored, regardless of what he has done in the past. Simultaneously, all those who are being detained in connection with the political situation should also be released, except for those who have committed treason or disturbed the national foundations;

(4) Human dignity must be respected and the basic rights of citizens should be promoted and protected as much as possible. Constitutional amendments should include all the strengthened basic rights clauses proposed by the DJP, including a significant extension of habeas corpus;

(5) To promote the freedom of the press, the Basic Press Law, which may have been well intended but has nonetheless been criticized by most journalists, should promptly be either extensively revised or abolished altogether;

(6) Freedom and self-regulation must be guaranteed to the maximum. Local councils should be elected and organized according to schedule. Colleges and universities—the institutions of higher learning—must be made self-governing and educational autonomy in general must be respected;

(7) A political climate conducive to dialogue and compromise must be created, with healthy activities of political parties encouraged. A political party should be a democratic organization that presents responsible demands and policies to crystallize the political opinion of the people. The state should exert its utmost efforts to protect and nurture political parties, so long as they engage in sound activities and do not contravene such objectives;

(8) Bold social reforms must be carried out to build a clean and honest society. In order that all citizens can lead a secure and happy life, crimes against life and property, such as hooliganism, robbery and theft, must be stamped out, and deep-seated irrationalities and improprieties that still linger in our society must be eradicated.

For the full text, see Manwoo Lee, *Odyssey of Korean Democracy*, 145–48.

35. Hyug-Baeg Im, "State, Labor and Capital," 12.

36. *Ibid.*

37. CISJD, *7–8 wŏl nodongja taejung t'ujaeng*, 47–51; Tong Ch'un Kim, *Han'guk sahoe nodongja yŏn'gu*, 104; Kŭm Su Kim, *Han'guk nodong undongŭi hyŏnhwanggwa kwaje*, 26; Ŏm, "Nodong undongŭi p'okpalchŏk koyanggwa minju nojo undongŭi kuch'uk," 165–67; No, "6 wŏl minju hangjaenggwa nodongja taet'ujaeng."

38. Ŏm, "Nodong undongŭi p'okpalchŏk koyanggwa minju nojo undongŭi kuch'uk," 48–49.

39. CISJD, *7–8 wŏl nodongja taejung t'ujaeng*, 43–69; Kŭm Su Kim, *Han'guk nodong undongŭi hyŏnhwanggwa kwaje*, 23–25.

40. For a summary of the June 29 Declaration, see note 34 above.

41. Dong, "Democratization of South Korea," 280.

42. Regarding the distinction between procedural democracy and substantive democracy, see Bobbio, *Democracy and Dictatorship*, 157–58; Choi, *Han'guk hyŏndae chŏngch'iŭi kujowa pyŏnhwa*, 255–70. Substantive democracy is similar to what O'Donnell and Schmitter call "socialization," which basically relates to "providing equal benefits to the population from the goods and services generated by society: wealth, income, education, health, housing, information, leisure time, even autonomy, prestige, respect, and self-development." O'-Donnell and Schmitter, *Transitions from Authoritarian Rule*, 12. It is also similar to "socioeconomic and cultural democratization," which O'Donnell distinguishes from "political democratization." O'Donnell, "Transitions, Continuities, and Paradoxes," 18. In a similar vein, Linz and Stepan mention "deepening of democracy," which encompasses gender equality and access to critical social services. Linz and Stepan, *Problems of Democratic Transition*, 457. Ho Ki Kim argues that the emergence of two different concepts and visions of democracy at the time was the result of the authoritarian regime's well-planned "two-people strategy" to fragment civil society. Ho Ki Kim, *Hyŏndae chabonjuŭiwa han'guk sahoe* 322–25.

43. Nam, *Korean Politics*, 313.

44. Hŭi Yŏn Cho, *Han'gugŭi kukka, minjujuŭi, chŏngch'i pyŏndong*, 281–85.

45. For a detailed analysis of why the opposition was defeated, see Yun, *1980 nyŏndae han'gugŭi minjuhwa ihaeng kwajŏng*, 176–97.

46. O'Donnell and Schmitter, *Transitions from Authoritarian Rule*, 19.

47. Hŭi Yŏn Cho, *Han'gugŭi kukka, minjujuŭi, chŏngch'i pyŏndong*, 165–81.

48. O'Donnell and Schmitter, *Transitions from Authoritarian Rule*, 56.

49. Hsiao and Koo, "Middle Classes and Democratization," 316.

50. Lipset, *Political Man*, 51.

51. Hsiao and Koo, "Middle Classes and Democratization," 316–17.

52. Moore, *Social Origins of Dictatorship*, 418.

53. Rueschemeyer, Stephens, and Stephens, *Capitalist Development*.

Chapter 6. Civil Society in Democratic Consolidation, 1988–

1. The discussion on the differences between the citizens' movement groups and the people's movement groups here is based on Chŏng, Kim and Yu, "Han'gugŭi simin sahoewa minjujuŭiŭi chŏnmang," 198–206; Lee, "Transitional Politics of Korea," 359.

2. Chŏng, Kim, and Yu, "Han'gugŭi simin sahoewa minjujuŭiŭi chŏnmang," 200 and n. 12; Uk In Paek, "Han'guk sahoe simin undong(non) pip'an," 58–83. Regarding the new social movements, see Offe, "New Social Movements"; Laraña, Johnston, and Gusfield, *New Social Movements*. For discussions on the new social movements in a Korean context, see Han and

Yang, *Sahoe undonggwa sahoe kaehyŏngnon.* Regarding social movements in general, see Tarrow, *Power in Movement;* Meyer and Tarrow, *Social Movement Society.*

3. Cha, "Politics and Democracy"; Heng Lee, "Uncertain Promise"; Lee and Sohn, "South Korea in 1994."

4. Song, "Munmin ch'unggyŏk, tae sasaege ppajin chaeya."

5. For an analysis of why people's movement groups regained unity and solidarity, see Sunhyuk Kim, "State and Civil Society in South Korea's Democratic Consolidation," 1140–44.

6. For example, in February 1999, a regional organization of the NADUK in north Chŏlla province officially left the NADUK and changed its name to "North Chŏlla Council of Civil Society Groups for Democracy," arguing that "people's movement should also adjust to the changing times." See *Han'gyŏre sinmun,* February 8, 1999.

7. "Han'guk sahoe, Hanch'ongnyŏn, kŭrigo haksaeng undong."

8. Song, "Hanch'ongnyŏn";; *Han'gyŏre sinmun,* April 9, 1995.

9. *Chungang ilbo,* June 14, 1997.

10. *Han'gyŏre sinmun,* January 21, 1998.

11. Diamond, "Toward Democratic Consolidation," 15.

12. Linz and Stepan, "Toward Consolidated Democracies," 15; Linz and Stepan, *Problems of Democratic Transition,* 5.

13. Diamond, "Is the Third Wave Over?" 33–34.

14. Regarding the issue of how to deal with the authoritarian past in Latin America and Eastern Europe, see Benomar, "Justice after Transitions"; Alfonsín, "'Never Again'"; Michnik and Havel, "Justice or Revenge?"

15. For details, see Cotton, "From Authoritarianism to Democracy," 256.

16. *Kwangju ilbo,* August 29, 1995; *Han'gyŏre sinmun,* August 30, 1995.

17. *Han'gyŏre sinmun,* October 25, 1995.

18. *Ibid.,* October 17, 1995.

19. *Chungang ilbo,* November 2, 1995.

20. *Han'gyŏre sinmun,* November 5, 1995.

21. *Chungang ilbo,* November 4, 1995.

22. *Han'gyŏre sinmun,* November 26, 1995.

23. Hŭi Yŏn Cho, *Han'gugŭi kukka, minjujuŭi, chŏngch'i pyŏndong,* 1138.

24. Hagopian, "Compromised Consolidation," 282; Choi, "'Pyŏnhyŏngjuŭi'wa han'gugŭi minjujuŭi," 187–99.

25. Regarding "birth defects" and the resultant delay in the consolidation of democracy in Brazil, see Hagopian, "Compromised Consolidation," 149.

26. For a good analysis of why Kim failed to institutionalize reforms, see Sang Hun Pak, "Minjujŏk konggohwaŭi silp'aewa kŭ kiwŏn."

27. CCFE, "Kongsŏnhyŏp chŏn'guk ponbu paltaesik"; CCFE, "97 nyŏn Seoul kongsŏnhyŏp hwaltongŭl chaegaehamyŏ.

28. *Han'gyŏre sinmun,* April 13, 2000.

29. *Chungang ilbo; Han'gyŏre sinmun,* April 16, 1999.

30. Regarding political reforms in the Kim Dae Jung government, see Sunhyuk Kim, "Politics of Reform in South Korea."

31. *Han'gyŏre sinmun,* December 11, 1995; *Ibid.,* March 31, 1999.

32. *Ibid.,* February 6, 1999; *Chungang ilbo,* February 6, 1999. Regarding the history and

applications of the National Security Law, see Wŏn Sun Pak, *Kukka poanbŏp yŏn'gu*, vols. 1 and 2.

33. *Han'gyŏre sinmun*, January 14, 1997.

34. For a general survey of environmental groups in Korea, see Eder, *Poisoned Prosperity*, 99–134.

35. Su-Hoon Lee, "Transitional Politics of Korea," 362–63.

36. *Ibid.*, 364.

37. CCEJ, "Urinŭn oe kyŏngje chŏngŭi silch'ŏn simin yŏnhabŭl palgihanŭn'ga?"

38. *Chungang ilbo*, January 2, 1998.

39. Su-Hoon Lee, "Transitional Politics of Korea," 364.

40. Hong Kyun Yi, "Simin undongŭi hyŏnjuso, kyŏngsillyŏn'gwa ch'amyŏ yŏndae."

41. *Han'gyŏre sinmun*, September 26, 1998.

42. *Chungang ilbo*, November 8, 1998.

43. *Han'gyŏre sinmun*, January 14, 1999; *Tonga ilbo*, January 18, 1999.

44. For a detailed analysis of the political origins of the current economic crisis in Korea, see Sunhyuk Kim, "Political Origins of the Korean Economic Crisis."

45. Eun Mee Kim, "Reforming the *chaebŏl*."

46. *Han'gyŏre 21*, September 15, 1994.

47. Hong Kyun Yi, "Simin undongŭi hyŏnjuso, kyŏngsillyŏn'gwa ch'amyŏ yŏndae," 90–91.

48. The Korean word "crisis" (*wigi*) consists of two Chinese characters, *wi* (crisis) and *gi* (opportunity).

49. Cho, *Han'gugŭi minjujuŭiwa sahoe undong*, 224–26.

50. Fukuyama, *End of History and the Last Man*.

51. *Han'gyŏre sinmun*, March 28, 1997.

52. *Chungang ilbo*, May 21, 1999.

53. Dryzek, "Political Institution and Dynamics of Democratization," 476.

54. *Ibid.*, 479–80.

55. *Ibid.*, 484–85.

56. Regarding the debate on the "soft-landing" and "hard-landing" of North Korea, see Harrison, "Promoting a Soft Landing in Korea"; Eberstadt, "Hastening Korean Reunification."

57. Tarrow, "Mass Mobilization and Regime Change."

Chapter 7. Conclusion: From Protest to Advocacy

1. Dryzek, "Political Institution and Dynamics of Democratization," 476.

2. Karl, "Dilemmas of Democratization," 8–12.

3. Rueschemeyer, Stephens, and Stephens, *Capitalist Development*, 6.

4. Many African experts also underline the distinctive nature of African civil societies, in contrast to Western cases. See Bayart, "Civil Society in Africa"; Lemarchand, "Uncivil States and Civil Societies"; Woods, "Civil Society in Europe and Africa."

5. Koo, "Strong State and Contentious Society," 246.

6. Rueschemeyer, Stephens, and Stephens, *Capitalist Development*, 46.

7. Koo, "Strong State and Contentious Society," 248–49.

8. Hagopian, "Compromised Consolidation," 164.

9. *Ibid.*, 151.

10. *Ibid.*, 165.

11. Schmitter, "Civil Society East and West," 247.

12. Diamond, *Democratic Revolution*, 7–15.

13. Byung-Kook Kim, "Korea's Crisis of Success." Jaung, "Elections and Political Parties."

14. Fish, "Russia's Fourth Transition."

15. Schmitter and Karl, "Conceptual Travels," 176.

16. For a comprehensive analysis of cultural aspects of Korean democratization, see Shin, *Mass Politics and Culture in Democratizing Korea.*

17. Chazan, "Africa's Democratic Challenge," 304.

18. Sunhyuk Kim, "Civil Society in South Korea." However, this is not to deny the value of oppositional social movement and to support exclusively interest group politics. The biggest problem with interest group politics is that it inevitably fails to reflect the lower classes' interests. As Schattschneider points out, "The flaw in the pluralist heaven is that the heavenly chorus sings with a strong upper-class accent." Schattschneider, *Semisovereign People*, 34–35.

Bibliography

Newspapers

Chungang ilbo (Chungang Daily).
Han'gyŏre sinmun (Han'gyŏre Daily).
Han'gyŏre 21 (Han'gyŏre Weekly).
Kwangju ilbo (Kwangju Daily).
Tonga ilbo (Tonga Daily).
Tonga yŏn'gam (Tonga Yearbook).

Public Documents, Statements, and Other Reports

CCEJ (Citizens' Coalition for Economic Justice). "Urinŭn oe kyŏngje chŏngŭi silch'ŏn simin yŏnhabŭl palgihanŭn'ga?" (Why do we launch the CCFE). Seoul: CCEJ, 1989.

CCEJ (Citizens' Coalition for Economic Justice)–*Chosŏn ilbo* (Chosŏn Daily). *Hwan'gyŏngŭl chik'inŭn han'gugŭi min'gan tanch'e* (Environmental Groups in Korea). Seoul: Chosŏn ilbosa, 1993.

CCFE (Citizens' Council for Fair Elections). "Kongsŏnhyŏp chŏn'guk ponbu paltaesik (Inaugural Ceremony of the CCFE)." Seoul: CCEJ, 1995.

———. "97 nyŏn Seoul kongsŏnhyŏp hwaltongŭl chaegaehamyŏ." (On resuming our activity for 1997). Seoul: CCFE, 1997.

EPB (Economic Planning Board). *Han'guk t'onggye yŏn'gam.* (Korea statistical yearbook). Seoul: EPB, Republic of Korea, 1969.

———. *Han'guk t'onggye yŏn'gam.* (Korea statistical yearbook). Seoul: EPB, Republic of Korea, 1973.

———. *Han'guk t'onggye wŏlbo.* (Monthly statistical report) Seoul: EPB, Republic of Korea, various dates.

FKTU (Federation of Korean Trade Unions). *Saŏp pogo.* (Business report). Seoul: FKTU, various dates.

IDD (Institute on Demography and Development). *Simin undong tanch'e hwalsŏnghwa pangane taehan yŏn'gu.* (A study on further development of citizens' movement groups). Seoul: IDD, Seoul National University, 1993.

KITA (Korea International Trade Association). *Han'guk kyŏngjeŭi chuyo chip'yo.* (Major statistics of Korean economy). Seoul: KITA, 1990.

KLI (Korea Labor Institute). *Pun'gibyŏl nodong tonghyang punsŏk.* (Labor trend analysis quarterly). Seoul: KLI, various dates.

NCCJDS (National Committee for Commemorating the 10th Anniversary of the June Democracy Struggle), ed. *6 wŏl hangjaeng 10 chunyŏn kinyŏm charyojip.* (Records of the June struggle). Seoul: Sagyejŏl, 1997.

NEC (National Election Commission). *Taehan min'guk sŏn'gŏsa.* (History of Korean elections). Seoul: NEC, 1964.

————. *Che 12 dae kukhoe ŭiwŏn sŏn'gŏ ch'ongnam.* (Overview of the 12th National Assembly elections). Seoul: NEC, 1985.

————. *Che 13 dae kukhoe ŭiwŏn sŏn'gŏ ch'ongnam.*(Overview of the 13th National Assembly elections). Seoul: NEC, 1988.

PSPD (People's Solidarity for Participatory Democracy). "PSPD: Solidarity and Hope for a Just Society." Seoul: PSPD, 1994.

"Han'guk sahoe, Hanch'ongnyŏn, kŭrigo haksaeng undong." (Korean society, the NCUSC, and student movement). *Mal* (Speech), May 1994.

"Pujŏng sŏn'gŏ wŏnhyung naemubu sagŏn p'an'gyŏlmun." (Verdict on the trial of the accused in connection with the rigged elections). In *4–19 hyŏngmyŏngnon.* (April 19 revolution) Vol. 2. Seoul: Irwŏl sŏgak, 1983.

Books and Articles

Ahn, Chung Si. "Economic Development and Democratization in Korea: An Examination on Economic Change and Empowerment of Civil Society." *Korea and World Affairs* 15 (1991): 740–54.

Alavi, Hamza. "The State in Post-colonial Societies: Pakistan and Bangladesh." *New Left Review* 74 (1972): 59–81.

Alfonsín, Raúl. "'Never Again' in Argentina." *Journal of Democracy* 4,1 (1993): 15–19.

Almond, Gabriel, and Sidney Verba. *The Civic Culture: Political Attitudes and Democracy in Five Nations.* Princeton: Princeton University Press, 1963.

Arato, Andrew. "Civil Society against the State: Poland 1980–81," *Telos* 47 (1981): 23–47.

Bayart, Jean-François. "Civil Society in Africa." In *Political Domination in Africa: Reflections on the Limits of Power,* ed. Patrick Chabal. New York: Cambridge University Press, 1986.

Bellin, Eva. "Civil Society: Effective Tool of Analysis for Middle East Politics?" *PS* 27,3 (1994): 509–10.

Benomar, Jamal. "Justice after Transitions." *Journal of Democracy* 4,1 (1993): 3–14.

Bernhard, Michael H. "Civil Society and Democratic Transition in East Central Europe." *Political Science Quarterly* 108,2 (1993): 307–26.

————. *The Origins of Democratization in Poland: Workers, Intellectuals, and Oppositional Politics, 1976–1980.* New York: Columbia University Press, 1993.

Bethell, Leslie. "From the Second World War to the Cold War: 1944–1954," In *Exporting Democracy: The United States and Latin America,* ed. Abraham F. Lowenthal. Baltimore: Johns Hopkins University Press, 1991.

Billet, Bret L. "The History and Role of Student Activism in the Republic of Korea: The Politics of Contestation and Conflict Resolution in Fledgling Democracy." *Asian Profile* 20,1 (1992): 23–34.

Bobbio, Norberto. *Democracy and Dictatorship.* Minneapolis: University of Minnesota Press, 1989.

Bratton, Michael. "Beyond the State: Civil Society and Associational Life in Africa." *World Politics* 41, 3 (1989): 407–30.

Bratton, Michael, and Nicholas Van de Walle. *Democratic Experiments in Africa.* New York: Cambridge University Press, 1997.

Bunce, Valerie. "Should Transitologists Be Grounded." *Slavic Review* 54, 1 (1995): 111–27.

————. "Paper Curtains and Paper Tigers." *Slavic Review* 54,4 (1995): 979–87.

Casper, Gretchen, and Michelle M. Taylor. *Negotiating Democracy: Transitions from Authoritarian Rule.* Pittsburgh: University of Pittsburgh Press, 1996.

Cha, Victor D. "Politics and Democracy under the Kim Young Sam Government: Something Old, Something New." *Asian Survey* 33,9 (1993): 849–63.

Ch'ae, Man Su, and Chang Han Kim. "T'ongil chŏnsŏn undongŭi chŏn'gae." (Development of unified front movements). In *Han'guk sahoe undongsa* (History of social movement in Korea), ed. Hŭi Yŏn Cho. Seoul: Chuksan, 1990.

Chamberlain, Heath B. "On the Search for Civil Society in China." *Modern China* 19,2 (1993): 199–215.

Chang, Tal Chung. "Chesam konghwagukkwa kwŏnwijuŭijŏk kŭndaehwa." (The third republic and authoritarian modernization). In *Hyŏndae han'guk chŏngch'iron* (Contemporary Korean politics), ed. Korean Political Science Association. Seoul: Pŏmmunsa, 1987.

Chazan, Naomi. "Africa's Democratic Challenge: Strengthening Civil Society and the State." *World Policy Journal* 9,2 (1992): 279–307.

Cheng, Tun-jen, and Eun Mee Kim. "Making Democracy: Generalizing the South Korean Case." In *The Politics of Democratization: Generalizing East Asian Experiences*, ed. Edward Friedman. Boulder, Colo.: Westview Press, 1994.

Cho, Hein. "The Historical Origin of Civil Society in Korea." *Korea Journal* 37,2 (1997): 24–41.

Cho, Hŭi Yŏn. "50, 60, 70 nyŏndae minjok minju undongŭi chŏn'gae kwajŏnge kwanhan yŏn'gu." (A study on the development of nationalist and democratic movement during the 1950s, 1960s, and 1970s)." In *Han'guk sahoe undongsa*. (History of social movement in Korea), ed. Hŭi Yŏn Cho. Seoul: Chuksan, 1990.

———. *Han'gugŭi minjujuŭiwa sahoe undong*. (Democracy and social movement in Korea). Seoul: Tangdae, 1998.

———. *Han'gugŭi kukka, minjujuŭi, chŏngch'i pyŏndong*. (The state, democracy, and political transformation in Korea). Seoul: Tangdae, 1998.

Ch'oe, Yŏn Ku. "80 nyŏndae ch'ŏngnyŏn undongŭi sŏnggyŏkkwa kŭ chŏn'gae." (The nature and evolution of youth movement in the 1980s). In *Han'guk sahoe undongsa*. (History of social movement in Korea), ed. Hŭi Yŏn Cho. Seoul: Chuksan, 1990.

Choi, Jang Jip. *Han'guk hyŏndae chŏngch'iŭi kujowa pyŏnhwa*. (Contemporary Korean politics: structure and change). Seoul: Kkach'i, 1989.

———. *Han'guk minjujuŭiŭi iron*. (Theory of Korean democracy). Seoul: Han'gilsa, 1993.

———. "Han'gugŭi minjuhwa: ihaenggwa kaehyŏk. (Korean democratization: transition and reform). In *Siminsahoeŭi tojŏn: han'guk minjuhwawa kukka, chabon, nodong*. (Challenge from civil society: state, capital, and labor in Korean Democratization), ed. Jang Jip Choi and Hyŏn Chin Im. Seoul: Nanam, 1993.

———. "Political Cleavages in Korea." In *State and Society in Contemporary Korea*, ed. Hagen Koo. Ithaca, N.Y.: Cornell University Press, 1993.

———. "'Pyŏnhyŏngjuŭi'wa han'gugŭi minjujuŭi." ('Transformism' and Korean democracy). *Sahoe pip'yŏng* (social review) 13 (1995): 183–221.

Chŏng, Hae Ku, ed. *Kwangju minju hangjaeng yŏn'gu*. (A study on the Kwangju popular uprising). Seoul: Sagyejŏl, 1990.

Chŏng, Ki Yŏng. "4 wŏl hyŏngmyŏngŭi chudo seryŏk." (Who led the April revolution?). In *Han'guk sahoe pyŏnhyŏk undonggwa 4 wŏl hyŏngmyŏng*. (Revolutionary movement in Korea and the April revolution).Vol. 1. Ed. Institute for the Study of the April Revolution. Seoul: Han'gilsa, 1990.

Chŏng, Tae Hwa. "Han'guk minjuhwawa chibae seryŏgŭi kyoch'e." (Korean democratization and changes in the ruling bloc). *Tonghyanggwa chŏnmang.* (Trends and prospects) 36 (1997): 174–98.

Chŏng, T'ae Sŏk, Ho Ki Kim, and P'al Mu Yu. "Han'gugŭi simin sahoewa minjujuŭiŭi chŏnmang." (Civil society and prospects for democracy in Korea)." In *Han'guk minjujuŭiŭi hyŏnjaejŏk kwaje: chedo, kaehyŏk mit sahoe undong.* (Current tasks for Korean democracy: institutions, reforms, and social movements), ed. Korea Council of Academic Groups. Seoul: Changjakkwa pip'yŏngsa, 1993.

CISJD (Christian Institute for the Study of Justice and Development). *Kaehŏn'gwa minjuhwa undong.* (Constitutional revision and democracy movement). Seoul: Minjungsa, 1986.

―――. *6 wŏl minjuhwa taet'ujaeng.* (Grand democracy struggle in June 1987). Seoul: Minjungsa, 1987.

―――. *7–8 wŏl nodongja taejung t'ujaeng.* (Labor struggle in July–August 1987). Seoul: Minjungsa, 1987.

Clark, Donald N. *The Kwangju Uprising.* Boulder, Colo.: Westview Press, 1988.

Collier, Ruth Berins, and David Collier. *Shaping the Political Arena: Critical Junctures, the Labor Movement, and Regime Dynamics in Latin America.* Princeton: Princeton University Press, 1991.

Cotton, James. "From Authoritarianism to Democracy in Korea." *Political Studies* 37,2 (1989): 244–59.

―――. "The Limits to Liberalization in Industrializing Asia: Three Views of the State." *Pacific Affairs* 64,3 (1991): 311–27.

Cumings, Bruce. "American Policy and Korean Liberation." In *Without Parallel,* ed. Frank Baldwin. New York: Pantheon, 1974.

―――. *The Origins of the Korean War: Liberation and the Emergence of Separate Regimes, 1945–1947,* Vol. 1. Princeton: Princeton University Press, 1981.

―――. "The Legacy of Japanese Colonialism in Korea." In *The Japanese Colonial Empire, 1895–1945,* ed. Ramon H. Myers and Mark R. Peattie. Princeton: Princeton University Press, 1984.

―――. "The Abortive Abertura: South Korea in the Light of Latin American Experience." *New Left Review* 173 (1989): 5–32.

―――. *The Origins of the Korean War: The Roaring of the Cataract, 1947–1950.* Vol. 2. Princeton: Princeton University Press, 1990.

―――. "The Corporate State in North Korea." In *State and Society in Contemporary Korea,* ed. Hagen Koo. Ithaca, N.Y.: Cornell University Press, 1993.

―――. "Civil Society and Democracy in Comparative Perspective." In *Civil Society in South Korea,* ed. Charles Armstrong. New York: Routledge, forthcoming.

Dahl, Robert A. *Polyarchy: Participation and Opposition.* New Haven: Yale University Press, 1971.

De Bary, Wm. Theodore. *Asian Values and Human Rights: A Confucian Communitarian Perspective.* Cambridge, Mass.: Harvard University Press, 1998.

Diamond, Larry. "Economic Development and Democracy Reconsidered." *American Behavioral Scientist* 35 (1992): 450–99.

―――, ed. *The Democratic Revolution: Struggles for Freedom and Pluralism in the Developing World.* New York: Freedom House, 1992.

―――. "Civil Society and the Development of Democracy: Some International Perspectives and Lessons." Unpublished manuscript. 1993.

―――. "The Globalization of Democracy." In *Global Transformation and the Third World* ed. Robert Slater, Barry Schultz, and Steven Doerr. Boulder, Colo.: Lynne Rienner Publishers, 1993.

————. "Toward Democratic Consolidation." *Journal of Democracy* 5,3 (1994): 4–17.

————. "Is the Third Wave Over?" *Journal of Democracy* 7,3 (1996): 20–37.

————. *Developing Democracy: Toward Consolidation.* Baltimore: Johns Hopkins University Press, 1999.

Diamond, Larry, and Marc F. Plattner, eds. *The Global Resurgence of Democracy.* Baltimore: Johns Hopkins University Press, 1993.

Diamond, Larry, Juan J. Linz, and Seymour M. Lipset, eds. *Democracy in Developing Countries: Comparing Experiences with Democracy* (2nd ed.). Boulder, Colo.: Lynne Rienner Publishers, 1995.

Doner, Richard D. "Limits of State Strength: Toward an Institutionalist View of Economic Development." *World Politics* 44,3 (1992): 398–431.

Dong, Wonmo. "The Democratization of Korea: What Role Does the Middle Class Play?" *Korea Observer* 22,2 (1991): 257–82.

Doyle, Michael W. "Kant, Liberal Legacies, and Foreign Affairs." *Philosophy and Public Affairs* 12,3 (1983): 205–35.

Dryzek, John S. "Political Institution and the Dynamics of Democratization." *American Political Science Review* 90,3 (1996): 475–87.

Eberstadt, Nicholas. "Hastening Korean Reunification." *Foreign Affairs* 76,2 (1997): 77–92.

Eckert, Carter J., Ki-baik Lee, Young Ick Lew, Michael Robinson, and Edward W. Wagner. *Korea, Old and New: A History.* Cambridge, Mass.: Harvard University Press, 1990.

Eder, Norman R. *Poisoned Prosperity: Development, Modernization, and the Environment in South Korea.* Armonk, N.Y.: M. E. Sharpe, 1996.

Ekiert, Grzegorz. *The State against Society: Political Crises and Their Aftermath in East Central Europe.* Princeton: Princeton University Press, 1996.

Fatton, Robert, Jr. "Democracy and Civil Society in Africa." *Mediterranean Quarterly* 2,4 (1991): 83–95.

Fine, Robert, and Shirin Rai, eds. *Civil Society: Democratic Perspectives* (*Democratization* 4,1). London: Frank Cass, 1997.

Finer, Samuel E. *Comparative Government.* New York: Basic Books, 1971.

Fish, M. Steven. "Russia's Fourth Transition." *Journal of Democracy* 5,3 (1994): 31–42.

————. *Democracy from Scratch: Opposition and Regime in the New Russian Revolution.* Princeton: Princeton University Press, 1996.

Frentzel-Zagorska, Zanina. "Civil Society in Poland and Hungary." *Soviet Studies* 42,4 (1990): 759–77.

Fukuyama, Francis. *The End of History and the Last Man.* New York: Free Press, 1992.

Gold, Thomas B. "The Resurgence of Civil Society in China." *Journal of Democracy* 1,1 (1990): 18–31.

Gunther, Richard, P. Nikiforos Diamandouros, and Hans-Jürgen Puhle, eds. *The Politics of Democratic Consolidation: Southern Europe in Comparative Perspective.* Baltimore: Johns Hopkins University Press, 1995.

Gyimah-Boadi, E. "Associational Life, Civil Society, and Democratization in Ghana." In *Civil Society and the State in Africa,* ed. John Harbeson, Donald Rothchild, and Naomi Chazan. Boulder, Colo.: Lynne Rienner Publishers, 1994.

Haggard, Stephan, and Robert R. Kaufman. *The Political Economy of Democratic Transitions.* Princeton: Princeton University Press, 1995.

Haggard, Stephan, and Chung-in Moon. "The State, Politics, and Economic Development in Postwar South Korea." In *State and Society in Contemporary Korea*, ed. Hagen Koo. Ithaca, N.Y.: Cornell University Press, 1993.

Hagopian, Frances. "The Compromised Consolidation: The Political Class in the Brazilian Transition." In *Issues in Democratic Consolidation: the New South American Democracies in Comparative Perspective*, ed. Scott Mainwaring, Guillermo O'Donnell and J. Samuel Valenzuela. Notre Dame, Ind.: University of Notre Dame Press, 1992.

Han, Sang Chin, and Chong Hoe Yang, eds. *Sahoe undonggwa sahoe kaehyŏngnon.* (Social movement and social reform). Seoul: Chŏnyewŏn, 1992.

Han, Sung-joo. *The Failure of Democracy in Korea.* Berkeley, Calif.: University of California Press, 1974.

———. "Chei konghwaguk." (The second republic). In *Hyŏndae han'guk chŏngch'iron.* (Contemporary Korean politics), ed. Korean Political Science Association. Seoul: Pŏmmunsa, 1987.

Harrison, Selig S. "Dateline from Korea: A Divided Seoul." *Foreign Policy* 67 (1987): 154–75.

———. "Promoting a Soft Landing in Korea." *Foreign Policy* 106 (1997): 57–75.

He, Baogang. "Dual Roles of Semi-Civil Society in Chinese Democratization." *Australian Journal of Political Science* 29 (1994): 154–71.

———. *The Democratic Implications of Civil Society in China.* New York: St. Martin's Press, 1997.

Higley, John, and Richard Gunther. *Elites and Democratic Consolidation in Latin America and Southern Europe.* New York: Cambridge University Press, 1992.

Hong, Sŭng T'ae. "Kwangju minjung hangjaengŭi chwajŏlgwa chinbojŏk nodong undongŭi mosaek." (Frustration of the Kwangju popular uprising and the search for a progressive labor movement)." In *1970 nyŏndae ihu han'guk nodong undongsa.* (History of labor movement in Korea since the 1970s) ed. Korean Alliance of Democratic Workers. Seoul: Tongnyŏk, 1994.

Hsiao, Hsin-Huang Michael, and Hagen Koo. "The Middle Classes and Democratization." In *Consolidating the Third Wave Democracies: Themes and Perspectives*, ed. Larry Diamond, Marc F. Plattner, Yun-han Chu, and Hung-mao Tien. Baltimore: Johns Hopkins University Press, 1997.

Huntington, Samuel P. *The Third Wave: Democratization in the Late Twentieth Century.* Norman, Ok.: University of Oklahoma Press, 1991.

Im, Hyug-Baeg. "State, Labor and Capital in the Consolidation of Democracy: A Search for Post-Authoritarian Industrial Relations in Korea." *Korean Social Science Journal* 18 (1992): 7–25.

———. *Sijang, kukka, minjujuŭi: han'guk minjuhwawa chŏngch'i kyŏngje iron.* (The market, the state, and democracy: democratic transition in Korea and theories of political economy). Seoul: Nanam, 1994.

Im, Yŏng T'ae, ed. *Singminji sidae han'guk sahoewa undong.* (Society and movement in colonial Korea). Seoul: Sagyejŏl, 1985.

Ishida, Takeshi, and Ellis S. Krauss, eds. *Democracy in Japan.* Pittsburgh: University of Pittsburgh Press, 1989.

Jaung, Hoon. "Elections and Political Parties." In *Institutional Reform and Democratic Consolidation in Korea*, ed. Larry Diamond and Doh Chull Shin. Stanford, Calif.: Hoover Institution Press, 2000.

Jones, David M. "Democratization, Civil Society, and Illiberal Middle Class Culture in Pacific Asia." *Comparative Politics* 30,2 (1998): 147–70.

Karl, Terry. "Dilemmas of Democratization in Latin America." *Comparative Politics* 23,1 (1990): 1–21.

Karl, Terry, and Philippe Schmitter. "Democratization around the Globe: Its Opportunities and Risks." In *World Security: Trends and Challenges at Century's End*, ed. Michael T. Klare and Dan Thomas. New York: St. Martin's Press, 1993.

—. "From an Iron Curtain to a Paper Curtain: Grounding Transitologists or Students of Postcommunism?" *Slavic Review* 54,4 (1995): 965–78.

Keane, John. *Democracy and Civil Society*. New York: Verso, 1988.

—. "Despotism and Democracy: The Origins and Development of the Distinction between Civil Society and the State 1750–1850." In *Civil Society and the State: New European Perspectives*, ed. John Keane. New York: Verso, 1988.

Kim, Byung-Kook. "Korea's Crisis of Success." In *Democracy in East Asia*, ed. Larry Diamond and Marc F. Plattner. Baltimore: Johns Hopkins University Press, 1998.

Kim, Dae Jung. "Is Culture Destiny?" *Foreign Affairs* 73,6 (1994): 189–94.

Kim, Eun Mee. *Big Business, Strong State: Collusion and Conflict in South Korean Development, 1960–1990*. Albany, N.Y.: State University of New York Press, 1997.

—. "Reforming the *chaebŏl*." In *Institutional Reform and Democratic Consolidation in Korea*, ed. Larry Diamond and Doh Chull Shin. Stanford, Calif.: Hoover Institution Press, 2000.

Kim, Ho Chin. *Han'guk chŏngch'i ch'ejeron*. (The Korean political system). Seoul: Pagyŏngsa, 1990.

Kim, Ho Ki. *Hyŏndae chabonjuŭiwa han'guk sahoe*. (Contemporary capitalism and Korean society). Seoul: Nanam, 1995.

Kim, Kŭm Su. *Han'guk nodong undongŭi hyŏnhwanggwa kwaje*. (Current status and future tasks of Korean labor movement). Seoul: Tŏksan, 1995.

Kim, Kwan-Bong. *The Korea-Japan Crisis and the Instability of the Korean Political System*. New York: Praeger, 1971.

Kim, Kwang Sik. "8–15 chikhu han'guk sahoewa migunjŏngŭi sŏnggyŏk." (Korean society immediately after the liberation and the nature of the USAMGIK). *Yŏksa pip'yŏng* (Historical review) 1 (1987): 49–72.

—. "4 wŏl hyŏngmyŏnggwa hyŏksin seryŏgŭi tŭngjanggwa hwaltong." (The April revolution and the emergence and activism of progressive forces). In *Han'guk sahoe pyŏnhyŏk undonggwa 4 wŏl hyŏngmyŏng*. (Revolutionary movement in Korea and the April revolution). Vol. 2. Ed. Institute for the Study of the April Revolution. Seoul: Han'gilsa, 1990.

Kim, Kyŏng Tae. "4 wŏl hyŏngmyŏngŭi chŏn'gae kwajŏng." (Development of the April revolution). In *Han'guk sahoe pyŏnhyŏk undonggwa 4 wŏl hyŏngmyŏng*. (Revolutionary movement in Korea and the April revolution). Vol. 2. Ed. Institute for the Study of the April Revolution. Seoul: Han'gilsa, 1990.

Kim, Nak Chung. *Han'guk nodong undongsa*. (History of labor movement in Korea). Seoul: Ch'ŏngsa, 1982.

—. "4 wŏl hyŏngmyŏnggwa minjok t'ongil undong." (The April revolution and movement for reunification). In *Han'guk sahoe pyŏndonggwa 4 wŏl hyŏngmyŏng*. (Revolutionary movement in Korea and the April revolution). Vol. 1. Ed. Institute for the Study of the April Revolution. Seoul: Han'gilsa, 1990.

Kim, Se Chung. "10 wŏl yusin'gwa minju hoebok undong." (October revitalization and the movement for the recovery of democracy). In *Han'guk hyŏndae chŏngch'isa.* (Contemporary Korean political history), ed. Korean Political Science Association. Seoul, Korea: Pŏmmunsa, 1996.

Kim, Sŏk Chun. *Han'guk sanŏphwa kukkaron.* (The state and Korean industrialization). Seoul: Nanam, 1992.

Kim, Sunhyuk. "Civil Society in South Korea: From Grand Democracy Movements to Petty Interest Groups?" *Journal of Northeast Asian Studies* 15,2 (1996): 81–97.

———. "State and Civil Society in South Korea's Democratic Consolidation: Is the Battle Really Over?" *Asian Survey* 37,12 (1997): 1135–144.

———. "Civil Society and Democratization in South Korea." *Korea Journal* 38,2 (1998): 214–36.

———. "Civic Mobilization for Democratic Reform." In *Institutional Reform and Democratic Consolidation in Korea,* ed. Larry Diamond and Doh Chull Shin. Stanford, Calif.: Hoover Institution Press, 2000.

———. "The Politics of Reform in South Korea: The First Year of the Kim Dae Jung Government, 1998–1999," *Asian Perspective* 24,1 (2000): 163–185.

———. "The Political Origins of the Korean Economic Crisis: Is Democratization to Blame?" *Democratization* (forthcoming).

Kim, Tong Ch'un. *Han'guk sahoe nodongja yŏn'gu: 1987 nyŏn ihurŭl chungsimŭro.* (A study on Korean workers: since 1987). Seoul: Yŏksa pip'yŏngsa, 1995.

Kim, Wang Sik. "Migunjŏng kyŏngch'arŭi chŏngch'ijŏk wisang." (The political status of the police under the USAMGIK). In *Han'guk hyŏndae chŏngch'isa* (Contemporary Korean political history), ed. Korean Political Science Association. Seoul: Pŏmmunsa, 1996.

Kim, Yong Pok. "Han'guk chabonjuŭiwa kukka, kwallyo." (Korean capitalism, state, and bureaucracy). *Yŏksa pip'yŏng* (Historical review) 43 (1998): 125–39.

Kim, Yŏng Myŏng. *Han'guk hyŏndae chŏngch'isa: chŏngch'i pyŏndongŭi yŏkhak.* (Contemporary history of Korean politics: dynamics of political change). Seoul: Ŭryu munhwasa, 1994.

Kim, Yŏng Rae. *Han'guk iik chiptan'gwa minju chŏngch'i palchŏn.* (Interest groups and Korean democratization). Seoul: Taewangsa, 1990.

KNCC (Korean National Christian Church Council). *1970 nyŏndae nodong hyŏnjanggwa chŭngŏn.* (Labor situation in the 1970s). Seoul: P'ulbit, 1984.

Ko, Sŏng Kuk. "4 wŏl hyŏngmyŏngŭi inyŏm." (Ideological basis of the April revolution). In *Han'guk sahoe pyŏndonggwa 4 wŏl hyŏngmyŏng.* (Revolutionary movement in Korea and the April revolution). Vol. 1. Ed. Institute for the Study of the April Revolution. Seoul: Han'gilsa, 1990.

Kong, Che Uk. "1950 nyŏndae han'guk sahoeŭi kyegŭp kusŏng." (Class structure in Korea during the 1950s). *Kyŏngjewa sahoe* (Economy and society) 3 (1989): 227–63.

Koo, Hagen. "Strong State and Contentious Society." In *State and Society in Contemporary Korea,* ed. Hagen Koo. Ithaca, N.Y.: Cornell University Press, 1993.

———. "The State, *Minjung,* and the Working Class in South Korea." In *State and Society in Contemporary Korea,* ed. Hagen Koo. Ithaca, N.Y.: Cornell University Press, 1993.

Krasner, Stephen D. "Approaches to the State: Alternative Conceptions and Historical Dynamics." *Comparative Politics* 16,2 (1984): 223–46.

Krizan, Mojmir. "'Civil Society'—A New Paradigm in the Yugoslav Theoretical Discussion." *Praxis International* 9,1–2 (1989): 152–63.

Kwŏn, Hŭi Kyŏng. *Han'guk hyŏksin chŏngdanggwa sahoejuŭi international*. (Progressive parties in Korea and the Socialist International). Seoul: T'aeyang, 1989.

Lapidus, Gail W. "State and Society: Toward the Emergence of Civil Society in the Soviet Union." In *Politics, Society, and Nationality inside Gorbachev's Russia*, ed. Seweryn Bialer. Boulder, Colo.: Westview Press, 1989.

Laraña, Enrique, Hank Johnston, and Joseph R. Gusfield, eds. *New Social Movements: From Ideology to Identity*. Philadelphia: Temple University Press, 1994.

Lee, Chong-sik and Hyuk-Sang Sohn. "South Korea in 1994," *Asian Survey* 35,1 (1995): 28–36.

Lee, Heng. "Uncertain Promise: Democratic Consolidation in Korea." In *The Politics of Democratization: Generalizing East Asian Experiences*, ed. Edward Friedman. Boulder, Colo.: Westview Press, 1994.

Lee, Manwoo. *The Odyssey of Korean Democracy: Korean Politics, 1987–1990*, New York: Praeger, 1990.

Lee, Su-Hoon. "Transitional Politics of Korea, 1987–1992: Activation of Civil Society." *Pacific Affairs* 66,3 (1993): 351–67.

Lemarchand, René. "Uncivil States and Civil Societies: How Illusion Became Reality." *Journal of Modern African Studies* 30,2 (1992): 177–91.

Lewis, Peter M. "Political Transition and the Dilemma of Civil Society in Africa." *Journal of International Affairs* 46,1 (1992): 31–54.

Linz, Juan J. *The Breakdown of Democratic Regimes: Crisis, Breakdown, and Reequilibration*. Baltimore: Johns Hopkins University Press, 1978.

Linz, Juan J., and Alfred Stepan. *Problems of Democratic Transition and Consolidation: Southern Europe, South America, and Post-Communist Europe*. Baltimore: Johns Hopkins University Press, 1996.

———. "Toward Consolidated Democracies." *Journal of Democracy* 7,2 (1996): 14–33.

Lipset, Seymour Martin. *Political Man*. Garden City, N.Y.: Doubleday, 1960.

Lowenthal, Abraham F., ed. *Exporting Democracy: The United States and Latin America*. Baltimore: Johns Hopkins University Press, 1991.

Mainwaring, Scott. *Transitions to Democracy and Democratic Consolidation: Theoretical and Comparative Issues*. Working Paper #130, Notre Dame, Ind.: The Helen Kellog Institute for International Studies, University of Notre Dame. 1989.

Mainwaring, Scott, Guillermo O'Donnell, and J. Samuel Valenzuela, eds. *Issues in Democratic Consolidation: The New South American Democracies in Comparative Perspective*. Notre Dame, Ind.: University of Notre Dame Press, 1992.

Mangwŏn Study Group on Korean History. *Han'guk kŭndae minjung undongsa*. (History of people's movement in modern Korea). Seoul: Tolpegae, 1989.

Maoz, Zeev and Bruce Russett. "Normative and Structural Causes of Democratic Peace, 1946–1986," *American Political Science Review* 87,3 (1993): 624–38.

Meyer, David S. and Sidney Tarrow, eds. *The Social Movement Society: Contentious Politics for a New Century*. New York: Rowman & Littlefield, 1998.

Michnik, Adam, and Václav Havel. "Justice or Revenge?" *Journal of Democracy* 4,1 (1993): 20–27.

Moore, Barrington, Jr. *Social Origins of Dictatorship and Democracy: Lord and Peasant in the Making of the Modern World*. Boston: Beacon, 1966.

Mun, Pyŏng Chu. "Han'gugŭi minjujuŭiroŭi ihaengrone taehan kŏmt'o." (Review of theories of democratic transition in Korea). *Tonghyanggwa chŏnmang*. (Trends and prospects) 33 (1997): 277–94.

Munck, Gerardo L. "Democratic Transitions in Comparative Perspective." *Comparative Politics* 26,3 (1994): 355–75.

Nakamura, Masanori. "Democratization, Peace, and Economic Development in Occupied Japan, 1945–1952," In *The Politics of Democratization: Generalizing East Asian Experiences*, ed. Edward Friedman. Boulder, Colo.: Westview Press, 1994.

Nam, Koon Woo. *Korean Politics: The Search for Political Consensus and Stability*. Lanham, Md.: University Press of America, 1989.

Ngo, Tak-wing. "Civil Society and Political Liberalization in Taiwan." *Bulletin of Concerned Asian Scholars* 25,1 (1993): 3–15.

No, Chung Ki. "6 wŏl minju hangjaenggwa nodongja taet'ujaeng." (The June democracy uprising and the great labor struggle). In *6 wŏl minju hangjaenggwa han'guk sahoe 10 nyŏn*. (Korean society ten years after the June democracy struggle), ed. Korea Council of Academic Groups. Seoul: Tangdae, 1997.

Oberdorfer, Don. "U.S. Policy toward Korea in the 1987 Crisis Compared with Other Allies." In *Korea–U.S. Relations: The Politics of Trade and Security*, ed. Robert A. Scalapino and Hongkoo Lee. Berkeley, Calif.: University of California Press, 1988.

O'Donnell, Guillermo. "Transitions, Continuities, and Paradoxes." In *Issues in Democratic Consolidation: the New South American Democracies in Comparative Perspective*, ed. Scott Mainwaring, Guillermo O'Donnell, and J. Samuel Valenzuela. Notre Dame, Ind.: University of Notre Dame Press, 1992.

O'Donnell, Guillermo, and Philippe Schmitter. *Transitions from Authoritarian Rule: Tentative Conclusions about Uncertain Democracies*. Baltimore: Johns Hopkins University Press, 1986.

O'Donnell, Guillermo, Philippe Schmitter, and Laurence Whitehead, eds. *Transitions from Authoritarian Rule: Prospects for Democracy*. Baltimore: Johns Hopkins University Press, 1986.

Offe, Claus. "New Social Movements: Challenging the Boundaries of Institutional Politics." *Social Research* 52,4 (1985): 820–32.

Ŏm, Chu Ung. "Nodong undongŭi p'okpalchŏk koyanggwa minju nojo undongŭi kuch'uk." (Explosive escalation of labor movement and establishment of the movement for democratic trade unions). In *1970 nyŏndae ihu han'guk nodong undongsa*. (History of labor movement in Korea since the 1970s), ed. Korean Alliance of Democratic Workers. Seoul: Tongnyŏk, 1994.

Owen, John M. *Liberal Peace, Liberal War: American Politics and International Security*. Ithaca, N.Y.: Cornell University Press, 1997.

Paek, Chong Kuk. "Han'gugŭi kukka, simin sahoe, kŭrigo chibae yŏnhabŭi pyŏndong." (State, civil society and changes in the ruling coalition in Korea). In *Han'guk chŏngch'i sahoeŭi sae hŭrŭm*. (New currents in Korean politics and society), ed. Institute for Far Eastern Studies. Seoul: Nanam, 1994.

Paek, Uk In. "Han'guk sahoe simin undong(non) pip'an." (A critical review of civil society (theory) in Korea). *Kyŏngjewa sahoe* (Economy and society) 12 (1991): 58–83.

Pak, Hyŏn Ch'ae. "79 nyŏn Puma sat'aeŭi yŏksajŏk paegyŏnggwa yŏksajŏk ŭiŭi." (The historical background and significance of the Pusan-Masan incident in 1979). In *Han'guk minjok minjung undong yŏn'gu*. (A study on nationalist and popular movement in Korea), ed. Nak Ch'ŏng Paek and Ch'ang Yŏl Chŏng. Seoul: Ture, 1989.

Pak, Sang Hun. "Minjujŏk konggohwaŭi silp'aewa kŭ kiwŏn." (Failure of democratic consolidation and its origins). *Tonghyanggwa chŏnmang*. (Trends and prospects) 34 (1997): 8–27.

Pak, T'ae Kyun. "Han'guk minjujuŭiŭi chudo seryŏk" (Leading forces of Korean democratization). In *Han'guk minjujuŭiŭi hyŏnjaejŏk kwaje: chedo, kaehyŏk mit sahoe undong.* (Current tasks for Korean democracy: institutions, reforms, and social movements), ed. Korea Council of Academic Groups. Seoul: Changjakkwa pip'yŏngsa, 1993.

Pak, Wŏn Sun. *Kukka poanbŏp yŏn'gu.* (A study on the National Security Law) Vol. 1: History of the National Security Law. Seoul: Yŏksa pip'yŏngsa, 1990.

———. *Kukka poanbŏp yŏn'gu.* (A study on the National Security Law). Vol. 2.: History of Applications of the National Security Law. Seoul: Yŏksa pip'yŏngsa, 1992.

Palais, James. *Politics and Policy in Traditional Korea.* Cambridge, Mass.: Harvard University Press, 1975.

Pelczynski, Z. A. "Solidarity and the Rebirth of Civil Society." In *Civil Society and the State: New European Perspective,* ed. John Keane. London: Verso, 1988.

Przeworski, Adam. *Democracy and the Market: Political and Economic Reforms in Eastern Europe and Latin America.* New York: Cambridge University Press, 1991.

Putnam, Robert D. *Making Democracy Work: Civic Traditions in Modern Italy.* Princeton, N.J.: Princeton University Press, 1993.

RGKP (Research Group on Korean Politics). *Han'guk chŏngch'isa.* (Korean political history). Seoul: Paeksan sŏdang, 1994.

Rowe, William T. "The Problem of 'Civil Society' in Late Imperial China." *Modern China* 19,2 (1993): 139–57.

Rueschemeyer, Dietrich, Evelyne Huber Stephens, and John D. Stephens. *Capitalist Development and Democracy.* Chicago: University of Chicago Press, 1992.

Russett, Bruce. *Grasping the Democratic Peace: Principles for a Post Cold War World.* Princeton: Princeton University Press, 1995.

Ryu, Sang Yŏng. "Han'gugŭi uik chiptan yŏn'gu." (A study on rightist groups in Korea). *Sahoewa sasang* (Society and thought) 14 (1989): 238–67.

Schattschneider, Elmer Eric. *The Semisovereign People: A Realist's View of Democracy in America.* Hinsdale, Ill.: Dryden, 1975.

Schmitter, Philippe C. "Still the Century of Corporatism?" *Review of Politics* 36,1 (1974): 85–131.

———. "Civil Society East and West." In *Consolidating the Third Wave Democracies: Themes and Perspectives,* ed. Larry Diamond, Marc F. Plattner, Yun-han Chu, and Hung-mao Tien. Baltimore: Johns Hopkins University Press, 1997.

Schmitter, Philippe C., and Terry Lynn Karl. "What Democracy Is . . . and Is Not." In *The Global Resurgence of Democracy,* ed. Larry Diamond and Marc F. Plattner. Baltimore: Johns Hopkins University Press, 1993.

———. "The Conceptual Travels of Transitologists and Consolidologists: How Far to the East Should They Attempt to Go?" *Slavic Review* 53,1 (1994): 173–85.

Schumpeter, Joseph A. *Capitalism, Socialism and Democracy.* 5th ed. New York: George Allen & Unwin, 1976.

Schwedler, Jillian. *Toward Civil Society in the Middle East?* Boulder, Colo.: Lynne Rienner Publishers, 1995.

Shils, Edward. "The Virtue of Civil Society." *Government and Opposition* 26,1 (1991): 3–20.

Shin, Doh Chull. "On the Third Wave of Democratization: A Synthesis and Evaluation of Recent Theory and Research." *World Politics* 47,1 (1994): 135–70.

———. *Mass Politics and Culture in Democratizing Korea.* New York: Cambridge University Press, 1999.

Sin, Myŏng Sun. "Han'gugesŏŭi simin sahoe hyŏngsŏnggwa minjuhwa kwajŏngesŏŭi yŏkhal."

(The formation of civil society in Korea and its role in democratization). In *Kukka, simin sahoe, chŏngch'i minjuhwa*. (The state, civil society, and political democratization), ed. Byŏng Jun An. Seoul: Hanul, 1995.

Skocpol, Theda. "Bringing the State Back In: Strategies of Analysis in Current Research." In *Bringing the State Back In*, ed. Peter Evans, Dietrich Rueschemeyer, and Theda Skocpol. New York: Cambridge University Press, 1985.

Sŏ, Kwan Mo. "Han'guk sahoe kyegŭp kusŏngŭi sahoe t'onggyejŏk yŏn'gu." (A social statistical study of class structure in Korea). *Sanŏp sahoe yŏn'gu*. (Research on industrial societies), ed. Korean Research Group on Industrial Societies. Seoul: Hanul, 1986.

Sohn, Hak-Kyu. *Authoritarianism and Opposition in Korea*. New York: Routledge, 1989.

Son, Ho Ch'ŏl. *Haebang 50 nyŏnŭi han'guk chŏngch'i*. (Fifty years of post-liberation Korean politics). Seoul: Saegil, 1995.

Son, Pong Suk. "Cheil konghwagukkwa chayudang." (The first republic and the Liberal Party). In *Hyŏndae han'guk chŏngch'iron*. (Contemporary Korean politics), ed. Korean Political Science Association. Seoul: Pŏmmunsa, 1987.

Sŏng, Kyŏng Ryung. "Han'guk chŏngch'i minjuhwaŭi sahoejŏk kiwŏn: sahoe undongnonjŏk chŏpkŭn." (Social origins of Korean democratization: a social movement approach). In *Han'guk chŏngch'i sahoeŭi sae hŭrŭm*. (New currents in Korean politics and society), ed. Institute for Far Eastern Studies. Seoul: Nanam, 1994.

Song, Mun Hong. "Hanch'ongnyŏn." (The National Coalition of University Student Councils). *Sindonga* (Tonga monthly), September (1993): 544–59.

———. "Munmin ch'unggyŏk, tae sasaege ppajin chaeya." (The civilian shock: dissident movement in profound agony). *Sindonga* (Tonga monthly), May (1993): 494–505.

Stepan, Alfred. *Rethinking Military Politics: Brazil and the Southern Cone*. Princeton: Princeton University Press, 1988.

Strand, David. "Protest in Beijing: Civil Society and the Public Sphere in Beijing." *Problems of Communism* 39,3 (1990): 1–19.

Tarrow, Sidney. "Mass Mobilization and Regime Change: Pacts, Reform, and Popular Power in Italy (1918–1922) and Spain (1975–1978)." In *The Politics of Democratic Consolidation: Southern Europe in Comparative Perspective*, ed. Richard Gunther, P. Nikiforos Diamandouros, and Hans-Jürgen Puhle. Baltimore: Johns Hopkins University Press, 1995.

———. *Power in Movement: Social Movements and Contentious Politics*. 2nd ed. New York: Cambridge University Press, 1998.

Valenzuela, J. Samuel. "Democratic Consolidation in Post-Transitional Settings: Notion, Process, and Facilitating Conditions." In *Issues in Democratic Consolidation: The New South American Democracies in Comparative Perspective*, ed. Scott Mainwaring, Guillermo O'Donnell, and J. Samuel Valenzuela. Notre Dame, Ind.: University of Notre Dame Press, 1992.

Wakeman, Frederic, Jr. "The Civil Society and Public Sphere Debate: Western Reflections on Chinese Political Culture." *Modern China* 19,2 (1993): 108–38.

Weigle, Marcia A., and Jim Butterfield. "Civil Society in Reforming Communist Regimes: The Logic of Emergence." *Comparative Politics* 25,1 (1992): 1–23.

White, Gordon. "Developmental States and Socialist Industrialization in the Third World." *Journal of Development Studies* 21,1 (1984): 97–120.

———. "Prospects for Civil Society in China: A Case Study of Xiaoshan City." *Australian Journal of Chinese Affairs* 29 (1993): 63–87.

White, Gordon, and Jude A. Howell. *In Search of Civil Society: Market Reform and Social*

Change in Contemporary China. New York: Oxford University Press, 1996.

Woods, Dwayne. "Civil Society in Europe and Africa: Limiting State Power through a Public Sphere." *African Studies Review* 35,2 (1992): 77–100.

Yang, Pyŏng Ki. "Han'guk chŏngch'iesŏŭi min–gun kwan'gyeŭi chŏn'gaewa sŏnggyŏk." (The development and nature of civil–military relations in Korean politics). In *Han'guk chŏngch'i tongt'aeron.* (Dynamics of Korean politics), ed. Hŭngsu Han. Seoul: Orŭm, 1996.

Yang, Tong An. "Hollan sogŭi kukka hyŏngsŏng." (State-building in the midst of turmoil). In *Hyŏndae han'guk chŏngch'isa.* (Contemporary Korean political history), ed. Tong An Yang. Seoul: Han'guk chŏngsin munhwa yŏn'guwŏn, 1990.

Yi, Chae O. *Han'guk haksaeng undongsa.* (History of student movement in Korea). Seoul: Hyŏngsŏngsa, 1984.

Yi, Chong Sŏk. "4 wŏl hyŏngmyŏng chudo seryŏgŭi pyŏnch'ŏn kwajŏng." (Vicissitudes of the leaders of the April revolution). In *Han'guk sahoe pyŏndonggwa 4 wŏl hyŏngmyŏng.* (Revolutionary movement in Korea and the April revolution). Vol. 1. Ed. Institute for the Study of the April Revolution. Seoul: Han'gilsa, 1990.

Yi, Chŏng Hŭi. "Chei konghwagugŭi chŏngch'i hwan'gyŏnggwa Chang Myŏnŭi leadership." (Political environment of the second republic and Chang Myŏn's leadership). In *Han'guk hyŏndae chŏngch'isa.* (Contemporary Korean political history), ed. Korean Political Science Association. Seoul: Pŏmmunsa, 1996.

Yi, Hong Kyun. "Simin undongŭi hyŏnjuso, kyŏngsillyŏn'gwa ch'amyŏ yŏndae." (The current status of citizens' movement, the Citizens' Coalition for Economic Justice and the People's Solidarity for Participatory Democracy). *Tonghyanggwa chŏnmang* (Trends and prospects) 35 (1997): 80–96.

Yi, Mok Hŭi. "10 wŏl Yusin'gwa minju nodong undongŭi oeroun ch'ulbal." (Yusin and the lonely beginning of the democratic labor movement). In *1970 nyŏndae ihu han'guk nodong undongsa.* (History of labor movement in Korea in the 1970s), ed. Korean Alliance of Democratic Workers. Seoul: Tongnyŏk, 1994.

Yi, Su In. "Chayudang chŏnggwŏnŭi yŏksajŏk sŏnggyŏk." (Historical nature of the Syngman Rhee regime). In *Han'guk sahoe pyŏnhyŏk undonggwa 4 wŏl hyŏngmyŏng.* (Revolutionary movement in Korea and the April revolution). Vol. 1. Ed. Institute for the Study of the April Revolution. Seoul: Han'gilsa, 1990.

Yi, T'aek Hwi. "Minjujuŭi t'och'akhwaŭi siryŏn." (The ordeal of sowing democracy in Korea). In *Hyŏndae han'guk chŏngch'isa.* (Contemporary Korean political history), ed. Tong An Yang. Seoul: Han'guk chŏngsin munhwa yŏn'guwŏn, 1990.

Youm, Kyu Ho. "Press Freedom under Constraints: The Case of South Korea." *Asian Survey* 26,8 (1986): 868–82.

Youm, Kyu Ho, and Michael B. Salwen. "A Free Press in South Korea: Temporary Phenomenon or Permanent Fixture?" *Asian Survey* 30,3 (1990): 312–25.

Yun, Sang Ch'ŏl. *1980 nyŏndae han'gugŭi minjuhwa ihaeng kwajŏng.* (Process of democratic transition in Korea in the 1980s). Seoul: Seoul National University Press, 1997.

Index

All-Nation Emergency Committee on
    Enacting a Special Law for Punishing the
    Perpetrators of the May 18 Massacre,
    115–16
anticommunism, 28, 30, 32–33, 69, 74, 102
Anticommunist Law, 54
anticommunist special law, 39
April Revolution Youth–Student Alliance, 37
Association of Anticommunist Groups, 41
Association of Families of Political Prisoners
    (AFPP), 121–22
Association of the Wounded in the April
    Revolution, 37
authoritarian breakdown (stage of
    democratization process), 11

Basic Press Law, 2, 68, 79, 96
"birth defect" (of Kim Young Sam and Kim
    Dae Jung regimes), 118, 119
"Bloody Tuesday," 35
Board of Audit and Inspection, 114
bourgeoisie. See capitalists.
Brazil, 146

capitalists, in Korean democratization, 91, 94,
    104, 144
Catholic Justice and Peace Mission, 79
Catholic Peasant Association, 87
Catholic Priests' Association for Justice
    (CPAJ), 59, 83, 88, 91, 116, 123
Central Council for Independent National
    Unification, 40
Ch'a Chi Ch'ŏl, 63
Ch'oe Kyu Ha, 64–65
Ch'oe Yŏl, 133
Ch'ŏnggye apparel labor union, 83
Chaebŏl reform, 127–28
Chaeya, 58–59, 61, 64, 71, 73, 84, 158n10,
    158n17
Chang Ha Sŏng, 128
Chang Myŏn, 31, 37–38

Chi Hak Sun, 59
Cho Pong Am, 32–33
Chŏn T'ae Il, 55, 70
Chŏng Sŭng Hwa, 65
Chosŏn Dynasty, 43–44
Chun Doo Hwan, 4, 65–68, 91, 113–114, 117
Chun Kyŏng Hwan, 113
Citizens' Coalition for Economic Justice
    (CCEJ), 106, 116, 123, 125–126, 128,
    131–33
Citizens' Council for Fair Elections (CCFE),
    120
citizens' movement groups, 106–8
Citizens' Solidarity for National Assembly
    Elections, 120
Citizens' Solidarity for Political Reform,
    120–21
civic community, 154n51, 154n60
civic culture, 8, 147
civil society: autonomy of, 13; coalition with
    political society, 39–40, 87–93, 151n15;
    definition of, 15; conflictual engagement
    with state, 24, 44–45, 71–72, 131, 146–48,
    155n1; and democratization, 4–5, 9, 19;
    diversity of, 14; dual autonomy of, 13;
    normative dimension (ND) of, 14–15;
    organizational dimension (OD) of, 12;
    pluralism of, 14; political societization of,
    133, 154n48; and political society, 13; and
    private units of production and
    reproduction, 13; publicness of, 12;
    relational dimension (RD) of, 12–13;
    resurrection of, 98, 144; self-governance of,
    14; self-organization of, 12; and the state,
    12–13, 24, 44–45, 71–72, 131, 146–48,
    155n1; statization of, 131–132, 154n48
civil society groups: alliance of, 86–87,
    151n15; associational explosion of, 26, 42,
    108
class structure, changes in, 69–70
Colombia, 146

Committee for Attaining Democratic
    Constitution, 87
Communist Youth Federation, 26
communists, 25–26
Confucianism, 43–44, 157n54
constitutional revision, 29, 32, 51, 56–57, 87
corporatism, 13, 42, 154n40
Council for the Promotion of Democracy
    Movement, 92
Council of Dismissed Professors, 59
Council of Movement for People and
    Democracy (CMPD), 83–84, 86, 101
Council of Writers for Practicing Freedom, 59
coup: military, 42, 65–66; multi-staged, 64, 67

Dahl, Robert, 10
democracy: definition of, 11, 151n1, 151n2;
    different conceptions of, in Korean civil
    society, 73; institutional requirements of,
    See procedural minimum of; mass-
    ascendant vs. elite-ascendant, 146;
    minimalist definitions of, 10, 153n29;
    procedural minimum of, 10; procedural vs.
    substantive definitions of, 95, 101–2,
    161n42
Democratic Charter to Save the Nation, 59
democratic consolidation (stage of the democ-
    ratization process), 11, 112, 147, 153n32
Democratic Declaration to Save the Nation, 59
democratic junctures, 16–19
Democratic Justice Party (DJP), 81, 90
Democratic Korea Party, 84, 86
Democratic Liberal Party, 118
democratic martyrdom, 92
Democratic People's Charter, 59
Democratic Republican Party, 51, 54
democratic transition (stage of the democ-
    ratization process), 11, 147
democratization: civil society paradigm, 4,
    8–9, 139; contingency paradigm, 4, 8, 139;
    definition of, 11; elitist paradigm, See
    contingency paradigm; preconditions
    paradigm, 8, 139; of Korea, compared with
    other cases, 5, 143–44, 146; stages of, 11;
    structuralist explanations, See
    preconditions paradigm; theories of, 152n8;
    voluntaristic explanations, See contingency
    paradigm
demonstration regulation law, 39
dictablanda (liberalized authoritarianism), 118

dissidence, vs. opposition, 59, 158n13
Dryzek, John S., 132

economic crisis, 55, 126–129
economic development, 52–53, 69, 81, 99
Economic Planning Board (EPB), 52
economic reform, 127–28
education (sunhwa) camps, 78
elites, 3–4, 139, 146
environmental movement, 124–25

February Revolution (Philippines), 89
Federation for the Promotion of National
    Reunification, 37
Federation of Farmers' Unions, 29
Federation of Korean Industries, 54, 91, 94
Federation of Korean Trade Unions (FKTU),
    29, 33–34, 40–41, 55, 80, 94, 109
Federation of Progressive Comrades, 38
founding elections, 96

garrison state, 69
global democratization, 9, 152n6
Great Labor Struggle, 93–95
gymnasium elections (ch'eyukkwan sŏn'gŏ), 1,
    85

Haggard, Stephan, 68
Ham Se Ung, 59
Ham Sŏk Hŏn, 59
Han Wan Sang, 59
Hanahoe, 2
hardliners. See softliners
Hŏ Chŏng, 36–37
Hyundai companies, labor disputes in, 93–94

Inch'ŏn Labor Federation, 89–90
Inch'ŏn Mass Rally, 89–90, 101
industrialization. See economic development.
International Monetary Fund (IMF), 127
intracampus democratization, 38, 65, 82–83

Japanese colonialism, 24
June 29 Declaration (adopting direct
    presidential election system), 93, 95,
    160n34

Kaufman, Robert, 68
Kim Chae Kyu, 63
Kim Chu Yŏl, 35, 92

Kim Dae Jung, 1, 57, 59, 61, 66–67, 79, 85, 90, 96–97, 119, 122
Kim Jong Pil, 54, 118–20
Kim Kyŏng Suk, 62, 92
Kim Sŏn Myŏng, 121
Kim Su Hwan, 88, 91, 111
Kim Yong Ch'ŏl, 113
Kim Young Sam, 61–63, 79, 85, 90, 96–97, 110, 114, 116, 118–19, 123, 128
Korea Association of Employers, 91, 94
Korea Central Intelligence Agency (KCIA), 2, 42, 53–54, 61, 63, 65, 69, 121–22
Korea Chamber of Commerce and Industry, 54, 91, 94
Korea Citizens' Council for Social Development, 121
Korea Coalition for National Democracy Movement, 108–9
Korea Confederation of Trade Unions (KCTU), 94, 127
Korea Council of Academic Groups, 111–12
Korea Council of Citizens' Movements (KCCM), 106
Korea Council of Professors for Democratization, 114
Korea Democratic Party, 29
Korea Economic Council, 41
Korea Ecumenical Youth Council, 60
Korea Federation for Environmental Movement (KFEM), 106, 125, 132–33
Korea Federation of Labor Unions, 41
Korea Federation of Peasants, 24
Korea Federation of Small and Medium Enterprise Associations, 91, 94
Korea Federation of Teachers' Associations, 109
Korea Federation of Workers and Peasants, 24
Korea Federation of Workers, 24
Korea International Trade Association, 54, 91
Korea People's Association, 29
Korea Socialist Party, 38
Korea Student Christian Federation, 60
Korea Trade Union Council (KTUC), of the 1960s, 33–34, 41, 156n24, of the 1980s, 109–10, 156n24
Korea Women's Association, 29, 54
Korea Women's Associations United, 116
Korea Youth Association, 54
Korea Youth Organization, 29
Korean Anticommunist Youth Association, 34–35

Korean Anti-Pollution Movement Association (KAPMA), 124–25
Korean Bar Association, 115
Korean Christian Academy, 60
Korean Communist Party, 25–26
Korean Council for Human Rights Movement, 59
Korean Council for Labor Welfare, 83, 87
"Korean Democracy," 57, 62, 74
Korean Democratic Youth Federation, 26
Korean National Christian Church Council, 91
Korean Nationalist Party, 84, 86
Korean Patriotic Women's Association, 26
Korean Peasant Movement Coalition, 109–10
Korean Teachers' and Educational Workers' Union (KTEWU), 109–10, 127
Korean War, 30
Korean Youth Association, 26
Korean-Japanese normalization, 51
Korean-United States economic agreement, 39
Kwangju Uprising, 67, 82, 116
Kye Hun Che, 59
Kyŏnghyang Daily, 32

labor movement, 29, 40–41, 55, 66, 70, 93–95
Lawyers' Association for a Democratic Society, 115–16
Legislative Council for National Security (LCNS), 2, 68, 79–80, 96, 109
legitimacy (in democratic consolidation), 112
liberal democracy, 28, 30, 33, 46, 73–74
Liberal Party (LP), 29
Lipset, Seymour M., 8, 99

March First Democratic Declaration, 59
martial law, 36, 63, 66–67, 72
middle class, 98–99, 129–30
monism, 42
Mun Ik Hwan, 59, 84

National Alliance for Democracy and Unification of Korea (NADUK), 109, 115–16, 122, 127, 162n6
National Assembly elections, 30, 38, 85–86, 113, 120
National Coalition for Democracy, 59, 61, 84
National Coalition for Democracy and Reunification, 59, 61, 64, 84
National Coalition for Democracy Movement, 88–89, 101

National Coalition of University Student
Councils (NCUSC), 110–11, 116
National Committee for Fighting against the
Antidemocratic Laws, 39
National Congress for Democracy and
Reunification (NCDR), 84, 86, 101
National Congress for the Restoration of
Democracy, 58–59
National Council of Labor Unions, 26–27, 34
National Council of Protestant Pastors for
Justice and Peace, 88, 91
National Council of University Student
Representatives, 108, 110
National Federation of Peasant Unions, 26–27
National Headquarters for Reconstruction, 54
National Independence League Party, 30
National Intelligence Service. *See* KCIA
National Movement Headquarters for
Democratic Constitution (NMHDC),
91–92, 96, 101
National Security Law (NSL), 30, 32–33, 54,
122
National Security Planning Agency. *See* KCIA
National Student Coalition for Democracy
Struggle, 83
National Women's Union, 26
New Democratic Party (NDP), 61–62, 73, 100
New Democratic Republican Party, 118
New Korea Democratic Party (NKDP), 85–90
New Korea Party, 122
new party tornado (*sindang tolp'ung*), 86
new social movements, 107
night schools, 70

opposition, *vs.* dissidence, 59, 158n13
Organizing Committee for the Reconstruction
of Korean Labor Groups, 55

Paek Ki Wan, 59
Pak Chong Ch'ŏl, 91–92, 121
Pak Hyŏng Kyu, 59
Park Chung Hee, 42, 51–52, 54, 57, 63
parochial groups, 12
Party for Peace and Democracy, 96
Path to Democratization, 83
people's candidate, 97
people's committees, 25
people's movement, 61, 84, 89–90, 106–12. *See
also* triple solidarity.
People's Movement Coalition for Democracy

and Reunification (PMCDR), 86–88, 90–91,
96–97, 108–09
People's Republic of Korea, 25, 27
People's Revolutionary Party, 54
People's Solidarity for Participatory
Democracy (PSPD), 116, 128
policy advocacy, 148–49
Political Climate Renovation Law, 68, 79
political reform, 121
political relaxation, during Chun regime
(*Yuhwa kungmyŏn*), 80–82, 84
Political Renovation Committee, 79
political society, 13; coalition with civil
society, 39–40, 87–93, 151n15
popular upsurge, 5, 9, 98
Prayer Meetings for the Nation, 60
Preparatory Committee for Establishing a
New State, 25
Preparatory Committee for the Korea
Confederation of Trade Unions, 115
presidential elections, 1, 31, 57, 95–97, 118–19
Presidential Emergency Measures, 59, 65
press guidelines, 79–80
Progressive Party, 32
Protestant Peasant Association, 87
Pusan-Masan Uprising, 62–63

quasi-civilianized government, 72

real name bank account system, 110
religious organizations, 60–61
Reunification Democratic Party (RDP),
90–91, 96, 118
reunification issue, 46–47, 74, 102, 133–34
reunification movement, 39–40
Reunification Revolution Party, 54
Roh Tae Woo, 3–4, 97, 113–18

Scientists' Alliance, 26
Second Nation-Building Campaign, 132
self-assertive diplomacy, 46–47
self-governing agricultural committees, 25
Seoul Labor Movement Coalition, 87, 97
signature collection campaigns, 59, 61, 88
Sin Ik Hŭi, 31
Sŏ Kyŏng Sŏk, 132–33
social purification (*chŏnghwa*) campaign,
67–68, 78–79
Socialist Mass Party, 38, 40
Socialist Party, 30

softliners, and hardliners, 3–4, 63, 98, 144
soldiers-in-mufti, 72
Song Yo Ch'an, 36
Special Committee for National Security
  Measures, 67–68
Special Committee on Constitutional
  Revision, 89–90
state and civil society, conflictual engagement
  between, 24, 44–45, 71–72, 131, 146–48,
  155n1
statements on the current situation (*Siguk
  sŏnŏn*), 88
Student Defense Corps, 30
students, university, 30, 33, 38, 43–44, 70–71,
  82–83, 85, 110–11, 116
Syngman Rhee, 28–29, 31, 36

Taegu incident, 41–42
Teachers' Labor Union, 38
Three *mins*, 89–90
trasformismo (transformism), 118
triple solidarity, 60–61, 68, 71, 73, 82, 87, 98

U Yong Kak, 121
Unification Socialist Party, 39
United States Army Military Government in
  Korea (USAMGIK), 26–30
United States, 2–3, 36, 68
university national reunification student
  fronts, 38
university national reunification student
  leagues, 38

Urban Industrial Mission, 60, 79
urbanization, 155n20

Venezuela, 146
Vietnam War, 51

Women's Alliance for Independence, 26
World Olympic Games, 82, 100
Writers' Alliance, 26

Y.H. Incident, 61–62
Yi Ch'ŏl Sŭng, 61
Yi Han Yŏl, 92
Yi Hoe Ch'ang, 114
Yi Ki Pung, 31
Yi Min U, 90
Yŏ Un Hyŏng, 25
yŏch'on yado (ruling party in the countryside
  and the opposition in the cities), 31
yŏso yadae (small ruling party *vs.* large
  opposition parties), 113, 118
Young Catholic Workers, 60
Youth Alliance for Democracy and
  Nationalism, 38
Youth Alliance for Reunification and
  Democracy, 38
Youth Coalition for Democracy Movement
  (YCDM), 83, 85, 96–97
Yun Po Sŏn, 59, 64
Yusin, 57–58; movement against, 58–61
Yusin Constitution, repeal of, 64–65